WOMEN AND WELFARE

Women and Welfare

Ten Victorian Women in Public Social Service

Julia Parker
Lecturer in Social Administration
University of Oxford

M
MACMILLAN
PRESS

First published 1989

Published by
THE MACMILLAN PRESS LTD
Houndmills, Basingstoke, Hampshire RG21 2XS
and London
Companies and representatives
throughout the world

Typeset by Wessex Typesetters
(Division of The Eastern Press Ltd)
Frome, Somerset

Printed and bound in Great Britain at
The Camelot Press Ltd, Southampton

British Library Cataloguing in Publication Data
Parker, Julia, *1931–*
Women and welfare: ten Victorian women
in public social service.
1. Women social reformers—Great
Britain—History—19th century
I. Title
362'.92'2   HN13
ISBN 0–333–46386–2 (hardcover)
ISBN 0–333–46387–0 (paperback)

For my daughters, Jane and Judith

Contents

Introduction

In Victorian England it was rare for women to have any kind of public career or position. Working-class women might go into domestic service or the mines or mills or factories to stave off destitution, but generally only until they married. Middle-class women had virtually no chance of paid work that was socially acceptable. If their families were able to support them they spent their youth preparing for marriage and their later years managing a household of servants and children and attending to the needs of more distant relatives. Only if family support failed, through death or bankruptcy or other misfortune, might unmarried daughters or widows be compelled to fend for themselves, but virtually the only form of respectable employment was teaching in a school or more commonly as a governess in a private household. Even the practice of women joining in the work of their own families on farms or in small business enterprises was becoming less common in the early nineteenth century. Increasing prosperity tended to the separation of family and business affairs and new notions of gentility emerged that required that women be dependent and confined to domestic matters.[1]

Opportunities for work outside their own families were limited by the scarcity of suitable jobs for women to do, by their own lack of appropriate education and training and by social conventions. Some battled for wider opportunities in the various women's movements, but this book is concerned with those who entered public social service. These were the pioneers of statutory welfare arrangements, and at the same time among the leaders of the movement of women out of private life into the public careers, jobs and professions occupied by men. Writing and speaking in public at a time when relatively high fertility still prevailed and when public life was virtually proscribed to respectable women, they are of crucial interest in showing how the shift from family life became possible. Their ambitions, the difficulties they faced in pursuing them, their near disasters and remarkable achievements form part of the story of the development of social work, and of other professions, and illustrate different strands in the middle-class response to poverty and distress during the later part of the nineteenth century. But the experiences of the early social workers are also interesting for what they reveal of the relations between men and women at that time, the

1

opportunities and constraints associated with particular kinds of family life and social and industrial organisation, and the significance of political culture and of fervent religious belief.

Why did certain Victorian women devote themselves to public social service? Powerful conventions governed the lives of women in the nineteenth century. Their place was assumed to be within their families and they were brought up to expect the domestic responsibilities of marriage and a household. Why did some leave their comfortable and cultivated homes, often in the face of family opposition and social disapproval, for work that was frequently physically, mentally and emotionally exhausting, among some of the most wretched of human beings?

There were of course a number of possible female positions outside the domestic role. Max Beerbohm notes three great women of the Victorian age; Victoria herself, Florence Nightingale and Marie Lloyd. The Queen had a unique public place in spite of her sex, ascribed by kinship, the outcome of the rules and politics of an hereditary monarchy. There was no family or social opposition to be overcome before she took on her public duties. On the contrary, she was carefully trained through her childhood and as a young woman for her royal responsibilities. Even in such circumstances, however, and with substantial wealth and the support of the Prince Consort, the Queen's role seems not always to have been an easy one. 'Oh! to be cut off in the prime of life – to see our pure, happy, quiet, domestic life, which *alone* enabled me to bear my *much* disliked position, CUT OFF, at forty-two', she wrote, on the death of Prince Albert.[2]

Florence Nightingale, by contrast, is an example of a woman obliged to make her own way into a male world of medical and army politics and administration. She came to personify feminine gentleness, care and devotion in her dedication to sick and dying soldiers. This was a thoroughly respectable female preoccupation and received public applause. But Miss Nightingale had a long and bitter struggle, especially with her mother and sister, before she was free to take up an independent nursing career, and she was constantly frustrated by the lack of opportunities for training. Her move into public work was a very difficult one; all the more so because for Miss Nightingale, unlike her sovereign, it involved the rejection of marriage. A sympathetic aunt wrote that her mother would have been 'most willing that you undertake a mission like Mrs Fry or Mrs Chisholm' had there been a Mr Fry or a Captain Chisholm to protect her. Official government support and public recognition did something to compensate for a missing husband. The invitation from Sidney Herbert, Minister at War, to organise a party of nurses to go to the Crimea and the popular acclaim for her work there both helped to reconcile the Nightingale family and the doctors, the army authorities and politicians, to her public activities.

The career of Marie Lloyd represented an even more difficult path into the public sphere in Victorian England. Actresses and entertainers had a precarious position of doubtful respectability. Their profession, unlike nursing or teaching, was a challenge to conventional assumptions about women's domestic responsibilities. The problems of reconciling this particular kind of public activity with family roles remain evident in the regular divorces and re-marriages associated with Hollywood film-making in the twentieth century.

The outrage aroused by behaviour that could be seen as defying the conventions of family life and the place of women within it is illustrated by Victorian attitudes to prostitution. If public entertainers were delicately balanced on the thin edge of respectability, the equally ancient profession of prostitution was the antithesis of conventional morality and of socially approved women's roles. In Victorian England it was not a matter that could be openly discussed in polite society, as Josephine Butler discovered in her fight against the Contagious Diseases Acts.

To transgress against the norms of sexual behaviour by bearing a child outside marriage also attracted severe punishment. Women with illegitimate children are the tragic figures of Victorian literature: Hardy's Tess, and Fanny in *Far from the Madding Crowd*, Mrs Gaskell's Ruth, George Eliot's Hetty, and Moore's Esther Waters. Their creators may be sympathetic but the women are destroyed by social prejudice and their own shame and guilt. Esther Waters was the most resilient, rejecting a proposal from the woman she paid to look after her child that the infant be quietly starved for a fee of £5. More often fictional illegitimacy led to death or crime, to the workhouse or to prostitution. This was so for women of the working class. The middle and upper classes with more ample resources could more easily maintain the appearance of social respectability.

The women who went into public social service were not, of course, offending against conventional notions of sexual morality. They were mostly doing what could be regarded as women's work, though outside instead of inside their families. Their great achievement was the display of high ability, enterprise, determination and courage, qualities more commonly attributed to men. Their lives were practical proof that women could be exceptionally capable and skilled in the most responsible managerial and administrative jobs, in political argument and debate and in the analysis of social problems and social institutions. Their example lent powerful support to the wider movements for female suffrage, for the right of married women to hold property, for higher education and more employment opportunities. The pioneers were, of course, a tiny minority of extraordinary people, but there were enough of them to discredit prevailing beliefs about any necessary or natural inequality between the sexes which unfitted women for public work.

So we return to the question raised earlier as to the circumstances that enabled or encouraged or compelled the move from private into public life. No doubt the drive to social service reflected a complicated mixture of motives, influences and experiences. But we have distinguished five factors which we have assumed to be specially important, and in the later part of this book we set out to test this assumption by examining the lives of a number of Victorian women famous for their public work.

First we consider family and social background. We have supposed that only women whose families could support them, and who could employ servants to take over domestic tasks within their own households would have the leisure to take on unpaid work outside. But we also thought that the character of the family culture would be important, especially the level of interest in political and social questions. Second is the quality of family relationships. We have assumed that strong ties of affection and sympathy with close kin, or the reverse, would be powerful encouraging or restraining forces. Third is a woman's conception of her own role and of the rights and responsibilities of women in general. We would expect that only those with considerable self-confidence would have the strength to challenge the social prejudices of their time. Fourth, even the slightest aquaintance with the literature suggests that religious belief might have a crucial effect on women's decisions about what they should do. But not all devout women turned to social service. Different denominations placed different emphasis on Christian duty to the poor and wretched. Finally, we have supposed that those who chose to intervene in public affairs would also have a keen sense of the injustice and misery in the world, and a confident belief in their own power and duty to remedy it.

No one of these factors is a necessary ingredient in the mixture of circumstances leading women into public work and some are uncertain in their consequences. They must be regarded, however, as possible elements in the explanation we seek. A reasonably prosperous background seems important, but Octavia Hill and her sisters had to make their own living. Marriage and family ties might either support or hinder outside activity. A home culture including active interest in social questions and social reform might encourage public service, but it was hardly characteristic of the Nightingale family. Both advanced education and faith in a 'calling' could give confidence in public work but did not always lead to it. Particular collections of family and social experiences offered obvious opportunities and incentives. They also helped to fashion a distinctive type of personality – highly educated, socially confident and aware, devout, with a strong sense of social obligation and public duty. It seems unlikely that such women would be willing to restrict themselves to conventional family roles, nor that they would find much interest in fashionable society.

Ten women have been chosen in the hope that their lives will illustrate different kinds of social service and its roots in family circumstances and individual personality. Very brief biographies appear in the appendix. Six women were primarily social workers in the various public institutions or in the homes of the poor. The interests of Florence Nightingale, Agnes Jones, Louisa Twining and Mary Carpenter with the sick, the destitute, and with neglected and delinquent children, could be seen as a more or less respectable extension of women's familial responsibilities. It might be expected, therefore, that their public lives would be relatively easy. On the other hand, none of them married and the neglect of this important female duty was a possible source of difficulty even while allowing more time for outside work. Elizabeth Fry, in her prison visiting, was dealing with women who were the outcasts of society and was therefore likely to encounter more opposition. Octavia Hill is of special interest as one of the most articulate proponents of voluntary effort and one of the most determined critics of state welfare. She had especially clear views about the nature of poverty and destitution and about the way in which it must be tackled.

The other four women were more involved in writing and research, in organising pressure groups and mounting political campaigns to forward their different causes. Mrs Webb stands in strong contrast to Miss Hill. Her passion and commitment was to social research not to casework, and her faith and hope were in collective action not private charity to remedy social injustice. Mrs Butler and Mrs Besant are examples of women facing great public hostility in pursuit of unpopular causes, the welfare of prostitutes and the right of women to practise birth control. Mrs Besant and Miss Cobbe rejected conventional religious belief, so they are particularly intriguing people to consider.

Most of this group of women came from large families of five or more children and most of those families were wealthy, affectionate and devout, with reformist and philanthropic traditions of social thought and action. Six of the daughters remained single and four married, though Mrs Besant left her husband after only a few disastrous years. But demographically they were highly distinctive in one crucial respect – their low fertility. Mrs Fry, herself a child of the eighteenth century, alone maintained the high birth rate which was the norm until the later years of the nineteenth. Only two of the others had children and all 10 together produced 17 offspring between them, compared with a total of 63 children in the families in which they grew up. With the exception of Mrs Fry, even the minority who married failed to bear the five or six live children usual in the mid-Victorian years.[3] To some extent, then, social service was an alternative to child-rearing.

One thing the ten women did have in common. All were 'ladies'. The term as it is used at the present time has an archaic flavour and often carries mocking or derogatory connotations. In this book it is intended to have no such overtones. It is used in the nineteenth-century sense to denote women whose family resources enabled them to live without paid employment in the households of their parents or husbands or independently, as Miss Nightingale and Miss Cobbe, but supported by income from their family. Paid work was crucial; to engage in it undermined the status of lady. The very suggestion of it was used as a threat to her mother by Esther Hargrave, when she was being urged to agree to a marriage distasteful to her. 'I threaten mamma sometimes, that I'll run away, and disgrace the family by earning my own livelihood, if she torments me any more; and then that frightens her a little. But I *will* do it, in good earnest, if they don't mind.'[4] Ladies only took paid employment if the death or impoverishment of father or husband left them without other means of support. And virtually the only work open to them which allowed them to retain any semblance of gentility was to take a position as a governess in somebody else's household.

Ladies were not employed but their style of life included the possibility and expectation of protracted holidays. Sometimes these were educational in the broad sense, foreign tours introducing young women to the political and intellectual society as well as to the scenery of European countries. Often they were prescribed for reasons of health. Doctors with only rather limited medical techniques were more disposed to order their ailing patients abroad or to country air in the Lake District or North Wales. No doubt such changes of scene were of great benefit for women working in the insalubrious parts of Victorian London, in insanitary institutions and among sick people where there was a constant threat of infection. At any rate, periods of recuperation and convalescence, often of many months, were a common experience of the women of this study.

A detailed discussion of the lives of the ten ladies follows in the second part of this book. But first, in the next two chapters, we consider more generally the employment and charitable work of Victorian women and the special character of social service. This should allow some appreciation of the peculiar histories of those chosen for special study, within the society to which they were so eccentric.

Part I
Women's Work

1 Employment and Charity

During the later years of the nineteenth century women were increasingly extending their activities beyond the traditional confines of their homes and families into a more public sphere.[1] What they actually did depended on a whole range of circumstances. Most importantly it depended on class, on social and family position and expectations, on their own education, religious experience and personal commitment.

The great majority of middle-class women did not expect either paid employment or any demanding occupation outside the domestic circle of family and friends. Nor were they equipped for it. The education of girls was widely neglected and extremely inadequate – even for marriage for which they were destined. After the 1850s, however, the preponderance of women in the population meant that marriage was not a realistic prospect for many of them. The imbalance between the sexes was partly structural and partly social. For every 1000 men there were 1050 women, reflecting higher child mortality among boys, the deaths of men in war and their loss through emigration. But marriage was also delayed, more than a quarter of men remaining unmarried at 30. The result was that two-thirds of all women between 20 and 24 and 30 per cent of those between 24 and 35 were single in 1871. For every three women over 20 who were wives, there were two who were widows or spinsters.[2] Such circumstances lent considerable force to proposals that women should therefore be educated to earn their own living. This, and the growing demand from industry and government for literate workers combined to strengthen the movement for reforms.

Women themselves were prominent in the agitation for better education for their sex, but the leaders were the remarkable exceptions and neither they, nor female champions of other feminist causes endeared themselves to the Queen.

> The Queen is most anxious to enlist everyone who can speak or write to join in checking this mad, wicked folly of 'women's rights' . . . *with all its attendant horrors*, on which her poor feeble sex is bent, forgetting every sense of womanly feeling and propriety . . . It is a subject which makes the Queen so *furious* that she cannot contain herself.[3]

The fury of the Queen may not have been equally shared by all her subjects, but the Victorian assumption that women would marry and occupy themselves within their families, or not marry and occupy themselves within their families, was common enough. Women of the upper classes with time to spare from family duties might enter 'society' or take up charity or some kind of literary work, but only paid employment in extreme misfortune. Among the newly rich the ability to keep their wives and daughters in idleness in imitation of the aristocracy was a mark of status which could have dire consequences for the women concerned, lacking either the education or tradition of social service that might have enabled them to fill their days. Such a woman was Mrs Carson, alarmed by her own carefully educated daughters and more comfortable in the company of her maid.

Mrs Carson was (as was usual with her, when no particular excitement was going on), very poorly, and sitting upstairs in her dressing room, indulging in the luxury of a headache. She was not well, certainly. 'Wind in the head', the servants called it. But it was but the natural consequence of the state of mental and bodily idleness in which she was placed. Without education enough to value the resources of wealth and leisure, she was so circumstanced as to command both. It would have done her more good than all the aether and salvolatile she was daily in the habit of swallowing, if she might have taken the work of one of her own housemaids for a week; made beds, rubbed tables, shaken carpets, and gone out into the fresh morning air, without all the paraphanalia of shawl, cloak, boa, fur boots, bonnet and veil, in which she was equipped before setting out for an 'airing', in the closely shut-up carriage.[4]

Mrs Gaskell's description is a nice illustration of Veblen's characterisation of bourgeois women, whose conspicuous idleness and impracticable dress redounded, he claimed, to the prestige of the head of the household.

the more expensive and the more obviously unproductive the women of the household are, the more creditable and more effective for the purpose of reputability of the household or its head will their life be. So much so that the women have been required not only to afford evidence of a life of leisure, but even to disable themselves for useful activity.[5]

Veblen goes on to point to high heels and corsets, among other items of dress, as evidence of incapacity for work and of female economic dependence on men. And Neff commenting on *Middlemarch* makes a similar point about the social constraints on female behaviour: 'Since she found opinions and intelligence an encumbrance, the wise girl like Rosamund Vincy got rid of them. . . In the process of trying to be what society expected she became unhealthy from lack of exercise and tight-lacing'.[6]

Opportunities for middle-class women to take paid work were developing rapidly, however, during the second half of the nineteenth century. The number in professional jobs – teachers, nurses and clerks – multiplied by four to reach nearly half a million in Great Britain by 1901.[7] Nevertheless, they were a small minority of all occupied women who numbered four and three quarter million compared with three million in 1851. Also, although nearly five million women were in paid employment at the turn of the century, more than twice as many remained unoccupied.

Although middle-class women did not normally take paid work, the most usual means of livelihood for those who wanted their independence, or who were obliged to support themselves, was to enter another household as a governess. In 1850 there were 21 000 women in such employment[8] and opportunities were increasing for those who were supposed to be of 'gentle birth' though often, in fact, themselves poorly educated.

The position of governess might be a respectable occupation for gentlewomen, but it was often extremely uncomfortable, uneasily poised between employers and domestic servants:

She is a bore to almost any gentleman, as a tabooed woman. . . She is a bore to most ladies . . . and a reproach too – for her dull, fagging, bread-and-water life is perpetually putting their pampered listlessness to shame. The servants invariably detest her, for she is dependent like themselves, and yet, . . . as much their superior in other respects as the family they both serve. Her pupils may love her, and she make take the greatest interest in them, but they can never be her friends.[9]

These remarks come from a contemporary review of *Vanity Fair* and

Jane Eyre. They suggest that the usual experiences of governesses
fell far short of the extravagant adventuring of Becky Sharp or the
more sober but still highly romantic history of Jane Eyre, whose
passionate plea to Mr Rochester no doubt expresses something of
Charlotte Brontë's own protest against the prevailing assumptions
and practices of the time:

> Do you think, because I am poor, obscure, plain, and little, I am
> soulless and heartless? – You think wrong? – I have as much soul
> as you, – and full as much heart! And if God had gifted me with
> some beauty, and much wealth, I should have made it as hard for
> you to leave me, as it is now for me to leave you! I am not talking
> to you now through the medium of custom, conventionalities, nor
> even mortal flesh: – it is my spirit that addresses your spirit. Just
> as if both had passed through the grave, and we stood at God's
> feet equal, – as we are![10]

Whatever the disadvantages, there were more women trying to find
work as governesses than there were households ready to receive
them, as may be seen by the various attempts to organise female
emigration. In the second half of the nineteenth century, however,
new possibilities of employment began to develop at home – not so
much in response to the various women's movements and pressure
from the early feminists but as a result of an expanding economy and
the changing demand for labour of an increasingly urban and industrial
society.[11] The growth of state education brought more posts in
elementary schools. At first these were largely filled by working-class
women for whom teaching offered better prospects and conditions
than either factory or domestic work. But as training became more
firmly established and schools more attractive, elementary teaching
rose in status and became acceptable for women of higher social
position.

Nursing too gradually changed to become a respectable female
profession. Up to the middle of the century it was regarded as a
'particularly repugnant form of domestic service'. Nurses were recruited from the poorest and the most disreputable classes to work
for fifteen hours at a stretch in appalling conditions in hospitals where
they divided their time between looking after the patients and cleaning
the wards, frequently neglecting both.[12] Early attempts to raise
professional standards often sprang from religious motives. In 1833
Pastor Fliedner established a refuge at Kaiserswerth and later

developed an orphanage, a school for female teachers and a hospital where protestant deaconesses were trained to nurse the sick poor. Elizabeth Fry, Florence Nightingale and Agnes Jones all visited Kaiserswerth, Mrs Fry returning to help to set up the Society of the Sisters of Charity in 1840 – the first institution for training nurses in England. Such opportunities for women were very few – especially among protestant sects.[13] In the 1850s Miss Nightingale was considering joining the Catholic Church for the sake of the training more readily available to women as nuns. She never did so but made several attempts to enter Catholic hospitals in Dublin and Paris for the nursing training they offered. A number of missions included nursing in their work among the poor but this tended to grow from their primary religious purpose and rarely involved training. It was the progress of medical science that underlined the need to establish professional education and discipline, the cause tirelessly pursued by Miss Nightingale after she returned from the Crimea.

Other possibilities of paid employment for women were developing fast in the last 30 years of the century in the distributive trades and in clerical work. In earlier years both shops and offices were commonly small family enterprises, carried on by family members or with the help of apprentices and demanding skilled workers with careful training. But social and economic changes altered these conditions. Industrialisation and growing wealth led to mass production of consumption goods, large-scale retail organisation, the disappearance of apprenticeships and the transformation of shop work into unskilled employment, thus opening it up to women.

In rather the same way clerical jobs in the middle of the century generally involved paying premiums and tended to be restricted to young men who had the necessary resources and education to read and write and do simple accounts. Middle-class parents rarely thought long and expensive apprenticeships suitable for girls who would be expected to marry. As industry expanded, however, so did associated activities in insurance, banking, advertising and so on. Shorthand and typing developed, work became more routine, and the spread of primary education and cheap commercial training opened clerical jobs to women who were in demand because they were less expensive than men. Office work was a traditional middle-class occupation, acceptable to middle-class women but also attractive to working-class girls, as it was easier than factory work as well as having higher social status.

It was not only industrial and commercial enterprises that flourished

in the nineteenth century. Government activity was also expanding
rapidly, a response in part to the economic and social conditions
exposed and engendered by population changes, industrial development and the growth of towns. This contributed to the increasing
supply of attractive clerical jobs offering secure employment and
relatively short working hours with generous sick leave, holidays and
pensions, even though low pay limited promotion prospects and, as
in many other jobs, a marriage bar obtained. Growing government
intervention in domestic affairs also offered opportunities, albeit
severely limited, for highly educated women to join the distinguished
band of men who worked as government inspectors under the poor
law and factory legislation and later in the public health and education
services. Jane Elizabeth Senior, sister of Thomas Hughes, daughter-
in-law of Nassau Senior, friend and correspondent of Octavia Hill
and Louisa Twining, was the first woman inspector of workhouses
and workhouse schools, appointed in 1874.[14] In 1883 and 1890 women
were appointed in the Education Department as Directress of
Needlework and Inspectoress of Cookery and Laundrywork respec-
tively. Two women were working as factory inspectors in 1883. By
1914 there were six women inspectors working for the Local
Government Board, 43 in the Education Department and 21 in the
women's branch of the Factory Inspectorate of the Home Office.[15]

The tiny number of women in the higher ranks of the civil service
in the early 1900s, representing as it did such a dramatic increase
over preceding decades, emphasises the very limited openings for
women in government departments. Nor were the professions easily
accessible to them. By the end of the nineteenth century there were
only a handful of women in higher education and in medicine – the
first woman physician, Elizabeth Blackwell, started her practice in
London in 1868. Government service and the professions, as well as
politics, were virtually the preserve of men.

Throughout the nineteenth century it was mainly working-class
women who entered paid employment, in various kinds of agricultural
and industrial labour and, most importantly, in domestic service.
Women of the industrial working class in the textile districts were
moving out of agriculture, out of unskilled trades and out of their
homes and small domestic workshops into the mills and factories as
industrial technology changed and the power looms turned weaving
to a greater extent into a woman's trade.[16] Other parts of the country
offered other kinds of industrial labour as well as agricultural work
and girls from poor urban and rural families found increasing openings

as domestic servants to confer respectability on the expanding middle classes. In 1901 by far the largest group of women were to be found in domestic service and laundry work – just over two million compared with half that number fifty years earlier. Many fewer, rather over three-quarters of a million, worked in textiles and a similar number in the clothing industry, but the increase in both these occupations had been much slower. Whatever the occupation to which they turned, working-class women were searching for paid work to maintain barely adequate standards of living for themselves and their families.

It was the factory women who attracted most attention. Their hours were long, often more than twelve a day, and their labour physically arduous and sometimes damaging to health. The position of women in the cotton mills was no worse than in other factories and workshops where hours might be longer, pay lower, and working conditions more unhealthy.[17,18] But the textile workers were a relatively large group, gathered together in relatively large institutions where they were peculiarly visible and they were the first to receive the notice of the legislators in the 1840s.

The factory employment of girls and women raised questions not only about their working conditions and the dangers of female competition for men's jobs, but also about the proper role and status of women and about the effects of outside work on family life. Such matters were discussed in commissions of enquiry, in the reports of the factory inspectors, in contemporary popular tracts and in parliamentary debates, and they have continued to arouse the interest of later historians. Dr Pinchbeck has pointed to the advantages of the development of factories and steam power in drawing machinery and workers out of the homes of operatives and permitting a pleasanter domestic environment. 'Now that the home was no longer a workshop, many women were able for the first time in the history of the industrial classes, to devote their energies to the business of home-making and the care of their children. . . .'[19] No doubt this was the case for some families. But the employment of women for twelve hours a day – the restriction imposed in 1844, reduced to ten in 1847 but easily evaded until the working day was limited to the hours between 6 a.m. to 6 p.m. in 1850 – left little time for child-care and home-making.

Childminding and baby farming flourished – often with disastrous consequences for the infants concerned. In the absence of any kind of maternity benefits or paid leave it was common for women to return to work nine or ten days after the birth of their babies, who were left in the care of older children or 'nurses'. Breast feeding was therefore difficult but special baby foods were unavailable and cow's milk expensive, so the rearing of infants 'by hand' – often on bread and water and a variety of 'preservatives' – was a dangerous substitute. Nevertheless, public intervention that could be seen as intruding into family life was not always welcome. An Infant Life Protection Bill of 1871 that would have provided for the registration of childminders was opposed by the National Society for Women's Suffrage on the grounds that it would interfere 'in the most mischievous and repressive manner with domestic arrangements'.[20] Registration was required a year later. A further Bill to exclude mothers from work for four weeks after the birth of a child was also challenged by some representatives of the women's movements. It should be a matter for individuals to decide when they would work, it was argued. Women needed the money and there was a danger of men driving them out of the labour market. In short, this was a time when industrial change gave rise to a complicated battle over the traditional sexual division of labour. Work for women outside their families created a need, if not an effective demand, for social services for mothers and children. The public response was mixed but to begin with was typically a conservative re-assertion of the primacy of family duty and the privacy of family arrangements.

High infant mortality rates and low standards of domestic management were neither universal among nor confined to the families of factory women; they were common among the poor and a result of poverty, ignorance and insanitary and overcrowded houses. Nevertheless, there does appear to have been an association between high infant mortality and the proportion of married and widowed women working, especially if the younger women are distinguished. Between 1896 and 1905 eight industrial districts with an average of 27 per cent of married and widowed women working had an average infant mortality rate of 182, which dropped to 150 in eight districts where only 7 per cent of married and widowed women worked. Differences in feeding habits had a more dramatic effect on differential death rates. In Salford in 1904 the infant mortality rate for breast-fed babies was 129, for those having cow's milk 264, and for those having 'other food' 439. In Birmingham the extremes varied from eight to 252.[21]

Some indication of the differences between the classes during the same period comes from Rowntree's early study of York. Here infant mortality in the poorest district, where 69 per cent of the population was living in poverty, was 247. The rate diminished where poverty was less intense, and dropped to 94 among the servant-keeping class.[22]

Although the growing number of working-class women in industrial employment provoked much discussion of its desirability, of their character and of their neglect of their primary family duties, only a minority of factory women were married – less than 30 per cent at any time during the second half of the nineteenth century, dropping to 24 per cent by 1901.[23] But factory work gave more publicity to behaviour and ways of living which challenged conventional middle-class assumptions about the things that women should do and aroused suspicions about the threat to feminine virtue and family responsibilities. The demonstration of independence involved in women maintaining themselves by their own labour offended Victorian sensibilities[24] and that factory work was often hard, dirty and dangerous, was an additional affront to conventional sexual stereotyping.

Despite the lack of public sympathy, it is doubtful whether factory workers were any more promiscuous or less careful of their children and households than other women of their class.[25] The suspicion of mill girls was often founded on ignorance and prejudice. Details of their lives were for the most part confined to the pages of government reports and enquiries and were rarely discussed by contemporary novelists who were unfamiliar with their circumstances and did not find them very attractive heroines. Those who did write with some knowledge of industrial work tended to show the more respectable women as avoiding factory employment if possible, like Mrs Gaskell's Mary Barton.

Industrial labour or domestic service was the usual resort of working class girls driven to supplement the family income, or by the desire for independence,[26] but dressmaking or millinery also offered a variety of employment in small workshops or as 'out' work, frequently in very poor conditions, but rather more respectable than factory work. Neff points out that sewing and making clothes was an occupation that was consistent with women's traditional roles and was, therefore, more socially acceptable and of higher status. Nor was it entirely closed to more educated women from middle-class families. Both Mrs Gaskell's Ruth and Dickens' Kate Nickleby as well as Mary Barton joined dressmaking establishments when obliged to work for money.

Paid work for middle-class women remained unusual, however,

throughout the century and social conventions continued to oppose
it. For those who lacked the opportunity, inclination or ability for
employment, some kind of charitable activity was an alternative way
of filling their leisure time that fitted the social ideal of the feminine
personality, with its attributes of self-sacrifice and compassion. For
many women philanthropic work sprang from religious commitment
and a strong sense of social obligation but, as Prochaska suggests, it
might also have offered something of an adventure and escape from
the routine sewing mornings based on home and church.[27]

There is no way of knowing precisely how many women engaged
in how much charitable effort. Much of it was informal and voluntary
and unrecorded. Prochaska quotes a survey by Louisa Hubbard and
Angela Burdett-Coutts in 1893 which estimated that 500 000 women
laboured 'continuously and semi-professionally' in philanthropy.[28]
This figure excluded nurses and the 5000 or so women in Sisterhoods.
It also excluded the numerous part-time workers – the 200 000
members of the Mothers' Union and the tens of thousands who
collected money and distributed tracts for the Bible societies. Charity
was conventional and expected for middle-class women and the
growing number of domestic servants allowed more leisure for it.
But, inevitably, some women gave more time to it than others. It
was far more important for Mrs Gladstone than for Margot Tenant,
and for Mrs Gaskell than for Charlotte Brontë. Opportunities and
incentives for voluntary or for paid work were very unevenly spread
both within and between social classes and also throughout the
country. Margaret Simey castigates the new middle classes in Liverpool who turned to philanthropy in imitation of the old merchant
families, but as a fashionable activity 'from which the underlying
integrity of purpose was sadly lacking' and remarks the unfortunate
consequences in 'ill-informed and ill-inspired meddling with the
working classes'.[29]

Charitable work, ill-informed or otherwise, was not the preserve
of women from wealthy families who had no need of paid employment
and who could rely on servants to relieve them of household
responsibilities. The educated women from the Victorian upper
classes are most remembered because they left letters and diaries and
books as evidence of their work. Many of them, moreover, numbered
writers, statesmen, politicians and civil servants among family or
personal friends so their efforts and their causes were more likely to
be successful.

The public service and charity to one another of the poor is less well documented and no doubt, as among the rich, it sometimes failed altogether. But there is also plenty of evidence of a pervasive and insistent sense of duty and responsibility among working-class people, especially women, to help the less fortunate among them. Often, as with women of other classes, the obligations lay primarily within the family. But the misery and destitution concentrated in the poor districts of the industrial towns were all the more apparent to the people who lived amidst them, and help to friends and neighbours in distress was an immediate response to obvious need.

As with middle-class women, religion was a powerful incentive to charitable action – even during the first part of the present century. In her attempt to discover the histories of working-class people in three industrial northern towns, Elizabeth Roberts stresses the importance of Christian upbringing – the good person was one who cared for family and neighbours; children were trained in the duty of obedience to parents and of help to neighbours without reward. Relations with kin outside the household were uncertain as it was difficult to give or receive help from those living far away, but solidarity existed among people living close to one another.

> The range of help provided by neighbours was immense: children were minded; the sick and dying were fed and nursed; clothes were passed on; funeral teas were prepared for the mourners; the dead laid out, shopping done for the elderly; and companionship and friendship provided for all ages.[30]

There are many examples in literature – and particularly in Mrs Gaskell's novels – of the help that the poor extended to one another. One of the few surviving histories of working-class philanthropy is the life of Catherine Wilkinson, born in Ireland in 1786 and migrating to Liverpool where she died.[31] Supported by a benefactress after the death of her father and sickness of her mother, she was sent to a cotton mill at the age of 11 where she lived, kindly treated by her employer, in an apprentice house. Leaving the mill to support an increasingly deranged and violent mother, she opened a school, at one time teaching 90 children sewing and reading, and later took work in the fields, charring, as a domestic servant, and in a nail factory to maintain a growing family. She had married a sailor and on his early death was left with two children to support, also taking in a destitute and handicapped woman who was denied the workhouse. In 1823 she married again, her husband Thomas

Wilkinson providing for the two children and two women dependants. Later the Wilkinsons added six orphans to their household and at another time five children of a drunken father. In the cholera outbreak of 1832 Mrs Wilkinson was in constant demand as a sick visitor and spent her time nursing the victims and looking after the children of dead and dying parents. She also attempted to check the spread of the epidemic by setting up a wash-house in her kitchen where neighbours could boil and disinfect clothes and bedding. In 1835 her own household contained, besides herself and her husband, two old women, four young women, two boys and four girls. The strictest economy permitted sufficient food of potatoes and broth and the evenings were occupied with music, games and reading aloud. In 1846, in recognition of their work, Mr and Mrs Wilkinson were appointed the Superintendents of Liverpool Public Baths.

Mrs Wilkinson's extraordinary life is a dramatic example of community service of the poor to the poor. The charity of the women of the middle and upper classes could not have the same basis in the local community. But in a society where religious observance was more common. Christian teaching could be a powerful reminder of the duty of charity for all social classes and for both men and women. The public exercise of that duty came more readily to those who had time and money to give to it and, for some at any rate, wealth and power carried an additional sense of moral and social obligation. The seventh Earl of Shaftesbury, at the beginning of his parliamentary life of labour on behalf of poor and afflicted people wrote of the purposes to which wealth should be put: 'Whether I shall ever be well off or not, God alone knows; but this I pray, that never asking for wealth, should it be sent me, I may receive at the same time a heart and spirit to lay it out for man's happiness and God's glory.'[32] Shaftesbury remains one of the most celebrated of the evangelicals. But less famous writers and speakers were drawing the attention of middle-class people to prevailing social problems and spreading knowledge of the social evils of the time beyond the readers of blue books and the papers of the Social Science Association and the local statistical societies.[33]

The response to poverty and distress, and to increasing knowledge of it, was as variable as the problems presented. In the earlier part of the nineteenth century charitable effort tended to be local in character. Women of the richer families visited and provided for the poor in their immediate neighbourhoods. For those who accepted such responsibilities it was a matter of course to devote some part of their income and their time to philanthropy. The sense of religious duty, of family responsibility and of social obligation of pious and well-to-do women is expressed by Mrs Gurney, mother of twelve children, one of whom later became Elizabeth Fry:

> In the morning endeavour, at first waking, to bring the mind into a state of silent waiting and worship, preparatory to the active employment of the day; when up visit the several apartments of the children . . . forget not the kindest attentions to my dearest companion . . . After walking with the little ones . . . begin with the necessary instructions for C and R; then attend to the kitchen and all family regulations, and to the claims of the poor.[34]

The remainder of Mrs Gurney's day might be spent in instructing her children, supervising household matters, writing letters or perhaps reading. The evening hours were to be devoted to 'the promotion of my husband's enjoyment and, if possible, to blend instruction and amusement for the elder children'. These remarks, Mrs Gurney recorded, were designed 'first, to promote my duty to my Maker – secondly my duty towards my husband and children, relations, servants, and poor neighbours'. As her daughters grew older they were encouraged to concern themselves with the poor people who lived around them – to take food to the destitute, to nurse the sick, to teach in the local schools. In later years Mrs Fry became famous for her prison work, though it seems her early efforts were not always very rewarding. In 1814 she wrote that she was affected by the 'distress of the poor' but hardly knew how to serve them:

> I am low, under a sense of my own infirmities, and also rather grieved by the poor. I endeavoured to serve them, and have given them such broth and dumplings as we should eat ourselves; I find great fault has been found with them, and one woman seen to throw them to the pigs.[35]

Exchanges between rich and poor that could develop relatively easily in the country tended to be lost in the towns where the streets of mean dwellings for industrial workers were set apart from the houses of the better off. In Liverpool the Toxteth Park population increased from 2069 in 1801 to 41 180 in 1841 and as more people crowded around the docks into insanitary courts and cellars, the merchant, trading and professional families moved out to more salubrious places, breaking the links with the people who had lived near them. Visiting the poor became a formal excursion into unfamiliar territory rather than a short walk to a neighbouring street.[36] This separation of the classes was later noted and deplored by Octavia Hill.

> We live upon the labours of the poor in districts far from our homes . . . we are content to draw our wealth from these [factories, offices, chambers]. Does this imply no duty? . . . It is our withdrawal from the less pleasant neighbourhoods . . . which has left these tracts what they are.[37]

With the changes in living habits came changes in habits of philanthropy. As the poor became less accessible, and perhaps more threatening, ladies' charitable activities tended to switch their emphasis from home visiting to all manner of fund-raising efforts – bazaars, sales of work, sewing parties and so on.[38] These endeavours were, of course, by no means restricted to relieving local or even national destitution or distress. Mrs Jellaby and her preoccupation with Borioboola-Gha was one of Dickens' more colourful caricatures but she indicates the remoteness of some philanthropic concerns.

The rapid growth of Liverpool was matched by the similarly rapid development of industrial towns throughout the country, exhibiting a degree of urban poverty which offered ample opportunity for charitable enterprise. Poor law policies after 1834 excluded the working poor and barely touched the sickness and destitution endemic among the urban working class which thus presented a formidable problem for voluntary effort.

One response was the drive to make charity more effective through attempting to co-ordinate the work of the many bodies and individuals involved in giving relief, and insisting that applications for help be investigated carefully to ensure that the poor were treated in the most appropriate way. It was this kind of concern that led to the founding of the Charity Organisation Society in 1866 and to the formulation of principles about the aims of charity, about who should receive it and in what circumstances, and about the relationship between statutory relief and voluntary action. It led to the devising of rules and methods of work to guide inexperienced volunteers and eventually to the organising of training for would-be social workers and the establishing of paid posts.[39] This drive for efficiency also meant attempts to distinguish the deserving from the undeserving poor to avoid wasting resources on those who would not or could not use the help that was offered for their betterment. The mass destitution of the industrial cities, however, especially evident in the years of recession in the later nineteenth century, defied attempts to separate sheep and goats and shifted the emphasis from moral character to social conditions as a more likely explanation of the prevailing poverty.

Thus a second response to the huge increase in the visible poor was to reconsider the relative responsibilities of voluntary effort and the state for the domestic affairs of the country. This raised fundamental questions about the duties and responsibilities of government and the duties and liberties of individuals. The political and economic costs, as well as the widespread individual distress arising when a tenth of the urban population were living below a bare subsistence level, had become more apparent by the end of the century after Booth's *Life and Labour of the People in London* and Rowntree's investigations into poverty in York. Nevertheless, the New Liberalism of the Christian Socialists and the Fabians, with its faith in the possibility of benevolent state intervention to advance personal welfare through collective action, was determinedly opposed by those who saw the way to individual and social progress through voluntary effort. Careful attention to particular cases of distress to adjust relief to need was considered the peculiar attribute of private philanthropy; this was the only way to encourage individual responsibility, the prerequisite of social well-being and advance, and avoid the demoralising effects of universal provision by the state.

The battle joined by the protagonists of more state welfare and the defenders of voluntarism was fought out within individual consciences as well as between people committed to opposing views about the proper bounds of government activity. It was a minority of five of the Poor Law Commissioners of 1905–9, led by Mrs Webb, who passionately argued the case for a minimum standard of living for all guaranteed by the state through universal services – a vision of collective responsibility that rejected the endeavour to restrict state support to the destitute on which the New Poor Law had been founded. But, in the 1880s, Beatrice Potter had still retained considerable doubts about the wisdom of government taking a larger part in planning.

In the meantime . . . I object to these gigantic experiments, state education and state-intervention in other matters . . . which flavour of inadequately thought-out theories. Neither do they seem to me to be the result of the spontaneously expressed desires of the people; but rather the crude prescriptions of social quacks seeking to relieve vague feelings of pain and discomfort experienced by the masses.[40]

The argument betwen the majority and the minority of the Poor Law Commissioners stemmed from their different conceptions of dependency or pauperism. For the majority it reflected some defect of moral character; for the minority, lack of economic opportunities and poor material circumstances. The debate had continued through the nineteenth century. But while in the earlier years poverty was widely regarded as a necessary aspect of human existence, calling for sympathy and kindness to those afflicted or for punishment for the undeserving, in the later years the more optimistic view that destitution might be prevented by appropriate government intervention was gaining ground. At the same time, as Simey has remarked, the problems of charity – of who should get what and how much – were changing to become a matter of relationships between classes rather than between individuals.[41]

This shift to a more impersonal form of charity was associated with the geographical separation of the social classes and with growing awareness of the importance of the social and economic circumstances that fashioned people's lives. But it was also associated with optimistic faith in the power of science and reason to resolve human problems, a belief not only in the desirability but in the possibility of benevolent government intervention in social arrangements. Mrs Webb recorded her faith in science as a means of sweeping away human misery and her own desire for training 'for research into the constitution and working of social organisation, with a view to bettering the life and labour of the people'.[42] She recalled her youth as passed in an atmosphere of intellectual ferment, when it was always assumed that in the end science could solve all problems. Such cheerful assumptions about the possibilities of social advance also sustained the philanthropic work of many of the women discussed in the second part of this book.

Looking beyond her family experiences Mrs Webb remarked that the middle of the nineteenth century was the period when 'the impulse of self-subordinating service was transferred consciously and overtly from God to man'.[43] This is perhaps a misleadingly simple observation. Many men and women in the earlier years expressed their commitment to service to God in dedicated service to people.

And many of the social workers and reformers of the later years, including Mrs Webb herself, were impelled to their investigations through a driving sense of and search for a 'calling' which can only be defined in religious or mystical terms, even though the conventional religious observances might be disregarded.

The search for religious truth continued to disturb many of those who were most enthusiastic in the pursuit of scientific method. But faith in a Deity who ordered the world in ways passing human understanding and submissive acceptance of personal misfortune conceived as God's will, particularly evident in the writing of Mrs Fry, but also of Mary Carpenter, was becoming less common in the later years of the century. The collection of large quantities of empirical data meant that social problems could be measured more accurately, and at the same time developments in engineering and sanitary science were offering possible solutions to them.[44] The demonstration of links between high mortality and insanitary and overcrowded dwellings and contaminated water supplies suggested the need for public action to secure a more healthy environment rather than the appointment of Fast Days of public humiliation on the appearance of cholera.[45] The realisation that 'primary poverty' was not always the choice of the feckless but might be the unavoidable consequence of low wages, sickness, old age or more than three children, suggested that it could be alleviated by public intervention and was not an inevitable disaster of human existence. Increasing knowledge, allied with religious commitment, was a powerful inspiration to efforts to deal with prevailing social distress. This did not always imply government action. State responsibility for or power to affect personal welfare remained a major question of political debate. It was in part an ideological debate conducted in terms of rights, duties and freedom; but the deplorable standards of staffing and accommodation and personal care in the various state institutions of the time must have lent considerable weight to the supporters of voluntary action.

If visiting the poor in their own homes was daunting and difficult, an alternative was visiting them in institutions – a largely female activity which gradually opened up these forbidding places to public scrutiny.[46] Mrs Fry was the most famous of early prison visitors but through the century increasing numbers of women organised themselves into ladies' committees and associations to carry on the work. Women volunteers also began to penetrate hospitals, asylums, the notorious general mixed workhouses of the poor law authorities, graphically described by the Webbs,[47] and their sick wards, children's homes and schools. Entry required considerable courage and determination. The managers and superintendents of the poor law establishments were often reluctant to expose conditions of life inside the institutions to outside observers, wanting no interference with procedures which were frequently inefficient, often inhumane and sometimes corrupt. It took many years for Louisa Twining to persuade local guardians and the central Poor Law Board that ladies should be permitted to visit paupers in workhouses. She herself had been admitted relatively easily as a visitor in Kensington in 1853 on the strength, she suggests, of her family connections. Before then she had not supposed such a thing to be possible, imagining the workhouse 'as an inaccessible fortress, which could only be entered through great difficulties and dangers'.[48]

The importance of involving women in the planning, organisation and daily routine of institutions for women and young girls, or for children of either sex, is now taken for granted. Even a hundred years ago such charitable work was relatively acceptable for women and offered an opportunity for public service and greater social recognition.[49] But they had to exercise their responsibilities with circumspection. Miss Twining noted critical comment about women in the 1890s, when 900 of them had been elected as poor law guardians to join a service previously run by 22 000 men, and pointed to their vulnerability, 'we must remember that it is just now a fierce light that beats upon women in a public capacity and every act is keenly watched and scrutinized'.[50]

At the same time, while philanthropic work with the poor and the sick may have been thought a suitable female occupation those very activities could lead far beyond the personal care of particular cases that is often seen as both the strength and weakness of voluntary work. The experience of Elizabeth Fry and Josephine Butler, of Mary Carpenter, Florence Nightingale and Octavia Hill in prisons, workhouses, ragged schools, hospitals and the homes of the London poor revealed evils which could not be remedied by individual effort, but required institutional reform and national legislation. For all these women local charitable activity developed into many forms of political agitation; research, writing, public speaking, organising committees and pressure groups, lobbying and petitioning members of parliament. Local problems turned into national and even international concerns, and the women involved in them displayed a toughness, determination and ability in their confrontations and negotiations with public authorities that was far removed from conventional notions of feminine behaviour.

The intrepid women who challenged the local guardians and the prison governors, who steeled themselves to give evidence to parliamentary commissions and committees of enquiry, who rose to their feet to address rowdy public meetings and who delivered papers to the British Association and the National Association for the Promotion of Social Science were *not* extending women's traditional domestic responsibilities into public life. They were crossing the occupational and social barriers to enter the male world of politics and professional activity, and so changing and redefining popular expectations about women's work and role and status.

This rarely represented a deliberate attempt to challenge male authority or to assert equality between the sexes. Feminist preoccupations of this kind were of secondary importance and treated with some disdain by such women as Miss Nightingale and Miss Potter, and it was a cause of anxiety to Mary Carpenter, even when she was nearly fifty, that her public behaviour might appear 'unwomanly'. Her biographer notes that she took no part in the discussions of a conference, in 1851, of workers concerned with the reformatory school movement even though she must have been one of the most experienced and informed people present. 'To have lifted up her voice in an assembly of gentlemen would have been, as she then felt, tantamount to unsexing herself.'[51] Women such as these were, above all, committed to the work they felt themselves called to do. If this required them to act in unusual ways they would brave opposition, often at considerable emotional and physical cost to themselves, not in order to assert women's rights but in order to advance the causes they had at heart.

Thus philanthropy not only led some women outside conventional female roles – Miss Carpenter later overcame her distaste for public speaking. It also made them a powerful force for reform in uncovering evils that could only be tackled effectively by some kind of collective action. Among the more able and dedicated women the initial charitable impulse quickly developed into tireless efforts to alter political and social arrangements to bring about the changes they desired.

There are two kinds of philanthropy. One, in tune with the conventional expectations of the day, was expressed by the many Victorian women who extended help and sympathy to the poor who lived around them and supported and patronised fund-raising events for a multitude of good causes. But the other goes far beyond normal expectations and requires outstanding physical, intellectual and spiritual effort. It is this second kind of activity, exhibited in the lives of the ten women chosen for this study, that we shall examine and try to explain.

2 The Nature of Social Service

We have already noted that social service was only one of a number of possible ways into public life for Victorian ladies. What was its distinguishing character and how easy a path was it?

Social service was partly an exercise in philanthropy directed towards the destitute and other casualties of nineteenth-century society. But it was also a particular expression of the women's movement that developed in different forms in the latter part of the century. Not that the women involved in public social service necessarily supported feminist causes; there was considerable ambivalence, especially towards female suffrage. Their interests tended to be focused on individual action to redress particular evils. They were less concerned with wider arguments about the rights and wrongs of their sex.

But the early social workers and researchers were by their very actions asserting their right, as women, to freedom of choice in their occupation and an independent life devoted to public matters rather than restricted to their own family affairs. Visiting the slums and workhouses and prisons they were responding to needs that they saw as urgent and immediate, but they were also demonstrating their assumption and conviction that women had a right and indeed a duty to take part with men in public life in pursuit of human welfare or social reform. They tended to favour reforms that would bring women more opportunities, such as the legal right of married women to hold property and, if separated from their husbands, to have custody of their children. Higher education for women, too, was enthusiastically supported as enabling those who remained single to lead a more satisfying life but also as a way of improving the quality of marriage, as Josephine Butler insistently argued.

The question of voting rights was of lesser interest to the women chosen for this study. Among them, only Frances Power Cobbe and Annie Besant took an active part in the campaign. Beatrice Potter was a signatory of the Appeal against female suffrage published in *The Nineteenth Century* in 1889[1] though she later made a public recantation. Florence Nightingale, rather dismissive of women and

31

their intellectual and moral frailties, thought they should have the vote but considered other issues more important. Mary Carpenter, initially sceptical, was finally persuaded of the justice of the cause by a personal letter from Mill.[2] None of the others seem to have given the matter much attention, though Octavia Hill remained opposed to votes for women to the end of her life.

A further characteristic of social service in the nineteenth century was its tendency to be linked to strong religious commitment. Most of the women in this study believed that there was some work or service that God was calling them to do. For some, such as Florence Nightingale, it was many years before they were sure about the exact nature of their vocation. But the recognition and acceptance of social obligation was linked to profound religious conviction that gave social service something of the flavour of a moral crusade. It required, first, untiring efforts to discover the will of God and then complete submission to it. Self-sacrifice, humility – to God if not to men – and great determination were the essential foundation for their work.

Nevertheless, in spite of the obstacles, social service offered in some ways, and for some women, a relatively easy step into public life. Delamont and Duffin have used Mary Douglas's notion of dominant and muted social groups to examine the position of women in nineteenth-century England, suggesting that the success of the various women's movements depended on their being able to express their ideas and aspirations in a form acceptable to men – the dominant group.[3] Whether the definition of women's roles prevailing in the nineteenth century can be attributed entirely to male dominance is arguable. Conceptions of feminine duty and responsibility also derived from a Christian tradition stretching back two thousand years, though Christianity itself, of course, is rooted in an ancient patriarchal culture that assumed the submission of children to parents and of women to men. But whatever the explanation of contemporary opinions about the position of women, the more female activities observed the conventions and expectations of the time, the less antagonism they were likely to arouse.

The underlying and pervasive constraint on women entering public life was the conventional division of power and responsibility between the sexes. But not only were women generally confined to family and domestic matters; also attributed to them was a distinctive personality, intellectually limited, physically delicate, but morally and emotionally sensitive and peculiarly fitted to cultivating civilised and affectionate relationships within the family, protected from the tough and competitive male world of business and politics and serious intellectual endeavour. Such a conception is familiar enough in Parsons' writing.[4] It was expressed more than a hundred years ago in Ruskin's more eloquent prose:

> But the woman's power is for rule, not battle – and her intellect is not for invention or creation, but for sweet ordering, arrangement, and decision. She sees the qualities of things, their claims, and their places. Her great function is Praise; she enters into no contest, but infallibly adjudges the crown of contest. By her office, and place, she is protected from all danger and temptation. The man, in his rough work in open world, must encounter all peril and trial; – to him, therefore must be the failure, the offence, the inevitable error: often he must be wounded, or subdued; often misled; and *always* hardened. But he guards the woman from all this; within his house, as ruled by her, unless she herself has sought it, need enter no danger, no temptation, no cause of error or offence. This is the true nature of home – it is a place of Peace; the shelter, not only from all injury, but from all terror, doubt, and division. In so far as it is not this, it is not home.[5]

Thus, another way of considering women's move from family to public life is in terms of the different expectations attaching to different roles. Parsons distinguishes five 'pattern variables' that he uses to analyse social relationships and social actions.[6] Certain motives and certain behaviour are conventionally expected of people in certain relationships to one another, or of actors within a social system. Indeed, a social system can only survive if there is agreement on and approval of the roles appropriate for the people within it. Parsons contrasts affective roles with those that are affectively neutral, self-oriented behaviour with that which is collectivity-oriented, universalism with particularism, achievement with ascription and specificity with diffuseness.

If we apply Parsons' scheme to behaviour inside and outside the family, the distinction between the different roles becomes sharper and the significance of the move from one system to another for Victorian women becomes clearer. For the most part, it involved a shift from one alternative to the other of Parsons' five pairs. Within the family position is ascribed by age and sex, and outside it rests on performance or achievement. Family relationships are particularistic, diffuse and affective. Public roles are universal, specific and affectively neutral. That is, the behaviour of family members to one another is governed by the particular relationship in which they stand as brother or wife or child, rather than by universal rules or moral precepts which might require the honouring of promises or respect for old people, for example. The interest of family members in one another tends to be all embracing, but outside the family relationships are more specific or restricted to particular purposes or particular activities. It is expected, if not always the case, that family members will feel affection for one another, but outside, in employment, or leisure, or philanthropy, there is no such expectation. Within families it is permissable to be self-interested in looking for personal affection or 'gratification'. Public roles require the yielding of personal interest to those of the collectivity.

Social roles outside the family, then, involve a different set of motives, rewards and expectations. Parsons makes this clear, and gives it a sexual dimension, in his essay on the American family, where men are social actors in the harsh world of industry and commerce, and receive only from their families affection that does not depend on achievement, and interest that extends to all aspects of their lives.

In this study of nineteenth-century social service we are concerned with women who adopted public roles, and so encountered the different set of expectations about how they should behave. Insofar as this meant a switching to masculine conduct it aroused considerable public hostility, as we shall see in later chapters. But the change of behaviour in terms of the pattern variables was not always complete. Josephine Butler and Florence Nightingale shifted from a particular to a universal role in their nursing of soldiers and prostitutes. But the range of attention and interest they gave to some of their patients was more akin to the 'diffuse' character of family relationships than to the 'specific' and limited interaction in work and professional exchanges. In other words, the novel roles into which women moved were modified by the behaviour to which they were more accustomed and which might well represent the alternative variable of Parsons' pair.

Parsons makes a similar point when he remarks that when women do take up outside careers they generally occupy positions where they are subordinate to men, and tend to choose work with the sick or with children that reflects traditional female family responsibilities. Women are more usually nurses than doctors and if doctors more likely to be paediatricians than surgeons. Women teachers are concentrated in schools for younger children and very few are found in the universities.

In examining the different ways into public life for Victorian women, social service must be distinguished from social reform. Social service, in its charitable aspects of concern for the poor and the sick, for errant parents and neglected children, called for qualities of gentleness, kindness and devotion which fitted well with the idealised stereotype of the feminine personality and involved no radical re-definition of roles. Nor did it directly threaten male interests. Men's involvement in social service was not so much in home or institutional visiting but more in organisation and administration and the management of financial affairs. The ladies' and gentlemen's committees that grew up in the nineteenth century in support of poor law institutions, prisons, hospitals and schools observed a nice distinction between women's work and the more important duties reserved for men.[7] The Charity Organisation Society, in its attempts to make relief more orderly and efficient, worked through district committees and visitors: the visitors mainly lady volunteers; and a few paid staff, collectors, enquiry agents and secretaries, usually working-class men. As the Society grew, more paid secretaries were appointed and recruited from a higher social class, but women were slow to establish themselves. By 1889 only 2 out of 10 district secretaries were women and by 1897 only 6 out of 14.[8]

Reform movements are by definition a challenge to existing values and institutions and while reformers may be concerned with the poor and the sick they are just as likely to be concerned with other forms of injustice and inequality. In this sense the 'philanthropy' of social service may emerge as 'self-help' in social reform, to use Beveridge's distinction between different forms of voluntary action. Thus in the nineteenth century middle-class ladies campaigned for property rights, or higher education, or the vote for themselves and for other middle-class ladies. Reformers tend to emphasis *rights*, be it for women, for the working class, for slaves or for religious freedom, rather than *duties*. They are more likely to express indignation than humility. In public action they are inspired by opposition to injustice in human arrangements rather than the search to discover and determination to carry out the will of God. The sense of a calling to service to individuals is overshadowed by commitment to a cause.

This distinction between social service and reform is somewhat artificial in that the two activities tend to merge in practice. Many of the nineteenth-century philanthropists were also reformers. But it is useful for purposes of analysis. Reforming zeal in its radical criticism of existing arrangements is always likely to provoke resistance and antagonism. When it involved Victorian ladies and working-class women appearing at public meetings to demand educational or political rights it aroused particular hostility. Such activities were assumed to require qualities of intellect, physical and mental endurance and determination that women either did not or should not possess. Perhaps more important, the universities, the professions and political life were established male domains and women's insistence on entering them was a threat to masculine power and influence and the prevailing notions about the appropriate division of labour between the sexes.

Discreet women among the reformers knew they must proceed with caution. When Elizabeth Garrett was elected to the London School Board in 1870 and, on the strength of enthusiastic support from the voters, remarked that she should like to be chairman, she received a rebuke from Emily Davies, also elected, though with fewer votes:

> I was a little sorry that you should tell people, whether in jest or earnest, that you would very much like a position which to my mind, would be incongruous even to the point of absurdity . . . It is not being a woman (tho' that probably enhances it) but your youth and inexperience that makes it strike me as almost indecorous to think of presiding over men . . . I should be sorry for you to do anything which might give colour to the charge of being 'cheeky', which has been brought against you lately. It is too true that your jokes are many and reckless. They do more harm than you know.[9]

Miss Davies was 40 at the time and Miss Garrett 35. At the first meeting of the board (where Miss Garrett was not elected chairman) the two women were asked to sit apart from the gentlemen. This they successfully resisted but Miss Garrett later remarked that she felt the atmosphere was 'decidedly hostile'.[10]

Nonetheless the difficulties of women taking their seat on school boards or boards of guardians were eased once the novelty wore off by the possibility of seeing this work with young children and the destitute as a natural expression of traditional feminine responsibilities, and indeed as positively requiring specifically female qualities as Miss Twining repeatedly argued.[11] By 1899 the Appeal against women's suffrage was pointing to fitting and suitable work for women on school boards and boards of guardians and in local government in contrast to the inappropriate agitation for votes. The suffrage movement, rejecting conventional feminine roles and trenching on an ancient male preserve, was another matter. In 1866 Emily Davies agreed to take part in the work of the London Suffrage Committee but asked that her name be kept out of sight so that her association with the agitation for the franchise should not damage her work in education.

We have noted that the distinction between social service and social reform is blurred. Within social service some women leaned more to social work, some to research, some to reform. But the nearer they moved to political activity and away from charitable work, the more opposition they encountered. Among the group discussed in this study, Octavia Hill is the purest example of the social worker, though she was also a writer, a contributor to the meetings of the Social Science Association, a witness to parliamentary committees and finally a member of the Royal Commission on the Poor Laws of 1905. Beatrice Webb comes nearest to the researcher, with apparently little inclination to social work but with some flair for public speaking and tireless in cultivating and lobbying political acquaintance. Josephine Butler represents the reformer, organising meetings, forming associations, writing pamphlets, famous as the leader of the agitation for the repeal of the Contagious Diseases Acts but also prominent in the campaign for women's education.

It was not only the political character of Mrs Butler's activities, of course, that aroused controversy. Her work on behalf of prostitutes was also an affront to Victorian sensibilities in its outspoken concern for women whose circumstances were generally regarded as too depraved to permit discussion in respectable society. Mrs Butler was championing women whose way of life defied and threatened the idealised feminine virtues of modesty, chastity and devotion to family relationships.

In general, then, the difficulties encountered by the social service pioneers were greater the more they challenged existing institutions and existing structures of power and authority. The ladies who fought and manoeuvred their way into prisons and hospitals and poor law institutions were resisted, perhaps partly because they were women, but also because they were threatening established practices. Sometimes they became involved in sectarian disputes as when the Liverpool Vestry forbade ladies to visit Brownlow Hill Workhouse because the chaplain objected to their reading the Bible to inmates.[12] Florence Nightingale ran into considerable trouble and opposition from Protestants because she was ready to work with Catholic nurses in the Crimea, and incurred the resentment of Catholics who were unwilling to accept her secular authority.[13]

At another level Miss Nightingale's Crimean reforms brought her into direct conflict with the soldiers and the War Office and the doctors. The administrative confusion, the dilatory bureaucratic practices of government servants and the hostility and rejection of many of the military and medical men were huge obstacles. She survived because of her extraordinary character; because she was able to use her personal income to buy the hospital supplies she needed; and because her social connections with leading members of the government, as well as her official appointment to organise nursing services, enforced some measure of co-operation from the hospital and army authorities at Scutari.

The circumstances of Miss Nightingale's success nicely illustrate the contrast between the social service of the nineteenth century and the professional social work of the twentieth.[14] The Victorian women received no payment for what they did and neither did they receive any formal training. There was no body of relevant, organised knowledge available to them nor any methods or principles of work established and tested by experience, to guide them. Instead they had the broad classical education that some wealthy, cultivated and liberal nineteenth-century families bestowed on their daughters as well as on their sons. Their work with the sick and the poor was inspired and guided by their reading of moral philosophy and the lives of the Saints, by the reports of government inspectors and commissions of enquiry, and by their individual hard-won understanding of the will of God.

This is one aspect of Victorian philanthropy. It could also be a refuge from a domestic life that some women found tedious, aimless and frivolous. But whatever the motive it depended on social position, on family wealth that made unpaid work possible, and on the social connections that helped to make it effective. It was status ascribed by birth that opened up opportunites for public work, rather than status achieved by the demonstration of competence that is required for modern professional practice.

Nevertheless, an assured social position lent the social service pioneers a confidence that comes less readily from professional training. A professional person is accorded special authority in recognition of specialised knowledge and experience, but narrowly restricted to professional matters. The nineteenth-century social workers assumed a measure of moral authority that might encompass any aspect of other people's lives. In this they were, perhaps, nearer to the priestly than the secular, and it is significant that several of the women in this study spoke of being called to their work by God. Present-day social work is less firmly based on faith, and the place of moral judgements in professional activity has become an awkward question.

The notion of 'service', however, is common to Victorian voluntary workers and present day professionals alike. Professional people are assumed to be disinterested, engaged not so much in the pursuit of profit but in offering a service to patients or clients.[15] As we have suggested, and shall show in later chapters, a similar sense of social obligation was associated with much of the charitable effort of the nineteenth century.

If the pioneers of social service had to rely on their social position and their own abilities and determination, some of them, at any rate, were keenly aware of the need for more formal preparation. Octavia Hill took great trouble over the instruction and training of her fellow workers and volunteer visitors and attached great importance to establishing principles to govern the giving of relief and to devising appropriate methods of work. On the whole, however, she assumed that right methods of work were essentially a matter of extending to the poor the sensitivity, courtesy and consideration that cultivated and educated Christians would normally display to one another. Again, one of Florence Nightingale's major interests was organising training for nurses. This inevitably meant the acquisition of some technical skill but for Miss Nightingale faith as well as natural interest was necessary to sustain professional activity:

the *natural motive* is the love of nursing the sick, which may entirely conquer . . . a physical loathing and fainting at the sight of operations . . . The *professional motive* is the desire and perpetual effort to do the thing as well as it can be done, which exists just as much in the Nurse, as in the Astronomer in search of a new star . . . I have seen this professional ambition in the nurse who could hardly read or write . . . But I do entirely and constantly believe that the *religious motive* is essential for the higher kind of nurse. There are such disappointments, such sickenings of the

heart, that they can only be borne by the feeling that one is called
to the work by God, that it is a part of His work.[16]

With the exception of Mrs Besant and Miss Cobbe all the women
in this study seemed to draw both strength and consolation from
their religious beliefs. Furthermore, if they lacked some of the
attributes of the professional as they are now understood, all possessed
to the fullest extent the professional motive as Miss Nightingale
defined it. It is the development of 'the desire and perpetual effort
to do the thing as well as it can be done' that we shall now try to
explain.

Part II
The Genesis of Social Service

The ten women who are the focus of this study went beyond the conventionally acceptable spare-time philanthropy of Victorian ladies. They committed their lives to social service. Their public work was an alternative to a private domestic existence bounded by family duties and the claims of social life. It meant rejecting the prevailing assumptions about feminine responsibilities and behaviour and braving varying degrees of family and public opposition. It meant, for many, renouncing considerable luxury and leisure for a life of intellectual effort or political campaigning or charitable labour among the most desolate people. Even the ladies who were primarily social workers rather than reformers, and who worked amongst the relatively 'respectable' poor, thus offending less against the social prejudices of the day, faced formidable difficulties.

> B court is something beyond expression awful . . . The scenes are perfectly indescribable. I am there almost daily now and it makes me very sick . . . I have to go at night to collect the rents; it is so awful groping about the pitch-dark stairs, surrounded by such people, with only thin walls to hide their hideous deeds.[1]

This was Octavia Hill describing her housing work in one of the worst of her London tenements where she used the opportunity afforded by collecting rents to try to encourage the tenants in a more orderly way of life. Twenty years later Beatrice Potter worked for a time as a rent collector in the same area and her observations echo Miss Hill's words, though her response to the conditions she found was very different:

> This East End life, with its dirt, drunkenness and immorality, absence of co-operation or common interests, saddens me . . . And practical work does not satisfy me; it seems like walking on shifting sand . . . Where is the wish for better things in these myriads of beings . . . even their careless, sensual laugh, coarse jokes, and unloving words depress one . . . It is not so much the

actual life . . . These buildings, too, are to my mind an utter failure . . . the meeting places . . . are the water closets! . . . they are the only lighted places in the building. . . . The lady collectors are an altogether superficial thing. Undoubtedly their gentleness and kindness bring light into many homes; but what are they in the face of this collective brutality . . ?[2]

Why then did they do it? What forces impelled Victorian ladies into social service and supported them in their efforts? We have already suggested a number of factors that might be important – social class, family background, the quality of family relationships, conceptions of their own position as women and of the rights and wrongs of women in general, religious experience, and, finally, the views they entertained about the nature of social problems and how they might be resolved.

In the following pages we try to assess the significance of such circumstances and attitudes by examining the biographies of ten famous women, renowned for their activities in public welfare. From this there should emerge a clearer picture of the experiences that influenced their work.

3 Family and Social Background

Most of the ten women grew up in families that were similar in several important ways. Apart from Annie Besant and Octavia Hill, whose father and step-father died in their childhood, all were relatively prosperous. All of them had a tradition of intellectual, moral and 'progressive' political interests which sustained informed discussion of the social and scientific issues of the time. Most contained between five and twelve children in the immediate family circle as well as numerous aunts, uncles and cousins all linked together by more or less close ties of affection and duty. All were acquainted, often through their membership of a numerous and cultivated family group, with men and women prominent in political, literary and religious affairs.

In short, childhood and early adult years were passed in circumstances of material ease and intellectual excitement informed by high moral purpose. Ample resources meant large houses, servants, frequent entertaining of family, friends and professional acquaintances, sometimes a London season and months of travel in Britain or Europe. Familiarity with the language and culture of other countries and friendships formed with people of other nationalities when they were young made it easy for Mrs Butler, Miss Nightingale and Miss Carpenter to extend their interests in British institutions to Europe, America and India as they grew older.

The Gurney, Nightingale and Potter families were especially wealthy and lived in considerable luxury, possessing at least one substantial country house and also apartments in London or relations with whom they could stay there when they wished to enter London society. John Gurney was a rich merchant, and a Quaker, as his family had been for over a hundred years. At first with houses in Norwich and a nearby village, he established his family at Earlham Hall in 1786, a large, old, irregular house in the centre of a well-wooded park.[1] There were twelve children, one of whom died in infancy. Mrs Gurney, cultivated, beautiful and 'disposed to scientific and intellectual pursuits', herself died when Elizabeth was 12. Until then she presided over the education of her daughters, her wishes reflecting her own accomplishments.

As piety is undoubtedly the shortest and securest way to all moral rectitude; young women should be virtuous and good, on the broad, firm basis of Christianity . . . it is necessary and very agreeable to be well informed of our own language and of the Latin, as being the most permanent; and the French as being the most in general request. The simple beauties of mathematics appear to be so excellent an exercise to the understanding, that they ought on no account to be omitted, and are perhaps scarcely less essential, than a competent knowledge of ancient and modern history, geography, and chronology. To which may be added a knowledge of the most approved branches of natural history and a capacity for drawing from nature, in order to promote that knowledge, and facilitate the pursuit of it. As a great portion of a woman's life ought to be passed, in at least regulating the subordinate affairs of the family; she should work plain work neatly herself, understand the cutting out of linen; also she should not be ignorant of the common proprieties of a table, or deficient in the economy of any of the most minute affairs of the family; it should be here observed, that gentleness of manner is indispensably necessary in women; to say nothing of that polished behaviour that adds a charm to every qualification; to both of which, it appears pretty certain, that children may be led without vanity or affection, by amiable and judicious instruction.[2]

Despite, or perhaps because of, this solicitude Elizabeth Gurney found childhood a painful time. Timidity, fear of the dark and of bathing, was so strong, she later observed, as 'greatly to mar the natural pleasures of childhood'.[3] As a young girl, she recalls, she was reserved and little understood except by her mother and one or two others. With little formal education, she was taught by her mother, to whom she was devoted, yet she still disliked her lessons. Physically delicate, subject to nervous attacks, she had a poor opinion of her own abilities. As she grew older her troubles and self-criticism centred on an anxious search for a right way of life, in face of her inclinations to be idle, wordly and vain. And above all, as we shall see, she sought for faith to protect her from the dissipation and unhappiness of the world and strengthen her to serve God as she should.

After her mother's death Elizabeth Gurney applied herself to her own education, but her intellectual interests soon turned to religion and particularly the question of whether or not she should join the plain Quakers. Social exchanges were mostly limited to the large family of brothers and sisters within, and aunts, uncles and cousins beyond, the household. Local society offered some excitements in the form of Prince William Frederick, later Duke of Gloucester, then quartered at Norwich. There were musical entertainments and military bands. Miss Gurney, at 17, took great pleasure in such events but the pleasure was mingled with remorse.

> I feel by experience, how much entering into the world hurts me; wordly company, I think, materially injures, it excites a false stimulus, such as a love of pomp, pride, vanity, jealousy, and ambition; it leads to think about dress, and such trifles, and when out of it, we fly to novels and scandal, or something of that kind, for entertainment. I have lately been given up a good deal to wordly passions; by what I have felt I can easily imagine how soon I should be quite led away. I met the Prince, it showed me the folly of the world; my mind feels very flat after this storm of pleasure.[4]

Several months later Mr Gurney took his daughter to London and left her there for some weeks with an 'old and faithful attendant' and 'under the protection and kind care of a relation' to become acquainted with the 'amusements and fascinations that the world offers to its votaries', as her own daughters put it. Miss Gurney, it seems, was interested and amused by this experience, but neither satisfied nor approving. Her distaste for society strengthened and was confirmed by later travels in other parts of England making and renewing the acquaintance of Quaker friends and relations. She started to abandon brightly coloured clothes and to adopt the sombre dress of the plain Quakers, the stricter group within the Society of Friends who observed careful rules of modesty and simplicity in dress, speech and behaviour. Her interest in local charitable work grew and by the time she was 18 she had a bible class of 70 children. At 20 she married Joseph Fry, from a strict Quaker family of rich merchants. Her daughters remarked of the marriage that her habits and education had rendered affluence almost essential to her comfort and that the prospect of living among Friends 'offered great and strong inducements'.

The affluence continued throughout Mrs Fry's life, though a banking failure necessitated the removal of the family from Plashet, the large country house passed down from her father-in-law, to a smaller establishment. The reversal of the family fortunes caused much distress to Mrs Fry, though the new dwelling seems to have continued to offer her considerable luxury.

The Nightingale family was perhaps the most cosmopolitan of the ten, moving freely in political and literary circles both in Britain and Europe. Mrs Nightingale, born Fanny Smith, was one of ten children of William Smith, a rich Unitarian, Whig MP for 46 years, fighter of lost causes for the weak and oppressed, friend of Wilberforce and Reynolds, collector of pictures. Mr Nightingale was himself rich and cultivated, a Unitarian, Whig and friend of Palmerston. After the marriage he and his wife spent three years travelling abroad, returning to England with two daughters when Florence, named after the town where she was born, was one year old.

Mr Nightingale had himself designed a house, Lea Hurst, in Derbyshire to which the family returned, but after a few years this was abandoned as a permanent dwelling for the large Embley Park in Hampshire. The family continued to spend the summer at Lea Hurst, considered by Miss Nightingale to be a small house as it had only fifteen bedrooms, visiting London twice a year during the spring and autumn seasons.[5]

The education of the two girls was largely undertaken by their father. There was a governess for music and drawing but Mr Nightingale himself taught his children Greek, Latin, German, French, Italian, history and philosophy. The elder sister, Parthenope, grew bored and rebelled; the younger was more able and interested. When she was nearly 20, discontented with social life, searching for some vocation, anxious to improve herself and working at mathematics with her Aunt Mai, her efforts to persuade her parents to agree to a mathematics tutor failed. So she continued to work alone at mathematics, philosophy and Greek.

In 1837 Mr Nightingale took his family abroad for some months while the house at Embley was enlarged to permit the entertaining necessary when his two daughters should 'come out'. As a result Embley was big enough to receive, in Miss Nightingale's words, 'five able-bodied females with their husbands and belongings'.[6] This first European tour introduced Miss Nightingale to Italian and French music, opera, balls and society but also to refugees working for Italian independence in Geneva, and to Mary Clarke and Madame Récamier in Paris and the circle of famous literary and intellectual men who surrounded them. A visit to Rome some ten years later with family friends after a period of ill-health led to a meeting and friendship with Sidney Herbert, later Secretary of State for War and

Miss Nightingale's ally in her expedition to the Crimea. It also enabled her to enter a convent for several days of meditation, an experience that strengthened her resolve to find her vocation in service to God, a determination taking clearer form the following year after more illness during further travels with friends in the East: 'Oh God, thou puttest into my heart this great desire to devote myself to the sick and the sorrowful. I offer it to thee. Do with it what is for thy service.'[7]

The Nightingale family were unusually wealthy but opportunities to develop social and intellectual acquaintances and interests were readily available for the other women. Mr Potter was a successful capitalist dealing in timber and railways and financial speculation. He is described by his daughter as a devout man who never doubted the divine government of the world, a lover of literature and poetry, a radical in politics, but thinking and acting in personal terms and without any clear vision of the public good. '"A friend", he would assert, "is a person who would back you up when you were in the wrong, who would give your son a place which he could not have won on his own merits".'[8]

The household was a prosperous one with houses in Westmorland, Gloucestershire and the Wye valley. Servants were taken for granted. When Martha Mills, Mrs Potter's 'lifelong companion and attendant', married, her husband became the family butler. Beatrice Potter claims that she and her sisters, nine daughters in all, were not conscious of superior riches; they were brought up to 'feel poor'. But what she, at any rate, did recognise was superior power. 'As life unfolded itself I became aware that I belonged to a class of persons who habitually gave orders, but who seldom, if ever, executed the orders of other people.'[9]

Family social life in the country Mrs Webb recalls as superficial and transitory: 'Our social relationships had no roots in neighbourhood, in vocation, in creed or for that matter in race; they likened a series of moving pictures – surface impressions without depth – restlessly stimulating in their glittering variety.'[10] But this was not the whole story. Although 'circumstances of life' did not permit a university education, Beatrice Potter and her sisters enjoyed one of the privileges of such an experience in associating on terms of conversational equality with gifted persons – 'not only with men of affairs in business and politics, but also with men of science and with the leaders of thought in philosophy and religion'.[11]

The most important intellectual influence on Beatrice Potter was

Herbert Spencer, an intimate family friend until his death. He was:

> [the] . . . only person who persistently cared for me – or rather
> who singled me out as one who was worthy of being trained and
> looked after . . . The amazing loyalty to a disinterested aim, the
> patience, endurance, the noble faith manifested in his daily life,
> sustained me through those dark years of discouragement, before
> success made continuous effort easy, and loving comradeship made
> it delightful.[12]

Later, Miss Potter's 'domineering curiosity into the nature of things'
was nourished by her own efforts to educate herself supplemented by
friendly intercourse with people of similar interests 'at reciprocal
dinner parties in London . . . and weekend parties in our respective
country houses'.[13] Politicians, philanthropists and social investigators
were numbered among her own family circle. Through her sister
Kate, who worked with Octavia Hill, she knew Miss Hill and the
Barnetts, and among her brothers-in-law were Henry Hobhouse,
C. A. Cripps and Leonard Courtney, Financial Secretary to the
Treasury under Gladstone. A cousin was married to Charles Booth.
Her own visits to more distant relations in Bacup in 1883, 1886 and
1889 confirmed her decision to devote herself to social research,
motivated, she insists, not so much by charity as by the desire to
understand how society worked.

> Unlike my sister Kate . . . I was not led into the homes of the
> poor by the spirit of charity . . . What impelled me to concentrate
> on the condition of the people . . . was the state of mind in the
> most vital centres of business enterprises, of political agitation and
> academic reasoning . . . Was the poverty of the many a necessary
> condition of the wealth of the nation and its progress in civilization?
> . . . was it desirable, was it even safe, to entrust them [the people]
> with the weapon of trade unionism, and, through the ballot-box,
> with making and controlling the Government of Great Britain with
> its enormous wealth and its far flung dominions?[14]

The Gurneys, Nightingales and Potters were the richer of the ten
families, cultivated, urbane, connected through kinship and friendship
with some of the leading politicians, writers and intellectuals of
their time. But although the other women had rather less affluent
backgrounds, most of them lived extremely comfortably, within

families with strong traditions of charitable and professional work
and active interest in politics and social reform. These were perhaps
the less 'wordly' households. With little pressure to enter society,
and probably without the resources to do so, the conflict between
frivolous and more serious pursuits seems to have been less marked
than with the three richer women. The same anxious searching for a
purpose to justify their lives is evident but the search was attended
with less anguish. On the contrary, family culture and family religion
tended to have an evangelical flavour and was congenial to the quest
for a vocation or calling that would satisfy the demands of duty both
to God and to men.

A strong sense of social obligation linked to religious commitment
was marked in Florence Nightingale and Beatrice Potter and Elizabeth
Gurney when they grew older, but it was something they had to
struggle to achieve. By contrast it pervaded the experiences of
Josephine Butler, Louisa Twining, Mary Carpenter, Frances Power
Cobbe, Octavia Hill, Annie Besant and Agnes Jones from earliest
childhood. Also, in these less wealthy households there existed a
readiness to treat women with a measure of equality unusual for the
time, and very high value was attached to education for women as
well as for men. For young girls this often took place at home under
the more or less close supervision of one or other parent, sometimes
with help from a governess as they grew older, occasionally inter-
rupted by attendance at a school. Later it was pursued with fierce
intensity by the ladies themselves in their search for a creed to live
by.

All the women wrote copiously, about themselves, about social
questions and also on many other subjects. In the nineteenth century
women spent much time writing journals and letters. But Mrs Butler,
Mrs Besant and Miss Cobbe as well as Mrs Webb and Miss Nightingale
also wrote on less personal matters, publishing works on religion,
art, philosophy, history and politics and other people's lives. Octavia
Hill helped with the illustrations for Ruskin's *Modern Painters*, Mary
Carpenter and Frances Power Cobbe both wrote poetry.

Josephine Butler grew up in a religious, liberal household which
frequently had visitors from all over the world. Her father, John
Grey, cousin of the prime minister, was himself active in the cause
of parliamentary reform, a free-trader and a committee member of
the anti-slavery society of Northumberland. He was a practised public
speaker, denounced by his opponents, according to his daughter, as
a political agitator haranguing mobs during the unrest following the

Napoleonic Wars. In 1831 his oratorical powers were turned against the House of Lords following the rejection of the Reform Bill in which all but two of the bishops concurred.

> As a friend of the Church of England I greatly lament this circumstance . . . The question so often asked, 'What will the Lords do?' has been woefully answered, and the question now is, 'What will the people do?' . . . I need not remind you that there is only one justifiable course to pursue. I need not caution you against any violation of the public peace, or opposition to the laws on which the welfare of society depends; but I will join you in seeking the accomplishment of this great object by every constitutional means. You may be assured that if the voice of the people of England shall be firmly but temperately and simultaneously raised in favour of Reform, it will speak throughout the land in a language which senators must heed and which legislators must obey . . . These, my friends, are the means by which we must seek to save our country from a fatal convulsion, and by which the very Peers themselves will be saved from the effect of their own infatuation.[15]

At this time Mr Grey was acting as campaign organiser for the prime minister's son, the member for Northumberland, and he was in close touch with Earl Grey himself who wrote for his advice about the likely public reaction to concessions to the Tories over Reform, 'provided the great principles of the Bill are maintained'.[16]

Mr Grey's reforming zeal extended beyond the parliamentary bill. In 1831 he had given evidence to the House of Lords Committee on the Poor Laws about the state of the poor in the north of England, and the following year he was expressing dissatisfaction with the slow progress of the anti-slavery movement. In her biography of her father, Mrs Butler recalls his conversation on that question with his children:

> And he very distinctly told us that a regard for the true welfare of our fellow-creatures, and a ready spirit of self-sacrifice towards that end, ought to be an international principle, as well as a guide for men of the same race in their conduct to each other, and that in this lay the best hope of all true progress.[17]

Political affairs took second place to his professional life, however, when John Grey was appointed in 1833 to take charge of the

Greenwich Hospital estates in Northumberland, a condition of the office being that he take no active part in politics. He held the position for 30 years, when he was succeeded by his son, winning the acclaim of the *Economist* for his work for British agriculture:

> That property has become known far and wide as a model of estate management, and a powerful stimulant to improvement, not only in that county but in other places also.

And again:

> Mr Grey is one of the leaders of . . . the economical school of landed proprietors, as distinguished from the semi-feudal school of landlords . . . His speeches and papers indicate the most advanced and sound principles in reference to the economical management of land.[18]

When Mr Grey retired from the Greenwich estates he occupied some of his leisure time by delivering lectures on poetry, startling his audiences, when nearly 80, by repeating long passages from the classics from memory. His reputation by the time he died extended far beyond professional expertise to that of a wise and benevolent man who exercised his considerable social influence for the public good.

> . . . a leading man in English agriculture, a leading exemplar of the duties of land owning, a leading teacher . . . He was the personal friend and adviser of . . . the population of a province . . . His wise advice will never be forgotten . . . Every class has been his debtor . . . The list merely of material results is but a scanty picture of it [his usefulness] . . . But it is the social influence of a good and wise and powerful man by which he is most effective, and we cannot doubt that this has been especially true of him . . . So that, though dead, his voice will yet be heard.[19]

Throughout her childhood, then, Josephine Grey was accustomed to discussion of political, social and intellectual matters. One of nine children, she and the other girls were largely educated by their parents. She became a talented pianist, taking part with her sisters in the events and entertainments of Northumbrian society. After she married and moved to Oxford she maintained her catholic interests, assisting her husband in all his projects. The Butlers established a house in St Giles for young men wishing to study in Oxford but not belonging to a college. Mr Butler was curate of St Giles church and a university examiner. Interested in university reform, he was associated with the movement to establish science in Oxford. He lectured on geography and also on art. With the help of his wife he catalogued the Taylor gallery's collection of Raphael and Michelangelo drawings and made a collection of Chaucer's poems from early manuscripts.[20] In later life, campaigning on behalf of prostitutes and women's higher education, Mrs Butler wrote on a variety of social issues, but she also published lives of her father and her husband, a biography of Catherine of Siena that won praise from Gladstone, and a history of the Salvation Army in Switzerland.[21]

The trouble-free Northumbrian upbringing, with earnest debate and argument on social and moral questions taken for granted, with a father who had liberal views about women's rights and women's education and an aunt, Margaretta Grey, who was a strong protagonist of the need for women of the upper classes to have the chance of useful occupation, gave Josephine Grey a view of the world that suffered a disagreeable shock when she moved, after her marriage, to Oxford. The shock, however, did not destroy her self-confidence and she continued to consider Northumberland's liberal society as infinitely superior to that of the ancient university town. She referred to the 'shadowside' of the pleasant life in Oxford as the celibate, male society with little or no leaven of family life. In male gatherings in her own drawing room Mrs Butler sat silent, the only woman, convinced of the truth of her own opinions but without the dialectics, as she claimed, to defend them. She noted the timidity of social intercourse: 'If on a splendid summer morning one remarked, "it is a fine day", the man addressed would hesitate to endorse the fact . . . simply from habit of holding everything in suspense; the unhappy philosopher sometimes not being sure that he himself existed.'[22]

She was offended by what she saw as unwillingness to take religion seriously and the prevailing scepticism that sometimes degenerated into cynicism among men whom she had supposed to be authorities on spiritual and moral matters. Especially objectionable to Mrs Butler were the conventional male judgements about women and sexual morality. She refers to the 'fatally false' assumptions evident in discussion of Mrs Gaskell's *Ruth*, that a moral lapse in a woman was immensely worse than in a man. She spoke to one of the 'wisest men – so esteemed – in the university' about a young girl 'bitterly wronged' in an attempt to find ways of bringing the man responsible to a sense of his wrong-doing, and was rebuffed.[23] She observed the indifference to the fate of a circus girl who attempted to escape and was re-taken – 'a world of sorrow, grief, injustices and crimes which must not be spoken of'.[24]

Louisa Twining was born eight years before Josephine Grey into a similarly prosperous, cultivated, religious and high-minded family.[25] She was the youngest of eight children. Her father, a businessman whose name survives as a familiar household word, was also a musician, a classical scholar and eventually a Fellow of the Royal Society. Mrs Twining, daughter of a clergyman, was an industrious woman who spent her time reading, making children's clothes, netting lace and drawing. The elder girls were taught by their mother and they in turn taught the younger ones. Later, they attended lectures at the Royal Institution. There were masters for different subjects, drawing lessons with the Nasmyth family and later Samuel Palmer, but no school and no governess.

The household contained five servants and a 'dear old nurse, who was one of the blessings of our lives'. The children, nevertheless, had plain clothes and plain food and, for the first 18 years of Louisa's life, holidays only in England. Her parents, however, encouraged visits to the theatre and to concerts, and musical parties and distinguished house guests were frequent events in the family. In the early 1850s Miss Twining travelled abroad, spending some time in Paris in the Louvre and the Bibliothèque Nationale, painting and collecting material for books. In 1852 she published a volume entitled *Symbols and Emblems of Early and Mediaeval Christian Art*. At this time Miss Twining was attending meetings of the British Association and of the Social Science Association, and the public lectures and sermons of Maurice and Kingsley, Wilberforce and Manning. By the middle of the 1850s her interests and activities in workhouses were established.

There was no very strong tradition of political activity nor of social reform within the Twining family; rather of intellectual and cultural interests, combined with piety and sustained by money from trade. Louisa Twining remembers her mother as superintending the Maternity Charity, one of two local charities (the other being charity schools) in the parish where the family lived. So Mrs Twining observed the conventional philanthropic habits of middle-class women of her time. Her daughter's interest in and visits to the local poor date from 1847 when she was already nearly 30 and started, Louisa

Twining herself suggests, 'perhaps owing to heavy losses and trials in our family circle'.[26] The nature of the family troubles is not, however, disclosed.

As she became more concerned with conditions in workhouses and the administration of the poor law, Miss Twining's reforming efforts brought her into touch with several of the other ladies in this study. In 1857 she visited Mary Carpenter: 'Her appearance was somewhat singular, with plain, old fashioned dress, and small grey curls on her forehead; her eyes were remarkable for expression and power, and her voice low and gentle.'[27]

Miss Carpenter was 50 at the time and already well known for her work with children from what she herself termed the 'perishing and dangerous classes'. She is the only one of the ten ladies whose father was a minister. But Dr Carpenter, a Unitarian, was also a lecturer and teacher, founder member of the local literary and philosophical institution in Bristol where the family moved in 1817. Mrs Carpenter was a devout woman, also from a non-conformist background, and joined her husband in teaching the schoolboys whom they received into the family: 'his house was long a centre of intelligent culture, which had a most quickening effect upon its inmates, the benefits of which Mary was the most fitted alike by position and powers to receive.'[28]

The religious tone of the household seems to have had a more sectarian flavour than that of the relatively free-thinking Nightingale or Grey families and the effects on the young Mary are described by James Martineau who, as well as his famous sister, went to Dr Carpenter as a pupil.

And I well remember the kind of respectful wonder with which . . . I was inspired towards the sedate little girl of twelve, who looked at you so steadily and always spoke like a book; so that, in talking to her, what you meant for sense seemed to turn into nonsense on the way . . . A certain want of suppleness and natural grace interfered with her proficiency in the usual feminine accomplishment with the needle, at the piano and in the dance. . . . The early maturity . . . was strongly marked in her countenance . . . by a certain fixity of thoughtful attention . . . There were traces upon that grave young face of an inward conflict.[29]

To his daughter, Mr Martineau continues, Dr Carpenter was prophet as well as parent and she reflected his 'absorbing veneration for the person of Christ as supernatural'.

Mary Carpenter was the eldest of six children, three girls and three boys. Taught by her father and mother, her education was unusual for girls at the time, including Latin and Greek, mathematics, physical sciences and natural history, Homer and Socrates, Shakespeare and Scott. She grew up in an atmosphere of scientific and political enquiry and debate, attending lectures at the local philosophical institution, herself a writer of verse, a painter, a critic of art, a teacher in the Sunday school attached to her father's church. In 1836 the British Association met in Bristol and though women were still excluded from the proceedings, the men adjourned to carry on their discussions in Dr Carpenter's house.

Earlier, in 1829, ill-health had obliged Dr Carpenter to give up his school and Mary and her sister Anna started a school for girls under the superintendence of Mrs Carpenter to supplement the family income. These appear to have been unhappy years. Letters and diaries reveal Miss Carpenter as self-reproachful and self-critical over her desire for admiration, her irritability and her vanity. They also express a keen sense of her own unworthiness and inefficiency. During this time, however, she began visiting the homes of Sunday school children and developed an increasing desire to work with the poor. In 1833 Dr Joseph Tuckerman and the Rajah Rammohun Roy had stayed in the household, two men whose work among the poor in America and India had a great influence on Miss Carpenter which was reflected in her later concerns with destitute children and with the 'regeneration' of India. In 1846 after she opened her first ragged school in Bristol she wrote in her diary, 'The desire of my heart for these twelve years – since I knew our beloved Dr Tuckerman – has been brought near its accomplishment; this has given me unspeakable joy . . .'.[30]

It is this part of her work for which she is particularly remembered and for Miss Carpenter herself it assumed an importance comparable with the anti-slavery movement, as she wrote to a friend in 1849.

My mind is now almost as much engrossed by our Ragged School as yours is by the abolition question. Indeed they are very kindred subjects . . . We are trying to free that divine nature from the still more than heathenish darkness in which it is growing to become a fiend, a worse than American slave. I feel this work inexpressibly glorious, nor have I ever felt the inextinguishable greatness of the human soul so much as I have at seeing it rise superior to such very degrading circumstances as it does in many of these children.[31]

Her interest in Indian affairs was slower to develop, but just before her first visit to that country in 1866, when she was already nearly 60, she recalled the early inspiration.

A grand and new life appears opening upon me. Heavenly Father . . . I believe that thou hast destined for me the unspeakable privilege before leaving this world, of going to our distant India and there working with the spirit of my beloved Father and the noble Rajah for the elevation of women.[32]

On the death of her mother in 1856 Miss Carpenter moved out of the family home to a house of her own near Red Lodge, a school for girls that she had opened a couple of years earlier. Shortly afterwards she was joined by Frances Power Cobbe.

Miss Cobbe went to Mary Carpenter to help in the ragged schools but also, after rejecting the evangelical Christianity in which she had been brought up, in hope of religious sympathy from a devout but unorthodox woman. She was a little taken aback by what she found. Mary Carpenter, she remarks, was a stoic, both by temperament and principle, quite indifferent to the comforts of life. Her prevailing characteristic 'was a high and strong Resolution, which made her whole path much like that of a plough in a well-drawn furrow, which . . . gently pushes aside . . . all intervening people and things'.[33] But her integrity was beyond question. Entirely single minded, her interest was 'in the children themselves in their very souls; and not (as such philanthropy too often becomes) an interest in *her Institution*'.[34] Miss Cobbe also comments on the way in which Miss Carpenter's immediate social work activities developed a strong reformist character as so frequently happened with the other ladies in this study. 'But Mary Carpenter was not only the Guardian and teacher of the poor young waifs and strays of Bristol when she had caught them in her charity-traps. She was also their unwearied advocate with one Government after another.'[35]

After twelve months Miss Cobbe left Red House to live independently, continuing to work in the ragged schools but developing a new interest in workhouse visiting, due partly to Miss Carpenter's influence. Relations between the two women remained 'cordial and pleasant'. Twenty years later they appeared on the same platform supporting women's suffrage.

Frances Power Cobbe was the youngest of five children and the only daughter in an Anglo-Irish landowning family. In her autobiography she paints an almost idyllic picture of her early life. Her ancestors were 'honourable specimens of country squires'. She herself, she says, enjoyed through life the advantage of being well-born in the true sense; her parents were good and wise, honourable and honoured, sound in body and mind. Mere existence was for her a positive pleasure; with cheerful spirits, untroubled by too much or too little money, as she puts it, life was pleasant and interesting even without marriage. This ebullience of Miss Cobbe, looking back on her life when she was over 70, is the more remarkable in view of the considerable vicissitudes of her childhood and youth.

The Cobbe family was wealthy and evangelical, with five arch-bishops among their near kin. Mr Cobbe was a careful and benevolent landlord who sold his pictures – a Poussin and Hobemmas – to improve his labourers' cottages at Newbridge, his Irish estate. Home life was happy. The four elder boys, though away at school, treated their sister kindly. She was devoted to her cultivated and beautiful mother who taught her until she was 7 years old. And there were large family gatherings at Christmas and in the summer.

Nevertheless for much of the time Frances was a lonely child. Her mother was lame and an invalid, her nurse very old. When she was 7 a nursery governess joined the household and at 14 she went to a fashionable girl's school at Brighton. Miss Cobbe described the education she received there as appalling, not concerned with things good, useful or delightful in themselves but only with 'that which would make us admired in society'. 'Everything was taught us', she adds, 'in the inverse ratio of its true importance. At the bottom of the scale were Morals and Religion, and at the top were Music and Dancing'.[36] She was not allowed to learn Latin and she was made to learn music for which she had no talent. In other words she fell victim to the conventional notions of the day about the duties and responsibilities of women:

> it was the universal opinion, that no gentlewoman could possibly earn money without derogating altogether from her rank (unless, indeed, by card-playing as my Grandmother did regularly!); and that housekeeping and needlework . . . were her only fitting pursuits. The one natural ambition of her life was supposed to be

a 'suitable' marriage; the phrase always referring to *settlements*, rather than *sentiments*. Study of any serious sort was disapproved, and 'accomplishments' only were cultivated.[37]

The constraints of her early youth did not, however, embitter Miss Cobbe. When she left school at 16 she set about educating herself, reading, writing and developing a keen desire to discover religious truth. Any resentment about missed opportunities may have been softened by the close affection existing between herself and her mother who helped her in her studies. She also had a liberal allowance that enabled her to buy books and she enjoyed the housekeeping that devolved upon her through her mother's illness.

Mrs Cobbe died in 1847 and the grief of her daughter, intensified by loss of religious faith, was for a time assuaged, she recalls, by the duties of running a household, looking after the sick and hungry in the two villages on the Newbridge estate and teaching in the village school. However, when her father learnt of her rejection of Christianity he dismissed her from the house. She went to her brother in Donegal, who was kind to her though thinking her father's behaviour quite natural, and there she spent ten months of 'utter loneliness'. She was then summoned back to her father's house and stayed with him for eight years until he died.

Miss Cobbe found herself relatively poorly provided for on her father's death. He had assumed that she would continue to live at Newbridge with her brother and his wife, and she received £200 a year in place of the £130 she had previously had as pocket money. But Miss Cobbe preferred to be independent. So she left Newbridge to her brother, cut off her hair since she could not manage it without a maid, and spent a year travelling in Egypt and the near East before going to Mary Carpenter in 1858.

After the end of the 1850s, however, she began to give up 'practical work among poor folk'. She travelled abroad a good deal and set up house in London with a friend, Miss Lloyd, devoting herself to intellectual and cultural interests, to social reform, including anti-vivisection and to women's rights movements. Without pretentions or the money to enter society, she had many friends including the Brownings, Kingsley and Mill. She admired Shaftesbury and corresponded with Jowett and knew, she claimed, all the most gifted women of the time with the exception of George Eliot and Harriet Martineau.

The three remaining women, Octavia Hill, Annie Besant (born

Annie Wood) and Agnes Jones, lived rather more quietly when they were young, their fathers dying in their adolescence or early childhood. For two of them this meant relative poverty compared with the other ladies in the study; both Mrs Hill and Mrs Wood supplemented their small incomes by paid work. The Jones family however were more wealthy and the death of Mr Jones brought little change in their fortunes or way of life.

More modest matcrial circumstances and the lack of a male head of household to link the family more effectively to the outside world of politics, science and literature, might be expected to have limited social intercourse and the development of cultural interests. But there is little sign of any such deprivation among the Hill sisters, nor with Annie Besant. Both Mrs Hill and Mrs Wood were educated, cultivated and devout women with the personal resources and strength of character to pass on these endowments to their children.

Octavia Hill was one of five daughters born to Caroline Southwood Smith, daughter of the sanitary reformer and third wife of James Hill. Mr Hill had five daughters and one son by his earlier marriages, and Caroline Southwood Smith first joined his household as governess on the death of his second wife. He was a corn merchant and banker, a radical, energetic in local municipal reforms and in philanthropic activities. He accumulated a substantial library, founded an infant school, started a paper to advocate various reforms, bought the local theatre and invited celebrated actors to perform in it. In 1840, however, two years after the birth of his eighth daughter, Mr Hill was made bankrupt and subsequently suffered complete mental and physical breakdown. His illness meant that his wife brought up his daughters alone, in an atmosphere of high principles and sanitary reform, with the support of her own father, Dr Southwood Smith. They lived in the country without servants and Mrs Hill taught her children herself. Her eldest daughter, Miranda, later wrote of her mother's remarkable character:

It is difficult to express to those who never knew Mrs Hill what her influence was on those who came in contact with her. On her children it left an indelible impression as deep as life itself, and as lasting. From her book 'Notes on Education' it will be seen how entirely she felt the *spirit* to be everything in education. She seldom gave a distinct order or made a rule; but her children felt that she lived continually in the presence of God, and that in her there was an atmosphere of goodness, and that moral beauty was a delight to her in the same way that outward beauty is to so many people. She was ardent and yet so serene that to come into her room was like entering a haven of peace where evil and bitterness could not live. Her children also learned from early infancy, from her attitude of mind, that if a thing was right it must be done; there ceased to be any question about it, and how great a help that feeling is to timid natures or weak wills only those know who have experienced it.[38]

In 1851 the family moved to London and Mrs Hill became the manager of the Ladies' Guild, a co-operative enterprise to provide suitable employment for ladies. Her daughters, too, took part in the work of the Guild and thus came to know Vansittart Neale, who supported it, and the group of Christian Socialists, especially F. D. Maurice, Charles Kingsley and later Thomas Hughes, with whom he was associated. A further experiment was started of providing work for ragged school children whom Octavia, while still a young girl, supervised. She also started lessons in drawing and painting with Ruskin. Listening to and reading the Christian Socialists and Mayhew's stories of London life, observing the ragged school girls and visiting their families, she became keenly aware of the poverty and degradation of many of the London poor. When she was only 14 she wrote to an elder sister:

Give my dearest love to Miss Graham. Tell her I never can thank her enough for all the noble and beautiful books she has lent me; that, as to the Christian Socialists, I never before read anything which inspired such earnest longing to do *something* for the cause of association; and it interested me so very much that the hours I have spent in reading *that* are never to be forgotten . . . I shall never forget . . . that it was to her that I owe the great happiness of first reading a Socialist book, which I consider one of the greatest happinesses which anyone can have.[39]

Letters to her mother, other sisters and close friends were full of similar enthusiasm; discussion of the books she read, of the lectures and sermons she heard, of her own developing religious convictions and her thoughts about her work with the children in the school.

It is a very wonderful work in which we are engaged. It is a very awful work, when you feel how easily you can reach their hearts, how hard it is to reach their consciences; they will do anything *for you*, they will do hardly anything because it is right. And tho' this is dangerous, because so false a ground to stand upon, yet this inclination testifies of a precious truth. It might teach us, if we would only learn, how much all human beings must crave for personality; how cold, how dead, how distant arc all abstractions.[40]

Before she was 20 she had developed an intense sense of duty and commitment; friends warned Miss Hill that overwork would damage her health, but to little avail:

and I told her just what I felt about it – that to leave off working was a privilege, to continue a duty – that I *dared* not claim *any* time as my own; that I had sometimes felt as if I had earned a time to rest or enjoy leisure; and then had been convinced that all time was God's and to be used for Him.[41]

In 1860 the family moved to 14 Nottingham Place and continued to co-operate in parish work, in sewing classes for poor women, in setting up a school. Here Octavia Hill began her housing work. It is for this which she is most famous and it was an interest closely linked to her grandfather's concerns. In 1859 she had joined the Ladies' Association for Sanitary Reform and heard the inaugural address by Lord Shaftesbury. She was also, with her mother and sisters, a keen advocate of higher education for women. Six girls from the Nottingham Place School were among the first to sit the Cambridge examinations in 1863 when they were experimentally opened to women for the first time. There is thus a marked continuity in Miss Hill's later work and her earlier childhood experiences.

Annie Besant was on the fringes of social service. She was primarily a writer and public speaker, devoting her life, as she saw it, to propaganda for free thinking and social reform even though this meant the loss of friends and of the custody of her child: 'But the desire to spread liberty and true thought among men, to war against bigotry and superstition, to make the world freer and better than I found it – all this impelled me with a force that would not be denied.'[42] Her association with Charles Bradlaugh as vice president of the National Secular Society and her support for free discussion of methods of birth control, a cause for which she was prepared to sacrifice her reputation in order to remedy the 'hopeless wretchedness of thousands', brought her notoriety. She qualified as a science teacher, but from the middle of the 1880s she was increasingly politically active in social reform; an advocate of free school meals, of shorter hours for young workers, of fair wages instead of doles and 'Christian charity', which she scorned. She dismissed the socialist party in England as made up of 'discontented foreigners, and of a few clever men playing on the suffering that exists'.[43] In 1885 she joined the Fabians, rejecting, she says, the Marxist doctrine that ends justify means, but lecturing on socialism with Shaw, Webb and Morris, and was elected to the London School Board. But four years later she became a Theosophist whereupon Bradlaugh, she reports, lost his faith in her judgement and reason. Much of the remainder of her life was spent in India where she became involved in the movement for Home Rule though retaining an interest in the development of women's suffrage in Britain. She is included in this study as one of the women who uncompromisingly rejected Christianity.

Mrs Besant was born Annie Wood. Her father, Irish, highly educated, a qualified doctor and with commercial interests, himself rejecting the Roman Catholic faith, settled with his family in London. But when his daughter was 5 and her brother 7, Mr Wood died leaving his wife and two children in poverty. Mrs Wood removed her family to Harrow so that she might pay for the education of her son at Harrow School by taking boys into her house as lodgers.

When she was 8, Annie went to Ellen Marryat, the rich charitable, evangelical sister of the novelist Frederick Marryat, to be educated by her with her only niece. There she joined in Miss Marryat's religious and charitable activities, a Sunday school, a Bible class, and visiting the poor. By this time, Mrs Besant recalls in her autobiography, she was a sensitive, imaginative and precocious child, reading *Pilgrim's Progress* and *Paradise Lost*. She was afraid of the supernatural, became a fervent evangelical and was confirmed in Paris in 1861 while travelling in France and Germany with Miss Marryat.

By the time she was $16\frac{1}{2}$ her formal education was over. She returned to her mother, to whom she was devoted, to a tranquil existence, a happy social life, continuing her studies of German and music and reading Christian literature. She began to consider her future as leading to some kind of religious vocation, deliberately looking for opportunities for service or sacrifice as with all those 'whose ears are opened to the wailings of the great orphan Humanity'.[44] Three years later she had her first doubts about the infallibility of the Bible. Nevertheless, with no outlet for her growing desire to be useful in her mother's house, a strong emotional feeling for religion and, as she puts it, 'idealising' clergymen, she became engaged to Frank Besant, deacon at a mission church in Clapham. Doubts about the marriage tempted her to break the engagement after only a few months but her mother, Mrs Besant later claimed, persuaded her it would be dishonourable to do so. So she married, a fatal blunder as it turned out, attracted by the notion of being a priest's wife and working among the poor.[45]

Annie Wood, then, grew up somewhat apart from the world in a quiet social milieu with fewer opportunities for intellectual intercourse than most of the other women in this study. Her desire to be of use seems to have sprung from her religious commitment and feelings rather than from any early acquaintance with public issues and social questions. In this regard she was similar to Agnes Jones, though the material circumstances of the two were very different.

The Jones family were Irish with a house in the country at Fahan.[46] There were three children, a boy and two girls. When Agnes was 5, however, her father, in the army with the rank of Lieutenant Colonel, was drafted to Mauritius. He was a pious man, and while living on the island the family, including Agnes, took a keen interest in missionary work and in the periodic persecution of Christians. There was regular Bible reading in the household.

On their return to Ireland the ill health of Mrs Jones led to a succession of governesses but Agnes appears to have been a slow learner. When she was 16 she went to school at Stratford rather briefly. Her father died two years later and the family moved to Dublin so that the children might be taught by masters. A year later Agnes Jones began to help in a ragged school and in 1853, during a six-month continental holiday, her interest in nursing was established by a visit to Kaiserswerth, following in the footsteps of Elizabeth Fry and Florence Nightingale.

Returning to Ireland she continued her ragged school work, helping in the school at Fahan and visiting the poor and the sick. A further visit to Kaiserswerth in 1860 enabled her to train to become a Sister and convinced her that nursing under Florence Nightingale was her vocation. On coming back to London, however, hospital work was temporarily put aside because of her own doubts about her abilities and her mother's strong objection to any training involving hospital residence, and instead Miss Jones worked as a Bible missioner.

After a few months, she was called to Rome by her mother to help to nurse her sister, ill with fever, and stayed to accompany them to Naples and Florence. She then left her family to visit various deaconess institutions on the continent. Her desire to devote herself to nursing revived and having won the consent of her mother she entered St Thomas's as a Nightingale probationer. Explaining her reasons for electing to train as a nurse she stated that she had long admired Florence Nightingale, that she was very happy in her home and work, but that she longed for 'greater power of usefulness'.[47]

The families in which the ten women grew up emerge with certain marked similarities but also important differences. All belonged to the educated middle class but they ranged from the well-to-do Nightingale and Potter families to the relatively impoverished households of Octavia Hill and Annie Wood. The former visited London for the season, presented their daughters at court, and entertained in their London and country houses their extensive acquaintance among the prominent intellectual and political figures of the day as well as men in business and trade. By contrast Mrs Wood and Mrs Hill led relatively quiet and secluded lives, obliged to earn money to support their children and with no opportunity to enter fashionable society.

Most of the women came from large families of brothers and sisters who provided a network of significant relationships throughout their lives, which might be more or less close and more or less friendly but which could not be ignored. This was especially true for Elizabeth Fry, Octavia Hill, Josephine Butler and Beatrice Potter and although Miss Nightingale had only one sister she had numerous cousins and aunts, to several of whom she was strongly attached. In contrast Agnes Jones and Annie Besant grew up in small families and apparently without close connections with more distant kin.

All the families encouraged the intellectual and artistic interests of their children, daughters as well as sons, though some more systematically than others. Family debate and discussion of social matters, of religion, of politics and science was taken for granted and many of the girls were offered the same classical education as their brothers, even if they were not expected to follow a profession or to take up public work or even to write books. Only Agnes Jones seems to have been relatively unresponsive to such opportunities, though we do not know much about her. All the other women developed outstanding intellectual ability. This and the social confidence drawn from their family upbringing made them formidable figures in their public work.

4 Family Relationships

Some general reference to the character of family relationships has already occurred in the discussion of the social and family background of the group of women who are the focus of this study. But it is worth trying to disentangle and describe more carefully the nature and intimacy of the ties between sisters, brothers, parents and more distant kin. It seems likely that family affection, respect and encouragement, or the lack of it, might be an important support, or obstacle, in the step out of domestic life into public work.

Strong family affection might nurture a desire to be useful and a sense of social obligation, but it also, perhaps, helped to form personalities that were confident of their own right as well as duty to 'meddle in the stuff of other people's lives'. If the Victorian ladies were tenacious and assertive, however, these were essential qualities for making their way in the outside world. They were also qualities which many learnt to disguise in order to minimise hostility to themselves and damage to their causes. Emily Davies displayed great discretion in her comments on a paper on women's suffrage by Barbara Bodichon:

> I find your paper capital . . . I don't think it quite does to call the arguments on the other side 'foolish'. Of course they *are*, but it does not seem quite polite to say so . . . the enemy always maintains that the disabilities imposed upon women are not penal, but solely intended for their good, and I find nothing irritates men so much as to attribute tyranny to them. I believe many of them really do mean well, and . . . it seems fair to admit it and to show them that their well-intended efforts are a *mistake* not a crime. Men cannot stand indignation, and tho' of course I think it is just, it seems to me better to suppress the manifestation of it.[1]

While family affection and support might ease the transition into public life, their absence, even in one parent, made matters much more difficult, as the experiences of Miss Nightingale make clear. Lack of sympathy for unconventional aspirations might also affect the direction of women's public activities. Hannah Mitchell is a good example of a woman whose fight for female suffrage was associated with a keen sense of the unfairness of the relations between the sexes and of the oppression of women that, she herself suggests, was rooted in her own childhood experiences. She was born in 1871 into a poor household, in a remote part of Derbyshire, one of six children who had little chance of education and who were expected to share the work of house and farm. Both parents were literate but Mrs Webster, who had been in service and disliked farm life, was a hard taskmaster:

> She never seemed to realise how small and weak we were. She made us sweep and scrub, turn the heavy mangle on washing days and the still heavier churn on butter-making days. Stone floors had to be whitened, brasses and steel fire-irons polished every week. On winter evenings there was sewing by hand, making and mending shirts and underwear. At eight years old my weekly task was to darn all the stockings for the household, and I think my first reactions to feminism began at this time when I was forced to darn my brothers' stockings while they read or played cards or dominoes.
>
> Sometimes the boys helped with rug making, or in cutting up wool or picking feathers for beds and pillows, but for them this was voluntary work; for the girls it was compulsory, and the fact that the boys could read if they wished filled my cup of bitterness to the brim.[2]

Little sympathy seems to have existed between Hannah and her mother:

> I never quite forgave her for my lack of education, and she never forgave me for my lack of interest in the things she considered important. Although she lived to the age of ninety, and in her latter years owed much of her comfort to me, she never showed any gratitude, never regarded me as anything but the one failure among her children, and always spoke contemptuously of my desire for culture.
>
> Work and cleanliness were her gods, but she disliked farm life so much she decided all her girls should learn a trade, and as she thought needlework was a ladylike and easy life we must all learn dress-making.[3]

Quarrels were frequent and at 14 Hannah left home to live with an elder brother. She worked as a domestic servant and later in various dress-making establishments for long hours and little pay.

She became interested in the ILP and in votes for women and in 1895, having left her brother's home, she married a fellow lodger in the house where she lived, a convinced and keen socialist. But married life was problematic for her, as had been her family life as a child.

> We were both tired of living in lodgings, and felt that our own hearth, however humble, would be more comfortable. . . . Perhaps if I had really understood my own nature, as I came to do later, I would not have married, for I soon realised that married life, as men understand it, calls for a degree of self-abnegation which was impossible for me. I needed solitude, time for study, and the opportunity for a wider life.[4]

Mrs Mitchell soon realised, she says, that the price of possessing her own home was very high. To begin with the Mitchells were poor and she took in sewing, working hard to meet the expense of an expected child. Although her husband passed his earnings to her she resented his failure to take any further financial responsibility: 'At first I tried to get him to reckon up the cost of living with me and keep a sort of weekly budget. But he refused, just handing his wages over and leaving all the worry to me.'[5]

The birth of her child was painful and she decided to have no more. Work for the suffragettes increasingly absorbed her time and interest, but it was an interest that she did not consider her husband shared, in spite of his enthusiastic socialism. In 1904 she was imprisoned for refusing to pay a fine for obstructing a public meeting. Although experiencing the awful conditions in Strangeways she was angry to be released almost at once after her husband paid her fine. He knew, she complained, that the suffragettes did not wish their fines to be paid and he was in sympathy with militancy,

> But men are not so single-minded as women are; they are too much given to *talking* about their ideals rather than *working* for them. . . . Most of us found that 'Votes for Women' were of less interest to our husbands than their own dinners. They simply could not understand why we made such a fuss about it.[6]

Two years later Hannah Mitchell had a nervous breakdown, a sad, bitter woman without the sense of family love and support to add satisfaction to her public work. She recovered to carry on with her

work for the feminists, as a poor law guardian, as a county councillor
and as a magistrate and lived to be nearly 90. Looking back towards
the end of her life she underlines her concerns with women's rights
and opportunities:

> More intensely than ever I believe in woman's right to equality,
> whether married or single, the right to her own individuality, her
> own soul. A lifetime of drudgery is too high a price to pay for
> following her natural instincts, a price no man is ever called upon
> to pay.[7]

It is of course too simple to attribute the militancy of Hannah
Mitchell to the lack of sympathy in her early family life. No doubt
the poverty of the Derbyshire farm was just as important. And there
was no liberal tradition within the family of respect for women's
rights, nor anything more than conventional religious observance to
soften the rigours of childhood.

In any circumstances girls growing up in a mixed family of brothers
might be expected to be more conscious and more resentful of the
different treatment accorded the two sexes. Seven of the ten women
who went into social service had brothers among their siblings; but
in no case is there evidence of jealousy or resentment. Such emotions
seem to have been averted in families well endowed with material
goods. Nor were they so likely where family culture was coloured by
evangelical faith, emphasising the social duties attached to social
position and linking charitable work to service to God and to personal
salvation. Moreover, any female sense of personal injustice was
mitigated by careful attention to the education of girls, by kindness
and affection, as recalled by Miss Cobbe and by explicit support for
women's rights, as in John Grey's household.

This does not mean that the ladies who grew up in families of girls
were innocent of the problems of a woman's position and moved
readily and easily into public lives of selfless and devoted service.
Both Florence Nightingale and Beatrice Potter, even though protected
by considerable wealth, were keenly aware of the disadvantages of
their sex and the restrictions it imposed on their personal ambitions.
Family affections were perhaps less strong and religious convictions
less firm in these two households. But demographic circumstances
were significant too. Florence Nightingale was one of only two
daughters and therefore more vulnerable to the claims of her many
relations for nursing and companionship. On several occasions her

attempts to train as a nurse in Paris and Dublin were thwarted by a call to nurse one or other member of her family. Beatrice Potter was the only unmarried daughter available on her mother's death to act as companion to her father, manager of his household and guardian of her younger sister. She observed these responsibilities, at some cost to her research activities, until her father died.

It is notable that Frances Power Cobbe, whose independence was sacrificed to family responsibilities until a similar age, expresses no similar sense of personal conflict. Perhaps her ambitions were less keen or less clearly formulated than in the case of Florence Nightingale or Beatrice Potter. Perhaps she was sustained by what she describes as a very happy childhood, and especially by the close affection existing between herself and her mother. Also of course her 'public' activities, writing, teaching in the village school, visiting the poor and sick on her father's estate, could more easily be carried on without leaving home. She had no need to enter an institution to train as a nurse, nor to travel to other places to investigate the life and labour of working people.

We can now examine in more detail the character of the family relationship of the ten selected social workers and social researchers to try to see how those relationships affected their public lives.

We have already noted for Florence Nightingale, and, to a lesser extent for Beatrice Potter, home circumstances while providing considerable wealth and cultural opportunities also impeded efforts to establish independence. Neither woman appears to have had a particularly close or sympathetic relationship with her mother or sisters. Both were more attached to their fathers, but Mr Nightingale did not support his daughter's ambitions consistently in the face of his wife's displeasure, and Mr Potter was away from home a great deal and seems to have shown little interest in his daughter's intellectual development.

Miss Nightingale had only one sister in her immediate family but numerous family connections through the brothers and sisters of her parents. When she was 14 her father reckoned she had 27 first cousins and nearly two dozen aunts and uncles related to her through blood or marriage. To some of these, especially her cousins Hilary Bonham Carter and Marianne Nicholson, her aunt Mai, her father's sister, and her father himself, Miss Nightingale was closely attached. But her relations with her mother and elder sister were very uneasy – if not through lack of affection, through differences in temperament, taste and values.

The large family circle meant for the Nightingales continuous activity in entertaining and exchanging news:

> Enormous numbers of letters were written. Not only major events, weddings, births, deaths, but the choice of a place for a holiday, the advisability of taking a holiday at all, the dismissal of a coachman or cook, the selection of a dress or a carpet provoked correspondence and consultations with aunts, uncles, cousins and grandmothers.[8]

The younger sister seems to have been increasingly uncomfortable with such a life. She recalls that as a child she was beset by many fears – that she was not like other people – that she was incapable of behaving properly. She was afraid of meeting strangers and refused to dine downstairs. By the age of 6, she claims, she had ceased to be afraid of the life at Embley and Lea Hurst but had come to dislike, despise and resist it.[9] By the time she was 14 she craved, she wrote, for 'something worth doing instead of frittering time away on useless trifles'.[10] As a child, though anxious to win her mother's affection, she never succeeded to her own satisfaction. As she grew older she developed at different times violent attachments to other people who appeared sympathetic, among them the cousins and aunt already mentioned, only to experience intense depression if those attachments were broken.

Whatever the reasons for the difficult relationship between Florence Nightingale and her mother and sister, the early lack of sympathy for her nursing aspirations caused her distress and resentment. By 1844, after alternating periods of energetic and successful social life, remorse for her own frivolity and sinfulness, illness and solitary work, she had decided that her vocation lay in hospitals with the sick. She had been encouraged by Dr Gridley Howe, the American philanthropist who had stayed at Embley, and she had learned from the Prussian ambassador of the work of Pastor Fliedner at Kaiserswerth, training deaconesses to nurse the sick poor. She was sustained by close friendship with a devout aunt, Hannah Nicholson, as well as with her aunt Mai. But when the refusal of a proposal of marriage from her cousin, Henry Nicholson, cost her the affection of his sister, Marianne, she was much distressed. Her biographer describes it as a catastrophe which brought Miss Nightingale near to mental breakdown.

Distracted a little from her own troubles by the illness of her grandmother and childhood nurse, both of whom she attended, she began to extend her nursing to the villagers around Lea Hurst. These experiences impressed upon Miss Nightingale the need for training. But her desire to go to Salisbury Infirmary to learn nursing, where the head physician was an old friend, was opposed by her mother and sister 'as if I had wanted to be a kitchen maid'. The objection may have been rational enough in view of the conditions in public hospitals at the time, but for Miss Nightingale it spelled despair:

> No advantage that I can see comes of my living on, excepting that one becomes less and less of a young lady every year . . . You will laugh, dear, at the whole plan I dare say; but no-one but the mother of it knows how precious an infant idea becomes; nor how the soul dies, between the destruction of one and the taking up of another. I shall never do anything and am worse than dust and nothing . . . oh for some strong thing to sweep this loathsome life into the past.[11]

The years after 1845 were a time of alternating periods of depression and near mental breakdown, of foreign travel to restore her health, of desperate attempts to educate herself and make herself fit to follow her vocation and of efforts to enter various institutions to train as a nurse. She began to detach herself from close relationships. In 1846 she wrote to Hilary Bonham Carter: 'Are not one's earthly friends too often Atalanta's apple, thrown in each other's way to hinder that course, at the end of which is laid up the crown of righteousness? So, dearest, it is well that *we* should not see too much of each other. . . . Farewell my beloved one.'[12] In a private note to herself she wrote, 'Oh God, no more love. No more marriage O God.'[13]

Society grew more distasteful to her, but in 1848 she was disappointed in expectations of going to Kaiserswerth. At Embley she incurred the displeasure of her mother and father by nursing the sick poor and, at her father's suggestion, tried teaching in a school instead. She did but disliked it. The family went to London for the season where Miss Nightingale taught in a ragged school in which one of her uncles was interested, but was effectively prevented from visiting the poor by her mother's insistence that a footman accompany her as it was not suitable that a young woman in her station of life should go out in London without a servant.[14]

Hard work, ill-health, increasing distress and family opposition to her plans brought Miss Nightingale to a point where, according to her biographer, she would have killed herself had she not thought it a mortal sin. She rejected a second proposal of marriage from Monckton Milnes in spite of strong attachment, for the sake of her calling. Mrs Nightingale was angry and resentful. 'What had begun as genuine maternal solicitude for her daughter's welfare turned into a contest of wills in which love and kindness were forgotten.'[15] A tour to the East to restore her health, however, permitted Miss Nightingale to visit Kaiserswerth and strengthened her resolve to dedicate herself to nursing. She returned to the anger of her family and to demands that she spend all her time at home.

After three months at Embley she described her life as 'suicide':

There is not a night that I do not lie down on my bed, wishing that I may leave it no more. Unconsciousness is all I desire. I remain in bed as long as I can, for what have I to wake for? . . . Oh, how am I to get through this day, to talk all through this day, is the thought of every morning . . . This is the sting of death. In my twenty-first year I see nothing desirable but death.[16]

Reproaches, however, were for herself, not for her sister or mother:

What is to become of me . . . I can hardly open my mouth without giving dear Parthe vexation – everything I say or do is a subject of annoyance to her.

And of her mother she wrote:

Oh dear good woman, when I feel her disappointment in me it is as if I were going insane . . . what a murderer am I to disturb their happiness . . . What am I that their life is not good enough for me? Oh God what am I? The thoughts and feelings that I have now I can remember since I was six years old . . . But why, oh my God cannot I be satisfied with the life that satisfies so many people? I am told that the conversation of all these good clever men ought to be enough for me. Why am I starving, desperate, diseased on it? . . . My God what am I to do?[17]

A few months later she had determined she would break away:

I must expect no sympathy or help from them. I have so long craved for their sympathy that I can hardly reconcile myself to this. I have so long *struggled* to make myself understood – been sore, cast down, insupportably fretted, at not being understood (at this moment I feel it even when I retrace these conversations in thought) that I must not even try to be understood. I know that they *cannot* . . . I must *take* some things, as few as I can, to enable me to live. I must *take* them, they will not be given to me . . . I have so long been treated as a child, and have so long allowed myself to be treated as a child.[18]

She went to Kaiserswerth for three months after emotional scenes with her sister and returned once again to the resentment of her family, remaining at home to nurse her father and sister. In 1852, in London for the season, she was still treated as a girl; closely supervised, her letters read, though she was over 30 and with her own circle of distinguished friends and acquaintance – Elizabeth Barrett-Browning, George Eliot, Lord Shaftesbury, Lord Palmerston, Arthur Stanley, Arthur Hugh Clough. Around this time Miss Nightingale recorded an imaginary conversation with her mother:

Why, my dear, you don't suppose that . . . I'm going to stay dangling about my mother's drawing room all my life! I shall go and look out for work . . . you must look upon me as your son. I should have cost you a great deal more if I had married or been a son . . . you were willing to part with me to be married.[19]

Efforts to enter hospitals for training in London, Paris and Dublin failed for various reasons, but eventually Mrs Nightingale agreed that at some future point her daughter should be allowed to do some kind of work. Bitter reproach followed from her sister, distraught to the point of a nervous breakdown, and whose doctor then advised that the two women be separated. Ten years later Miss Nightingale wrote a sardonic comment: 'A very successful . . . physician once seriously told a sister who was being Devoured that she must leave home in order that the Devourer might recover health and balance which had been lost in the process of devouring.'[20] The obligation to stay at home, however, had vanished. With her mother's agreement and Manning's help she arranged to go to a Catholic hospital in Paris but the plan was cancelled as she was required to nurse a great aunt. She eventually reached Paris in 1853 and was about to enter the *Maison de la Providence* of the Sisters of Charity when she was recalled to England by the illness of her grandmother.

Nevertheless the battle was now won. In the summer of 1853 Miss Nightingale became Superintendent of the London Hospital for Sick Gentlewomen, the appointing committee first assuring themselves that the position had the approval of her parents. The post was unpaid, but she was able to take rooms away from her family with an independent allowance from her father. She had the support of Mr Nightingale but not of her mother and sister who wished that while they were in London she should continue to live with them. A suggestion to this effect from Mme Mohl provoked a reply that left Miss Nightingale's feelings about the matter in no doubt

> I have not taken this step . . . without years of anxious consideration . . . *I have* talked matters over . . . with Parthe, *not once but a thousand times* . . . It has been . . . with the deepest consideration and the fullest advice that I have taken the step of leaving home and it is a *fait accompli*.[21]

How far Miss Nightingale's tempestuous emotional life is to be attributed to her own personality and unshakeable ambitions, how much to the restrictive demands made upon her by her mother and sister, need not detain us here. Whatever the case, family relationships were such as to intensify rather than to soften the conflict likely to arise for any lady trying to make a public career in early Victorian England. Mrs Nightingale's opposition to her daughter's ambitions reflected the conventions of the time. It arose out of anxiety for her welfare as well as a wish that she observe the accepted customs of her class.

> Your mother would, I believe, be most willing that you undertake a mission like Mrs Fry or Mrs Chisholm, but she thinks it necessary for your peace and well-being that there should be a Mr Fry or Captain Chisholm to protect you and in conscience she thinks it right to defend you from doing anything which *she thinks* would be an impediment to the existence of Mr F or Captain C.[22]

Perhaps not surprisingly in view of their highly charged relationship, her sister emphasised the ambition rather than the charity in Miss Nightingale's character. When the younger sister was about to visit Mme Mohl in Paris in 1853 the elder wrote bitterly of the ten months or so Florence had spent away from home during the preceding year:

> so that I hope she has passed a very pleasant year, but meantime these eternal poor have been left to the mercies of Mamma and me, both very unwell . . . I believe she has little or none of what is called charity or philanthropy, she is ambitious – very and would like well enough to re-generate the world with a giant *coup de main* or some fine institution, which is a very different thing. Here she has a circle of admirers who cry up everything she does or says as gospel and I think it will do her much good to be with you, who, though you love and admire her, do not believe in the wisdom of all she says *because* SHE says it. I wish she could be brought to see it is the intellectual part which interests her, not the manual. She has no *esprit de conduite* in the practical sense. When she nursed me everything which intellect and kind intention could do was done but she was a shocking nurse.[23]

A more detached observer, Mrs Gaskell, came to rather similar conclusions, though emphasising Miss Nightingale's 'perfect grace and lovely appearance' and remarking that she had a great deal of fun and was a capital mimic.

> She has no friend – she wants none. She stands perfectly alone, half-way between God and His creatures. She used to go a great deal among the villagers here, who dote upon her. One poor woman lost a boy seven years ago . . . and FN went twice a day . . . The mother speaks of FN . . . as of a heavenly angel. Yet the father of this dead child – the husband of this poor woman – died last 5th of September and I was witness to the extreme difficulty with which Parthe induced Florence to go and see this childless widow *once* while she was here; and, though the woman entreated her to come again she never did. She will not go among the villagers now because her heart and soul are absorbed by her hospital plans . . . She and I had a grand quarrel one day . . . she said if she had influence enough not a mother should bring up a child herself; there should be crêches for the rich as well as the poor. If she had twenty children she would send them all to a crêche . . . but then this want of love for individuals becomes a *gift* and a very rare one, if one takes it in conjunction with her intense love for the *race*: her utter unselfishness in serving and ministering . . . but she

is really so extraordinary a creature . . . that anything like a judgement of her must be presumptuous.[24]

The iron will and apparent lack of compassion might exacerbate the relations between Miss Nightingale and her mother and sister and cause Mrs Gaskell some dismay. But they were also the qualities that enabled her to introduce a measure of humanity, cleanliness and efficiency into the military hospitals in the Crimea.

Moreover, although family conflicts were sometimes bitter, they did not destroy the underlying attachments. During the public acclaim for her work in the Crimea Miss Nightingale wrote to her parents that if anything she had done had given them pleasure, that was real pleasure to her. 'I shall *love* my name now, and shall feel that it is the greatest return that you can find satisfaction in hearing your child named. . . . Life is sweet after all.'[25] When her sister died her brother-in-law, Sir Harry Verney, wrote that Lady Verney's love for Miss Nightingale was intense. 'You contributed more than anyone to what enjoyment of life was hers . . . It was delightful . . . to see her face, perhaps distorted with pain, look happy when she thought of you!'[26] After her sister's death, the Verney's house, Claydon, become Miss Nightingale's country home.

Compared with the stormy relationships of Miss Nightingale, the family experiences of the other nine ladies seem to have been relatively tranquil. For the most part, with the exception perhaps of Annie Besant and Beatrice Potter, sympathy and encouragement from their families played an important part in easing the troubles of their public lives.

Miss Potter's family relationships were less emotionally charged than those of Florence Nightingale, though she too had a long struggle to establish her independence. She was born into a family of nine daughters, an only son dying when he was three years old. One of her strongest attachments was to her father, whom she describes as 'the central figure of the family life – the light and warmth of the home'.

How well I remember how we girls raced to the front door when we heard the wheels on the carriage drive . . . He worshipped his wife, he admired and loved his daughters; he was the only man I ever knew who genuinely believed that women were superior to men, and acted as if he did . . . he made his wife and daughters his confidantes in all his under-takings, or at any rate he seemed to do so. In spite of his business preoccupations he had retained a love of poetry, of the drama, of history and idealistic philosophy; he was a devout student of Dante (in the original), of Shakespeare and of Plato; he taught us to appreciate the eighteenth-century humorists and the French encylopaedists and the novels of Jane Austen and Thackeray; he was a fanatical admirer of Burke and Carlyle and John Henry Newman – an oddly assorted trio, proving, I think, that his preferences were inspired by emotional thought rather than by pure reason. He always talked to us as equals; he would discuss with his daughters, even when they were young girls, not only his business affairs, but also religion, politics and the problems of sex, with frankness and freedom . . . He delighted in the beauty of moor and mountain, in wild winds and the changing hues of cloud and sea. But his peculiar charm lay in his appreciation – his over-appreciation of the intellect and character of those with whom he lived. We girls thought him far too long-suffering of Mother's arbitrary moods; she thought him far too acquiescent in his daughter's unconventional habits.[27]

Others saw Mr Potter in a different light, dubious in his business dealings, sometimes violent and unfeeling in his treatment of his family, and with limited and conventional intellectual and literary interests.[28] As with the Nightingale family, there was a nurse, 'a saint' who remained a lifelong friend, companion of Mrs Potter and chaperon to Beatrice on her visits to her relations in Bacup.

Childhood, however, was an unhappy time. Mrs Webb recalls a lonely existence, with little formal education, considerable ill-health and largely brought up by servants. She remained distant from her mother, a scholarly, devout, withdrawn woman, until a few years before her death. Her daughters, we are told, were not the kind of women of whom Mrs Potter approved. 'She had been brought up "a scholar and a gentlewoman"; her daughters refused to be educated and defied caste conventions.'[29] Beatrice she appears to have admired least of all, considering her the only one of her children of below average intelligence. For her daughter she was a remote person:

a source of arbitrary authority whose rare interventions into my life I violently resented. I regarded her as an obstacle to be turned, as a person from whom one withheld facts and whose temper one watched and humoured so that she should not interfere with one's own little plans.[30]

It seems that intimacy and affection only developed between the two women in the few years before Mrs Potter died, and it was only after her death that her daughter fully discovered her benign influence.

These latter days I constantly think of mother: sometimes the feeling of her presence is so strong that I am tempted into a kind of communion with her. We knew each other so little in her lifetime. Strangely enough I love her better now, I feel that she at last knows me, tries to cheer my loneliness and to encourage my effort. She seems now to belong more to me than to the others; the others have their husbands and children, I have nothing but my work and the fitful warmth of friendship. So mother seems to stand by my side, to be watching me, anxious to reach out to me a helping hand; at any rate to bless me . . . I can fight through the rest of the battle of life with courage.[31]

When his children were young Mr Potter was frequently away on business tours and the family led a nomadic and rather rootless existence moving between their various country houses and a furnished house in London. Beatrice Potter found social life in the country dull and empty but later was even more scathing about London society. Foreign travel started in 1873 when she went to America with her father and sister and already there are signs in diary entries of the desperate search for a 'creed' and for work to give meaning to her life. 'Perhaps I shall find some day a solution to this great difficulty, of, how I ought to employ my time.'[32] There are also somewhat patronising remarks, from a girl of 15, about her sisters:

One thing I want to do, when I get home, that is to make more a friend of Maggie. Hitherto I have lived a great deal too much apart from my sisters, partly from indolence, and partly from my unfrank disposition. Dear Kitty, I have got quite fond of her, she has been such a dear kind devoted sister. I can't think why she does not get on better at home. Though we lived on the most intimate relationship for the last three months or more, I really have not found out one serious fault.[33]

Back in England and in the absence of her father, Miss Potter set about educating herself, continuing her search for a religion which would satisfy her. The instinct for careful social enquiry is already there.

> I am really trying to gain a firm belief for myself. I think it is no good going to others to have your belief cut out for you; you must examine, study, both the Bible and the lives of those who follow the Bible and those who don't. It is no sin to doubt, but it is a sin after you have doubted not to find out to the best of your capability why you doubt, and whether you have reasons to doubt . . . I must make a faith for myself and I must work, until I have.[34]

It was a lonely existence. She writes of time spent with Mrs Potter and two of her sisters as follows:

> Here we are alone, Mother, Blanche and myself. Poor Mother, she has two rather broken crutches to lean upon. Blanche is a dear girl but she is unpractical and rather inclined to bore you; and as for me, I am as Mother says, too young, too uneducated, and, worst of all, too frivolous, to be a companion to her. But, however, I must take courage, and try to change, and above all I must guard against that self-satisfaction which I consider is one of my worst faults. If I give in to it, it will prevent my ever improving myself.[35]

Poor health was followed by a period in a girls' boarding school in 1875, by more earnest attempts to understand religion, by Confirmation, and by continuing battles with her own tendencies to vanity and frivolity:

> I hope that when I return home I shall not lose the little earnestness I have gained; that I shall be diligent in the study of Religion. I do not want to 'come out' and I hope I shall have enough determination and firmness to carry my point . . . I wish my aim in life to be the understanding and acting up to Religion.[36]

The determination not to 'come out' did not endure and at 18 Miss Potter joined her sisters in what she describes as the customary pursuits of the girls of her class – riding, dancing, flirting and dressing-up. But the self-doubt and the self-criticism, also characteristic of Miss Nightingale, persisted and were intensified by similar conflicting desires to enjoy the social entertainments and excitements of a London season and the fears that such pleasures were unworthy distraction from a serious purpose. It was during these years that she first developed an intimate friendship with one of her sisters, Margaret, a few years older than herself.

> Maggie left this morning. I feel her loss terribly. We are perfectly intimate and at one with each other and when I am with her I want no other society. We have had a very happy time here together – have read, talked, walked and slept together, and now she has gone it is a dreary blank.[37]

After her mother's death in 1882 domestic responsibilities began to interfere with her personal ambitions. Doubting the sympathy of her sisters, she concealed her plans for self education and self improvement from family and acquaintance. She rose at five in the morning to read and work until eight and described these hours as the happiest of the day. In 1883 however, she decided to devote herself to the social duties of a London hostess. Her later observations about the character of London society suggest this must have been a distasteful experience. She describes this period of her life as a time of unreality and of dissemblement to her family and the world, her life divided into thoughtful and active parts. She began to withdraw from society, searching for training for social investigation. She started work as a rent collector and became a visitor for the Charity Organisation Society. Between 1883 and 1889 she made three visits to Bacup to examine the lives of her own working-class relations at first hand. 'My first chance of personal intimacy, on terms of social equality, with a wage-earning family', Mrs Webb later remarked.[38] Above all she began to work with Charles Booth on his statistical enquiry into the life and labour of the people of London.

The attempt at scientific social enquiry along with the 'assiduous study of Blue Books, social histories and economic treatises' and continual arguments with politicians and philanthropists over these years, served to determine Miss Potter's future.

> From being a lively and, at times, good-looking society girl, assumed to be ready to follow her elder sisters' example in making a happy and otherwise satisfactory marriage, I was transformed into, I will not say a professional, but a professed brain worker, overtly out for a career of my own.[39]

But the transformation did not banish uncertainty and doubt. Like Miss Nightingale, Beatrice Potter found herself obliged to choose in the early 1880s between the possibility of a happy marriage and the pursuit of intellectual work.

> I saw myself as one suffering from a divided personality; the normal woman seeking personal happiness in love given and taken within the framework of a sucessful marriage; whilst the other self claimed, in season and out of season the right to the free activity of 'a clear and analytic mind'. But did the extent of my brain power – I was always asking myself – warrant sacrificing happiness, and even risking a peaceful acceptance of life, through the insurgent spirit of a defiant intellect? For in those days of customary subordination of the woman to the man – a condition accentuated in my case by special circumstances – it would not have been practicable to unite the life of love and the life of reason.[40]

The need to choose arose out of Miss Potter's attraction to Joseph Chamberlain and caused great personal unhappiness. When Mr Potter became paralysed in 1885 his daughter largely gave up her attempts at social investigation to nurse him and the combination of circumstances added to her distress. Doubts in her own capacity persisted but hopes and doubts alike were hidden even from her closest friends. And she was still torn by the desire for both social and intellectual life.

> I do not wish to forgo the society of my own class – and yet to enjoy means wasted energy. Late hours, and excitement, stimulants and unwholesome food, all diminish my small stock of strength available for actual work. And society has another drawback; it attracts one's attention away from the facts one is studying, so that the impression is not so keen and deep.[41]

By 1888, however, with growing experience of dock labour and the tailoring trade, which involved training as a 'plain hand', Miss Potter seems to have regained her confidence in herself and her work.

> I am more than ever assured that *I have capacity* . . . and now there are no conflicting desires and few conflicting duties. 'Society', even now it is unusually gracious and flattering, has no charm for me.

And two months later:

> My work is now all in all to me . . . prayer is a constant source of
> strength . . . my painstaking study of detail will help towards the
> knowledge of the whole, towards which I am constantly striving; I
> shall leave steps cut in the rock, and from it man will eventually
> map out the conquered land of social life.[42]

All this was in spite of a dire warning from Alfred Marshall that
women must not develop their faculties in a way unwelcome to men,
that strength, courage and independence were not attractive in
women and that rivalry in men's pursuits was positively unpleasant.
'If you compete with us we shan't marry you', he told Miss Potter in
1889.[43]

However, in 1890 she met Sidney Webb. Two years later, after
the death of her father, she married him, and the famous partnership
began. The special character and crucial importance of the marriage
of Mrs Webb emerges clearly from her own writing. From the
beginning it was a working arrangement. She later described their
plan of life. There were eight or nine months in London, working
together in the mornings, Sidney spending the afternoon on LCC
administration, the evenings either alone together with periodicals
and light literature or discussing research, municipal administration
or Fabian propaganda with friends and associates. The other months
were spent in the countryside working on their material or in
provincial towns carrying on their investigations. Every two or three
years there were a few weeks complete holiday on the continent.[44]

Each co-operated in research and writing and also encouraged the
other's independent activities, as when Sidney joined his wife's
investigations into the working of the poor laws and the campaign
for reform. Mrs Webb relied on her husband for the strength to carry
on with her work and separation caused painful anxiety:

> if it were not for my reliance on Sidney's strength, I should almost
> retire from business. I tremble to think how utterly dependent I
> am on him – both on his love and on his unrivalled capacity for
> 'putting things through'. When he is late, I get into a panic of fear
> lest some mishap has befallen him. This fear of losing each other
> is always present – more with me, I think, than with him.[45]

These words were written in 1907 in the middle of Mrs Webb's work on the Poor Law Commission, but her diaries contain many expressions of similar feelings. A couple of years later, on the seventeenth anniversary of her marriage, she reflected on the likelihood of her and Sydney dying together.

> If only we could look forward to going out together, hand in hand, as we have pressed through the active period of our lives, trying each day to complete some little part of the common task, but always close together in body and mind, day and night, night and day. This union in death is too great a prize to win – in nature's way?[46]

She recalled the complete comradeship, not only in research and writing but also in organising and speaking in the campaign to break up the poor laws. Sidney had been 'extraordinarily generous' in according her the front place as the leading Minority commissioner. 'Fortunately' she added, 'in spite of his modesty, everyone knows that he is the backbone of the "Webb" firm, even if I do appear, on some occasions, as the figurehead.'[47]

In 1926 when Mrs Webb began to prepare the second volume of her autobiography she set down her impressions of her husband. Work on the book was slow, and publication delayed until after her death, but in 'advanced old age' she retained the sketch to insert as an introduction to *Our Partnership*. It ends with the following sentence. 'The days of his absence are weary to get through; and the sleepless hours of the night are haunted, not by the fear of death, but by the dread of life without him.'[48]

The conflict between family and social obligations and their own aspirations seems to have been muted, or entirely absent in the lives of the other ladies in this study. All grew up in families where relationships appear to have been close and affectionate, a source of strength and encouragement rather than frustration and restraint. Inward uncertainty and self-criticism were common enough, but tended to be soothed rather than exacerbated by family attachments.

Elizabeth Fry is the earliest born of all the women, spending her first 20 years in the eighteenth century. She seems to have been a lonely, timid, delicate child, and her mother's death when she was 12 robbed her of the person whom she thought best understood her. As she grew older she took great pleasure in family entertainments and activities, in the companionship of her brothers and sisters and more distant relations, though her father remains a rather shadowy, if benevolent, figure. To some of her family she was especially attached, especially an uncle, Joseph Gurney, and a cousin, Priscilla Hannah Gurney, who was a Quaker minister. Her journals are full of affectionate references to all her siblings but she was particularly close to her sister Rachel and brother John who sympathised in her determination to give up music and dancing so that she might become a plain Quaker. To another cousin, Joseph Gurney Bevan, she turned for advice about her marriage. In later life her sense of family affection and support remained strong. In 1807 on the marriage of a sister she noted, 'A very serious and interesting time to us all. My father, all of us eleven, my husband and Samuel Hoare. . . . All appeared unity and love; rather remarkable to see so large a family all so nearly sympathising, and closely united.'[49] On one occasion when Mrs Fry found that her work at Newgate required more money than she could conscientiously ask from her husband she appealed to other relations. All responded and asked her to apply to them whenever assistance was needed.[50]

She fully subscribed to the common assumption of her time that a woman's most important duties lay among her immediate family. On the death of a sister-in-law, in 1822, she wrote in her praise: 'She was, I believe, one who loved and feared the Lord . . . she was an excellent wife, mother, daughter and sister; a great friend to the poor and remarkably generous.'[51] And she was meticulous in her attentions to her own children. To her eldest daughters of 13 and 15 staying away from home, she wrote as follows:

I anxiously hope that you will now do your utmost, in whatever respects your education, not only on your own account, but for our sake. I look forward to your return with so much comfort, as useful and valuable helpers to me . . . I mean that you should have a certain department to fill in the house, amongst the children and the poor, as well as your own studies and enjoyments; I think there was not often a brighter opening for two girls. Plashet is after all such a home, it now looks sweetly, and your little room is almost a temptation to me to take it for a sitting room for myself, it is so pretty and so snug . . . The poor, and the schools, I think, will be glad to have you home, for help is wanted in these things. Indeed if your hearts are but turned the right way, you may, I believe, be made instruments of much good; and I shall be glad to have the day come, that I may introduce you into prisons and hospitals. 'Therefore, gird up the loins of your mind and be sober'.

This appears to me your present business – to give all diligence to your present duties; and I cannot help believing, if this be the case, that the day will come when you will be brought into much usefulness.[52]

When two of her sons went away to school she sent to each the following Rules for a Boy at a Boarding School.

1st BE REGULAR; strict in attending to religious duties; and do not allow other boys around thee to prevent thy having some portion of time for reading, at least a text of scripture, meditation, prayer . . .

2ndly. I shall speak of moral conduct, which, if religious principles be kept to, we may believe will be good; but I shall give certain hints that may point out the temptations to which schools are peculiarly liable. I have observed a want of strict integrity in school-boys, as it respects their school masters and teachers, a disposition to cheek them, to do that behind their backs which they would not do before their faces; and so having two faces. Now this is a subject of the utmost importance – to maintain truth and strict integrity upon all points.[53]

Her own immediate family was sympathetic to her public work, her husband and one or more children frequently accompanying her on her travels as a Quaker minister and in her visits of inspection to prisons in England and abroad. In spite of this accord, leaving home occasioned considerable distress.

It is no doubt a sacrifice of natural feeling, to leave the comforts of home, and my beloved husband and children: and to my weak nervous habits, the going about, and alone (for so I feel it in one sense without my husband) is, I have found from experience, a trial greater than I imagined: and my health suffers much . . . This consideration of its being a cross to my nature, I desire not to weigh in the scale . . . What I desire to consider most deeply is this: Have I authority for leaving my home and evident duties?[54]

Sometimes sharper conflicts arose. In 1817, pleased by the success of her prison work, she went on to point to less happy domestic experiences:

but there are also deep humiliations for me. My beloved children do not appear sufficiently under the influence of Religion. I am ready to say; oh! that I could prosper at home in my labours, as I appear to do abroad. Others appear to fear for me that I am too much divided, but alas! what can I do, but follow the openings. I think that I do also labour at home.[55]

And again, during the following year:

My prison engagements have gone well . . . Although I have had much support . . . yet I believe many Friends have great fears for me and mine; and some not Friends, do not scruple to spread evil reports, as if vanity or political motives led me to neglect a large family. I desire patiently to bear it all, but the very critical view that is taken of my beloved children, grieves me much.[56]

It is hardly surprising that with a family of 11 children, however affectionate, Mrs Fry found difficulties in reconciling her public and private duties. But the conflict she faced shows that the urge to public work needed to be very strong to overcome the personal inclination and social pressure to regard domestic responsibilities as properly absorbing a woman's time. Mrs Fry was fortunate in that throughout her life her sisters, brothers, cousins, uncles, husband and children offered continuing support.

The other ladies in the study may have had fewer close kin but most seem to have drawn strength and encouragement from secure family relationships. The experiences of the different women are more or less well documented, but Josephine Butler, Mary Carpenter and Octavia Hill stand out as having especially close and affectionate ties. For Mrs Butler this was perhaps particularly important, given the public suspicion and hostility aroused by her work with prostitutes.

The life that Mrs Butler wrote of John Grey testifies to the amiability of the Grey household in which she grew up and to her own respect and admiration for her father.

I believe that his political principles and public actions were alike the direct fruit of that which held rule within his soul – I mean his large benevolence, his tender compassionateness, and his respect for the rights and liberties of the individual man. His life was a sustained effort for the good of others . . . He had no grudge against rank or wealth, no restless desire of change for its own sake . . . but he could not endure to see oppression or wrong of any kind inflicted on man, woman or child.[57]

She continues to justify the biography:

Men of great integrity and purity of life, who have no thought of pushing into any ambitious spheres, but only of doing with all their might the work which their hands find to do, are the salt of society, the strength of a nation and it is not well that such should be forgot.[58]

Mr Grey was sympathetic to the views of his sister on the need for more educational and occupational opportunities for women, and his attachment to the women within his own family is explicit in a letter to a daughter in Naples, who had just given birth to a girl, referring to the Italian practice of hanging out a black flag on the birth of a daughter to indicate the bad news:

I marvel to hear of anything so unnatural and unwise as the great preference that is given in your new country to boys, and the little estimation that girls are held in . . . What gives warmth to the affections, and strength to the principles of the rising generation, compared to the early influence and attachment – the inherent power of a mother's love? Looking back to the invaluable blessing of an excellent mother, and the happiness of a family of daughters . . . I can speak and feel practically on that subject.[59]

The six girls in the Grey family were largely educated by their parents. Apart from her mother and father Josephine was especially close to her sister Harriet, and remained so throughout her life. Also in the Grey household was a family nurse, the figure familiar to the more wealthy ladies of this study.

Though a poorly educated woman, her Christian thoughtfulness and sustained communion with God gave her a wisdom which made her the sought adviser of many beyond our own family. My father or mother would often visit her alone in the nursery at night . . . in order to confer with her on matters of difficulty, or of the deepest concern to the family.[60]

In her later life the most important support for Mrs Butler in her work seems to have come from her husband. George Butler was a Liberal and academic, a sportsman, mountain walker, lecturer at Durham University and subsequently lecturer and examiner at Oxford where he was ordained in 1853. In Mrs Butler's words he was more than a helper in her work:

> He had a part in the creation of it, in the formation of the first impulse towards it. . . . The idea of justice to women, of equality between the sexes and of equality of responsibility of all human beings to the Moral Law seems to have been instinctive in him.[61]

Mrs Butler recalls her shock on encountering the conventional prejudices of Oxford masculine society but also the disdain of her husband for the 'one-sided arguments' of the men around him, 'they know no better poor fellows', he remarked. For Josephine Butler this was a new light on affairs. Oxford men she had supposed would be authorities on spiritual and moral matters. George Butler was equally gifted, intelligent and learned but with him the 'blessed gift of common sense came to the rescue'.[62]

After only a few years the Oxford climate had undermined Mrs Butler's health. Back at her father's house her husband wrote to her: 'The only earthly anxiety I have is that your health may be sufficiently restored to you to enable you to do the work for which you are so well fitted.'[63] The following year her doctors advised Mrs Butler to leave Oxford for good and within a few months her husband was appointed Vice-Principal of Cheltenham College, ten years later moving to become Principal of Liverpool College. It was here that Mrs Butler began to visit destitute girls and prostitutes in the workhouse oakum sheds and hospital, bringing them first into the cellar and garrets of her own house, later establishing a separate House of Rest and Industrial Home. A widowed sister came to help her in this 'work without a name' and her husband acted as chaplain, friend and adviser to the women inmates.

In 1869 Josephine Butler was asked to lead the campaign against the Contagious Diseases Acts. Middle age and married status gave a measure of freedom and social respectability that made it more possible for women to speak in public about prostitution. Mrs Butler was, it seems, preferred to Florence Nightingale or Harriet Martineau as leader of the Ladies' National Association because she was married and with children.[64] But the prospect was a grim one. The revulsion aroused by the subject of prostitution may be gauged from Mrs

Butler's careful delicacy when she later wrote about this part of her work: 'in consideration for some who may open this book with a fear in their minds lest it should contain painful details I shall say at once that not one word shall occur in its pages which might offend the most fastidious reader'.[65]

George Butler gave his unqualified support, but desiring not to neglect his college duties he limited his appearances at meetings with his wife to vacations. Nonetheless his public association with the campaign cost him his chances of promotion, a sacrifice, according to his wife, that was deliberately accepted. Nor did he escape the censure of church dignitaries. In 1872 the Church Congress met to discuss 'The Duty of the Church in reference to the Moral State of Society in various Classes at the Present Time', but refused to hear a paper from George Butler protesting against the contagious diseases legislation, and he was later rebuked by the Archbishop of York for attempting to raise the subject.[66]

The debt that Mrs Butler owed her husband is summed up in a letter from the sister with whom she was most intimate: 'There breathes no woman on earth who would miss her husband more were he taken first – not one who depends more upon him. Next to God he is the strength for good in you; you stand rooted in his calm faith and deep quiet sympathy and approval.'[67]

Neither Miss Carpenter nor Miss Hill married, so the important family relationships were with parents and siblings, cousins, uncles and aunts. These seem to have been affectionate and reliable for both women, a help rather than a hindrance in their public activities. Although neither married each appeared at some time either to have wished or intended to do so, but there is little evidence that disappointment caused lasting bitterness.

Miss Carpenter's strongest ties seem to have been to her father. 'To his daughter he was prophet as well as parent, and her whole mood and demeanour reflected his.'[68] When Dr Carpenter died in 1839 his daughter suffered from prolonged depression, finding it necessary even three years later to take a continental holiday to gain some relief. But rather like Miss Potter's memories of her mother, Miss Carpenter retained after her father's death, according to her biographer, the sense of encouragement that she had received from him when he was alive.

The companionship of study, of philanthropic interest, of worship and affection, was thus exchanged for an inward fellowship, transcending the conditions of her daily work, and mingling with ever higher aspiration. Not only in the pursuits with which he had been associated, but in each new enterprise he led the way for her; even amid the sickening moments of failure and defeat . . . a spiritual sympathy gave strength and light.[69]

As Miss Carpenter's work with ragged schools and reformatories expanded some conflicts of duties arose. She did not entirely escape opposition from family and friends over the growth of outside commitments.

I feel that I have a work which *I must do* . . . I have now an idea to develop in acts . . . which my friends would dissuade me from. I feel that I must try to do it. Heavenly Father do thou help me and by the Spirit of Christ . . . may I overcome them that oppose themselves.[70]

Such problems, however, seem to have been insignificant by comparison with the family affection and sympathy maintained throughout her life. Holidays were frequently spent with brothers or sister. She was her mother's companion and nurse until she died. The death of her sister brought great grief, and condolences from Florence Nightingale. 'But I must have two hearts, one to rejoice with her who is now in the Joy of her Lord, and who we are very sure does not wish to come back . . . and one to grieve with you over this insupportable and touching loss.'[71] Four years later Miss Carpenter spoke of her continuing sense of loss in a letter to a friend: 'But the journey [to America] did nothing towards filling the void caused by the depature of my sister Anna, my loved companion for 62 years . . . There is no one who cares for me as she did . . . excuse this personality. But you know that I am *essentially* a woman . . .'[72] Similar feelings were aroused by the death of the brother in America whom she had earlier been visiting. 'This is a great blow to me . . . a love of 57 years since I nursed by brother as an infant.'

With Octavia Hill there is little sign of any family opposition to the work she set herself to do and her public life was smoothed by continuing domestic sympathy. The support of her family was complete as was hers for them. From time to time the health of one or other failed and holidays in Europe or in Wales or in the Lake District followed to recover strength. The mutual affection is evident in the letters exchanged and also in the easy co-operation in family activities. By 1870 her sisters were doing most of the teaching in the Nottingham Place school as Octavia Hill became more involved with housing work. In 1877, when illness caused her doctor to order a prolonged foreign tour, her sisters and 'fellow workers' and friends took over all her responsibilities. Her mother wrote to express affection and encouragement:

> I feel it a great blessing that you have no anxiety about your work. I am glad, both for its sake, and for yours; for I am sure you could not recover, as we wish you to do, if you felt things were likely to go ill. I hope this change will prove an improvement in its organisation, and the beginning of an easier life for you. You have climbed the hill far enough to look back, and survey the road passed over; and reflection will suggest to you by what future paths the goal you set for yourself is most likely to be reached. Accept this interval, as the precious time lent you for retrospect and prospect and for renewing the bodily health that you have expended so unsparingly.[73]

And a letter from Miss Hill to her mother on her birthday underlines the strength of the ties between them all.

> I think of you so, and shall think of you on the day . . . how you are all doing, and have done so much, and how little I am doing to combat the difficulties that every day brings. I do hope you all know that I am better; *that* will make one anxiety less. How I think of you all . . . Among them all, however, you seem to me to have the heaviest weight, who have to care for us and think for and of us, and be our centre and head.[74]

The family experiences of the remaining four women are less easy to penetrate. Only Annie Besant married, and that for but a few unhappy years. As a child and young girl, closely attached to her mother, she appears to have had a peaceful and affectionate life, in spite of the death of her father and the modest material circumstances of the household. Later, family support meant less to her than her search for a faith to replace Christianity, her interest in free thought and her friendship with Bradlaugh. After she left her husband in 1873 her brother offered her a home on condition that she give up her heretical friends and 'keep quiet'. She rejected it, but arrangements to set up house with her mother foundered when Mrs Wood died. She retained and prized the affection of her children, but she chose to continue with propaganda for free thinking and social reform even though this meant the loss of custody of her daughter. After a time right of access was granted her, but when she found her visits disturbed the child she stopped them and determined that '. . . robbed of my own, I would be a mother to all helpless children I could aid, and cure the pain of my own heart by soothing the pain of others.'[75]

Political zeal seems to have been the impetus that drove Annie Besant into her public activities, and family relationships took second place. Whether this demonstrates the strength of her principles or the weakness of her affections is not clear, nor for present purposes is it important. The significant thing is that Mrs Besant led a public life in pursuit of extremely unpopular causes without the support of conventional family affections. Possibily her friendship with Bradlaugh that developed after 1874 provided some substitute.

Frances Power Cobbe, Agnes Jones and Louisa Twining all appear to have had reasonably happy family lives. Miss Cobbe speaks of the great affection between her and her mother and the kindness of her father and brothers, though she also recalls a lonely childhood. Apart from her mother, who encouraged her early attempts to educate herself, Miss Cobbe pursued her ambitions with little support and some opposition from her family though her attachments remained secure. Her father sent her out of the house when he learned of her 'heresy'. The brother to whom she went and where she spent months of 'utter loneliness' was kind to her, though thought her father's behaviour quite natural. She was summoned back to her father's house after nearly a year only to live in a 'sort of moral coventry'. Running the household, teaching in the village school and visiting the sick left little time for her own work. Her reading and writing had to be at night and in the early morning. When she completed her *Essay on the Theory of Intuitive Morals* her father was displeased that she should publish a book, even though she wrote anonymously to save him annoyance. After her father's death she lived independently, though continuing to visit all her brothers and after some years the elder increased her allowance.

Knowledge of the family life of Agnes Jones comes from the biography written by her sister, which suggests tranquil and affectionate relationships sustained on the part of Agnes by a strong sense of religious commitment to her family as well as to a nursing career. Her sister records that Agnes was especially fond of her father and suffered greatly at his death when she was 18. Affection and a sense of duty led her to accede to her mother's objection to her training as a nurse and delay her entry to St Thomas's as a Nightingale probationer without bitterness and she readily responded to a call to nurse her sister in Rome.

Little is known of Miss Twining's family experiences. In her autobiography she is extremely reticent about personal matters. The family was liberal, cultivated and devout but we cannot judge the strength of their attachments nor of the encouragement or otherwise offered to Miss Twining in her public work.

For most of the women, then, family ties were very significant in the move into public life. Generally, they provided support and consolation, sometimes they aroused bitter conflict, occasionally they led to both. But they could not be ignored. They offered some measure of continuing emotional security even to Florence Nightingale. Only Annie Besant ended an unhappy marriage. All the others contrived a compromise between duty and affection for their families and their personal ambitions. But the conceptions that they and their families held of women's rights and responsibilities significantly affected the quality of the relationships and the character of the compromises. It is to the various views about a woman's place that we now turn.

5 A Woman's Place

The character of the public work they chose presented varying obstacles for the ten women in this study. That they chose such work at all implies a rejection of the conventional views that limited women to domestic and family responsibilities. How then did they perceive their own role and that of others of their sex?

Their conception of right and duties, their hopes and aspirations, grew out of certain common experiences of social background and family upbringing. These were ladies who inherited family traditions of active interest in public affairs, in social reform, in church matters, science and literature. They also shared a family tradition that confidently assumed leadership of movements and of opinion, and that took for granted both the right and the duty to engage in public debate and public action. Their class and social relationships, family culture and religious faith, combined to mould a special kind of social personality.

To this extent the early social workers and reformers drew great strength from their class position. But they were also vulnerable, both within their families and in the outside world, to prevailing ideas about how they should behave as women. Josephine Butler claimed that the radical politics of the Grey family, particularly of her father, extended to a belief in equality between the sexes and that she suffered no sense of inferiority or lack of opportunity as a young woman before her marriage. And in general the ladies came from educated and cultivated families with liberal and reformist political leanings that protected them personally from extreme forms of discrimination. Frances Power Cobbe remarks several times in her autobiography that she never experienced injustice or unkindness from father or brothers. When she became a 'woman's rights woman', she says, it was not because she in her own person had been made to feel a 'woman's wrongs'. Rather, the knowledge of the oppression of *other* women lay heavy on her mind.[1]

Family pressure to observe a particular kind of feminine behaviour varied. Florence Nightingale was particularly unfortunate and Josephine Butler especially lucky. But for the majority of the nineteenth-century pioneers, and for most of the time, their families were a source of strength in their public work rather than repressive institutions from which they had to break free. Thus most of the ladies placed a high value on the family and on a woman's special place within it. Their support for women's rights generally extended only so far as such wider opportunities could be shown to present no threat to family life, no hostility to men, no sacrifice of 'womanly' qualities. Few believed in equality between the sexes and most accepted that women had or should have certain attributes of character and personality that fitted them for particular sorts of activity.

To be 'lady-like' was extremely important for the women who moved into public life, both for their own self-esteem and to turn aside the wrath of more conservative opinion. In 1869 Elizabeth Garrett, fighting to win her rights to medical education on the same terms as men, wrote indignantly to Emily Davies about the unsuitable behaviour of one of their acquaintance.

> I do wish the D's dressed better . . . she looks awfully strong-minded in walking dress . . . she has short petticoats and a close round hat, and several other dreadfully ugly arrangements . . . it is abominable, and most damaging to the cause. I will not have her visit me at the hospital in it . . . Experience is modifying my notions about the most suitable style of dress for me to wear at the hospital. I feel confident now that one is helped rather than hindered by being as much like a lady as lies within one's power.[2]

This is a good example of the endeavours of the 'muted group' to observe the prejudice of the dominant group but there were many more. Miss Clough, Principal of Newnham, was well aware of the suspicion aroused by women students in Cambridge and anxious to demonstrate that the pursuit of higher education need involve no departure from conventional proprieties. After a complaint that Newnham students had been seen buttoning their gloves on the streets she gently remonstrated. 'I know, my dears, that you have a great deal to do, and have not much time; but I don't like people to say such things about you, and so, my dears, I hope you'll get some gloves that don't want buttoning.'[3] The women who supported the franchise faced particular hostility and some, at any rate, were at pains to disarm it.

> It was evident that the audiences came expecting to see curious masculine objects walking on to the platform, and when we appeared, with our quiet black dresses, the whole expression of

the faces of the audience would instantly change. I shall never forget the thrill which passed through us when, on one occasion, a Nonconformist minister assured the audience in his speech from the chair, that we were 'quite respectable' – meaning to convey that we were people with some position, and not merely seeking notoriety or earning money by our speaking.[4]

In some cases of course women might find their sex an advantage, as Florence Nightingale realised. 'A woman obtains from military courtesy (if she does not shock either their habits of business or their caste prejudices) what a man, who pitted the civilian against the military, effectually hindered.'[5] This sensitivity to 'habits of business and caste prejudices' induced a caution in her reforming efforts which was probably essential for their success. In a rather different way, but still attempting to disarm male antagonism, Mrs Butler was at great pains to argue that the repeal of the Contagious Diseases Acts was in the interests not only of women but also of men and would thus benefit the whole community.

The women's views on a woman's place may be discussed in terms of their position as daughters within their families, their experiences of and attitudes to marriage and to society, and their opinions about women's rights in general.

WOMEN AS DAUGHTERS

The weight of conventional opinion bore particularly heavily on Florence Nightingale and Beatrice Potter in their youth. In diaries and letters they inveigh against their restricted lives, the demands made upon them by their families and by society, their inability to establish their independence. Florence Nightingale wrote especially bitterly:

Women don't consider themselves as human beings at all. There is absolutely no God, no country, no duty to them at all, except family . . . but I know nothing like the petty grinding tyranny of a good English family . . . What I complain of the Evangelical Party for is the degree to which they have raised the claims upon women of 'Family' – the idol they have made of it. It is a kind of Fetichism. There is no duty, no right, no happiness for a woman beyond her Fetich. They acknowledge no God, for all they say to the contrary, but this Fetich . . . It is only in the lives of the upper classes that you see this.[6]

The Nightingale family circumstances offered great privileges of wealth, education and a wide circle of distinguished and cultivated friends and acquaintances. But for a woman who wanted independent life and work they contained fatal flaws. Mrs Nightingale's ambitions for her daughters required that they attend to household and family duties, acquire accomplishments, take their place in society and make successful marriages. Even as a child Florence appeared ill at ease in the social world of her mother and elder sister, inclining more to the intellectual and literary tastes of her father. As she grew older, the dissatisfaction sharpened. Clever and cultivated, charming and elegant, she moved easily in the intellectual and political circles of Europe and London. But unable to reconcile herself to what she conceived to be an aimless existence, her sympathy with her sister and parents grew increasingly limited. Mr Nightingale was a careful landlord and Mrs Nightingale took an interest in village schools and charities but these activities were rather 'graces rightly incidental to their station, than the main business of life'.[7] About her own youth Mrs Nightingale had written, 'We Smiths never thought of anything all day long but our own ease and pleasure.'[8] Home life for her daughters supplied comfort and security, affection, intelligence and companionship but little freedom. Miss Nightingale's desire for a vocation made such circumstances intolerable. In 1852 she wrote an autobiographical sketch, *Cassandra*, of the life of a girl in a prosperous family. Subject to incessant frivolous and trivial demands and unable to follow any serious interest, Cassandra eventually dies, unable either to find happiness in her life or to alter it.

My people were like children, playing on the shore of the eighteenth century. I was their hobby horse, their plaything; and they drove me to and fro, dear souls! never weary of the play themselves, till I, who had grown to woman's estate and to the ideas of the nineteenth century lay down exhausted, my mind closed to hope, my heart to strength, 'Free – free – oh! divine freedom, art thou come at last? Welcome beautiful death!'[9]

With such a sense of the destructive and intrusive character of family relationships and with so keen a desire for independent work, it is not surprising that Florence Nightingale rejected marriage as a possible escape from the constrictions of home life. Teaching, more socially acceptable than nursing, she had tried and disliked. Writing, for which she had some gift, she regarded as a poor substitute for action. 'I had so much rather live than write; writing is only a substitute for living.'[10]

Mrs Webb's autobiographical writings also describe a troubled and unhappy childhood within a similarly wealthy and cultivated family. Her closest ties as a girl appear to have been with her father. Her mother, preferring others among her children, remained remote and little sympathy developed between the two women until a year or two before Mrs Potter's death.[11] It was at this point that family expectations about female responsibilities weighed most heavily on Beatrice Potter. As the only unmarried adult daughter she became the manager of the Potter household, meeting place of seven married sisters, her father's counsellor and the guardian of her younger sister. The companionship of her father and young sister was pleasant to her, but other family duties and the conventional assumptions of the time threatened her efforts to form her own life.

> But there were other assumptions with regard to the whole duty
> of woman that I refused to accept. According to the current code,
> the entire time and energy of an unmarried daughter . . . was
> assumed to be spent, either in serving the family group, or in
> entertaining or being entertained by the social circle to which she
> belonged.[12]

Determined to avoid this fate and doubting the sympathy of her sisters, she concealed her plans for self-education from family and acquaintance. As we have seen, she rose early in the morning to read and work and described those hours as the happiest of the day.

Such efforts to prepare for their future while living more or less conventional lives were common to Miss Potter and Miss Nightingale. Both rejected the normal social diversions and preoccupations of women of their class but family claims could not be altogether denied. Ties of duty and affection were strong. Both women looked after various members of their families during sickness and death, Florence Nightingale delaying her nursing training and Beatrice Potter postponing her social research. Neither was free to embark on her independent work until they were thirty-three or thirty-four years old. The conflicts for Miss Potter were less acute, the bitterness about the position of women in English middle-class families less evident.

Indeed she later explained her initial opposition to female suffrage by claiming that she was conservative by temperament, anti-democratic by social environment and without personal experience of the disadvantages of being a woman. Nor, in the end, did she reject marriage.

None of the other women in the study experienced such severe constraints in their childhood and youth. On the contrary, family relationships seem to have been unusually close and affectionate and filial duty willingly rendered. Neither the social opportunities nor the pressure to enter society and make good marriages evident in the wealthy Nightingale and Potter families appear among the others. These were distinguished by more explicit parental religious commitment – frequently expressed in family prayers and Bible reading – and by stronger family traditions of radical political interests and philanthropic work. Only Agnes Jones postponed her nursing training in deference to her mother's opposition. The question at issue was whether she should continue work in London as a 'Bible Woman', which she enjoyed, or become a Nightingale probationer nurse, which she had come to feel she was called to do. But the opposition only lasted for a year and the delay occasioned no bitterness, Miss Jones accepting her mother's authority and the power of God to determine the best outcome: 'Trustfully and prayerfully have I left it in the hands of my Heavenly Father, and if He incline not my Mother's heart to allow of my going to St Thomas's, I shall thank him that he has provided me with another field of labour.'[13]

This letter was written when Agnes Jones was nearly 30.

WOMEN AND MARRIAGE

The position of daughter involved a set of responsibilities to parents and brothers and sisters and to more distant relations. It was also a sort of apprenticeship for girls to prepare them for marriage, conventionally the most important and respected feminine achievement. For the most part, however, the assumption that the first duty of a woman was to provide sympathy, support and care for husband and children fitted ill with a life dedicated to public social service. It is true that Mrs Gladstone among many others was notable for her philanthropic work.[14] Nursing cholera victims and setting up a home for orphans whose parents had died from the disease were among her many charitable activities. These however were not permitted to infringe on her observance of the responsibilities of the prime minister's wife. A spectator gave a malicious description of Mr and Mrs Gladstone at a meeting in the 1880s:

> He is followed by a simply dressed woman who busies herself in warding off the hands of enthusiasts eager to touch him. This is Mrs Gladstone, with the soft face, high coloured like a girl's, and tremulous mouth, intent on one thing only in this life – her husband. They step up to the platform by a reporter's stool. A dozen willing hands would aid him but it is hers which grasped his ankles to steady him lest in his eagerness he should slip. She begs a seat immediately behind him. Forth he stands and begins at once, 'Mr Chairman!' She pulls at his overcoat and one sleeve comes free; impatiently he stops while she tugs at the other sleeve. Two more sentences and he is fairly launched upon a sea of passion regardless of Mrs Gladstone who sits behind, placidly folding her husband's overcoat.[15]

Among the women deeply committed to social service, marriage, if it occurred, tended to have an unusual character. Mrs Fry, Mrs Butler and Mrs Webb all had marriages that gave them enormous support in their outside work but which for that very reason were extremely unconventional.

Elizabeth Gurney was born and married into old Quaker families. But Quakers believed in and practised an unusual degree of equality between the sexes. No promise of obedience was required of the woman at the marriage ceremony and women were recognised by the Friends as ministers. 'Their independence is equal, their dependence mutual, and their obligations reciprocal.'[16] Mrs Fry had become a plain Quaker before her marriage at 20 and four years later she came to believe that God wished her to be a minister. After another seven years she was so acknowledged in 1811. The respect and freedom accorded to women within the Quaker community no doubt made it easier for them to assume responsibilities outside their families. Certainly for Mrs Fry her religious faith and prison work were inextricably bound together. Both took her away from her home, and this was matter for some distress for her. In 1806 she wrote that she desired above all things to have a life in doing the will of her creator. The difficulty was to know what that might be:

> but some lowness and discouragement have been my portion lately,

fearing from so many objects of duty, I should become perplexed; and also others fear for me, that I should in consequence neglect my home duties. May this not be the case. Oh! may I be directed what to do, and what to leave undone, and then I may humbly trust, that a blessing will be with me in my various engagements.[17]

As we have seen, such conflicts of duty were eased by the loyalty and affection of her large family as well as by ample material resources. In the conclusion to their memoir of Elizabeth Fry, her daughters write that she considered domestic duties the first and greatest earthly claim on women. But she also believed, in accordance with the tenets of the Quakers, that occasionally individuals were called to leave their home and families for other work.[18]

Josephine Butler also attached great importance to women's domestic responsibilities. Only three of her four children survived infancy, so she could combine public and family life more easily than Mrs Fry. Moreover, her husband was prepared to sacrifice his own work to hers and he provided constant affection and support. Thus, for Mrs Butler personally there was little conflict. And she generalised her own experiences in joining her pleas for more rights for women with insistence on the fundamental importance of family life: 'for I believe that Home is the nursery of all virtue, the fountain-head of all true affection, and the main source of the strength of our nation.'[19]

Mrs Webb was a third woman who combined marriage with her public work and again it was a marriage of a peculiar kind. It was postponed until after her father's death when she was 34 and it was childless. It was conceived from the first as a partnership in research and writing and is anticipated in her diary a year before her wedding.

We are both of us second-rate minds; but we are curiously combined. I am the investigator and he the executant; between us we have a wide and varied experience of men and affairs. We have also an unearned salary. These are unique circumstances. A considerable work should be the result if we use our combined talents with a deliberate and persistent purpose.[20]

Earlier Miss Potter had rejected any possibility of marriage with Joseph Chamberlain because she feared the customary subordination of the woman to the man would have made it, in that case, impossible 'to write, to unite the life of love and the life of reason'. But the

conflict between the desire for a normal and successful marriage and
the right to free activity was acute.

> Life seems to my consciousness a horrible fact . . . I am never at
> peace with myself now; the whole of my past looks like an
> irretrievable blunder. I have mistaken the facts of human life as
> far as my own existence is concerned. I am not strong enough to
> live without happiness . . . I struggle through each new day waking
> with suicidal thoughts early in the morning; I try by determined
> effort to force my thoughts on the old lines of continuous enquiry,
> and to beat back feeling into the narrow rut of duty . . . eight and
> twenty, and living without hope![21]

To marry, then, for a woman committed to some form of social
service, or, indeed, to any independent public career, required careful
arrangement and the deliberate choice of a partner who shared her
intellectual or philanthropic interests. Beatrice Potter comments on
the rather incongruous marriage of the Barnetts:

> At 19 years of age, pretty, witty, and well-to-do, Henrietta Rowland
> married the plain and insignificant curate who was her fellow-
> worker in the parish of St. Marylebone; not solely . . . because he
> had won her admiration and affection, but also as a way of
> dedicating her life to the service of the poor.[22]

Mrs Barnett herself has described her feelings on receiving Mr
Barnett's proposal. She was very surprised, she recalls, as she had
thought his 'many communications' represented his anxiety for the
success of Octavia Hill's social experiment which required the careful
supervision of new young workers. Moreover, he looked so much
older than his 27 years that Miss Rowland had accepted his interest
'as that of a kindly elderly gentleman, with small sensitive hands, a
bald head and shaggy beard'.[23] She goes on to recount Mr Barnett's
eccentricities of dress and behaviour and his parsimonious habits in
small matters that were entirely contradictory to his 'real generosity
of heart' but were unattractive to a girl reared in a luxurious home
and accustomed to lavish living and entertaining. She was troubled
by his proposal of marriage and was first inclined to refuse it, but
realised that if she did, one or other must 'give up Miss Octavia's
work'. Unwilling to damage Miss Hill's plans, she delayed a decision

for six months, endeavouring to look behind the 'irritating manner-isms' and eventually 'realised that his gift of love was too holy to refuse'.[24]

In a rather similar way Annie Besant also claimed that she married her husband, a deacon at a mission church in Clapham, as a way of realising her desire to work among the poor. But she married without love, after a brief acquaintance and 'with no more idea of the marriage relation than if I had been four years old instead of twenty'.[25] The result was disaster and finally separation when, after six years and the birth of two children, Mrs Besant's doubts over Christian belief led her to refuse to take communion. Told by her husband that she must conform to the outward observances of the church or leave the house, she left the house. Her description of her experiences and her reaction to them illustrate the conflict between conventional domestic assumptions and arrangements and a woman's desire for independence.

> We were an ill-matched pair, my husband and I . . . he, with very high ideas of a husband's authority and a wife's submission, holding strongly to the 'master-in-my-house' theory, thinking much of the details of home arrangements, precise, methodical, easily angered and with difficulty appeased. I, accustomed to freedom, indifferent to home details, impulsive, very hot-tempered, and proud as Lucifer. I had never had a harsh word spoken to me, never been ordered to do anything, had had my way smoothed for my feet, and never a worry had touched me. Harshness roused first incredulous wonder, then a storm of indignant tears, and after a time a proud, defiant resistance, cold and hard as iron.[26]

But it was not only her husband with whom Mrs Besant was at odds. She lived, she claimed,

> with strangers about me with whom I had no sympathy; visited by ladies who talked to me only about babies and servants – troubles of which I knew nothing and which bored me unutterably – and who were as uninterested in all that had filled my life, in theology, in politics, in science, as I was uninterested in discussions on the house maid's young man and the cook's extravagance in using 'butter when dripping would have done perfectly well, my dear'.[27]

With such expectations attaching to marriage, it is not surprising that many women who were publicly active remained single. Some had little opportunity to do other, as women outnumbered men throughout the later part of the nineteenth century. But for most of the middle-class ladies of this study, comfortable circumstances, social and family connections, cultural interests and activities and the public acclaim they increasingly received for their work meant that spinsterhood was a perfectly acceptable alternative to conventional marriage.

Miss Nightingale and Miss Potter both on occasion rejected marriage as a constraint on their independence, and in spite of strong emotional attachments. But whereas Beatrice Potter later accepted Sydney Webb, Florence Nightingale remained single. Of her refusal of Monckton Milnes she wrote:

> I have an intellectual nature which requires satisfaction and that would find it in him. I have a passionate nature which requires satisfaction, and that would find it in him. I have a moral, an active nature which requires satisfaction, and that would not find it in his life . . . I could not satisfy this nature by spending my life with him in making society and arranging domestic things . . . to be nailed to a continuation and exaggeration of my present life, without hope of another, would be intolerable to me . . . would seem to me like suicide.[28]

Several years before the proposal from Monckton Milnes was ever made she had written of marriage as depriving women not of what 'at their festivals the idle and inconsiderate call life', but as in reality bringing the end of life and the chill of death.[29] Nevertheless the passionate attacks on marriage and the 'grinding tyranny' of family life were tempered by anguish over what she had lost. Perhaps the stormy relationships with her mother and sister and the highly emotional personality that grew out of them, exacerbated by periods of illness, made Miss Nightingale more vulnerable than the other single women in this study. In 1862 she wrote to her mother in despair:

> I have lost all. All the others have children or some high and inspiring interest to live for – while I have lost husband and children and all. And am left to the dreary hopeless struggle . . . I am glad

to end a day which never can come back, gladder to end a night, gladder still to end a month.[30]

In contrast, people like Octavia Hill, Mary Carpenter, Louisa Twining, Agnes Jones and Frances Power Cobbe seemed to have had sufficiently close and affectionate ties with parents, siblings and other relations to provide them with all the family they needed and also to imbue them with a profound respect for what Josephine Butler called 'home elements'.

Miss Cobbe remarks in her autobiography that life had been pleasant and interesting even without marriage. She enjoyed acting as housekeeper for her father, and grief on her mother's death was assuaged by household duties. As we have seen, she displeased her father by writing and publishing her *Essay on the Theory of Intuitive Morals*, and displeased him more seriously by becoming an agnostic. Her only leisure for writing and reading were at night and in the early morning. Otherwise she carried on the 'feminine correspondence' of the household, taught in the village school and visited the poor and the sick. 'Like most women I was bound hand and foot by a fine web of little duties and attentions which men never feel.'[31] None of this, however, disturbed Miss Cobbe's willing absorption in domestic responsibilities or her own writing – largely on morals and religious duty. Her interests in social and political reform developed after her father's death when she left the family home.

Nor does Agnes Jones appear to have contemplated marriage. Extremely devout, she lived in Ireland until she was nearly 30, teaching in the village school and visiting the sick and the poor but searching for a 'life-work to employ the faculties which God has given me: they are not many or great mentally but they are His gift, and I desire to devote them to His service.'[32] When she finally decided that nursing should be her vocation it was relatively easy for her to leave home as her widowed sister was able to act as companion to her widowed mother. Her total commitment to nursing is evident in her reaction to the appalling conditions in the Liverpool workhouse where she died of typhus in 1868.

I sometimes wonder if there is a worse place on the earth than Liverpool, and I am sure its workhouse is burdened with a large proportion of its vilest. I can only compare it and Sodom, and I wonder how God stays his hand from smiting. Then, so little effort is made to stem the evil. All lie passive, and seem to say it must be. The attempt at introducing paid workers has certainly not met with any sympathy from clergy or laity. In the nearly ended two years of our work, how few have ever come for the work's sake to wish us God speed in it! I do not mean to say that I am discouraged. I believe we have had the blessing of the poor; I never regret coming and I never wish to give it up.[33]

Of the other women in the study Octavia Hill rejected an offer of marriage, though apparently without the anguish felt by Miss Nightingale. There is no record of either Miss Twining or Miss Carpenter having considered it, and little evidence of their personal feelings about it. Through Mary Carpenter's diaries, however, there runs a thread of wistful desire for some form of companionship closer than any she experienced. When she was 40 and had opened her first ragged school in Bristol she wrote of her unspeakable joy but continued, 'yet still there seems a want of my nature unsatisfied. . . . But if my God knew that it would be good for me to have such a companion in my pilgrimage . . . he would not withhold the blessing. Be still then, my soul . . .'.[34]

WOMEN AND SOCIETY

Apart from the claims of their families Victorian women also had to come to terms with expectations about appropriate feminine behaviour in the outside world. For those wishing to devote their lives to social service, or indeed any other public work, this inevitably meant some measure of withdrawal from the social life normal to their class and position. George Eliot refused to make visits because she found herself trapped in futile conversation and preferred to limit her social intercourse to people whom she actually wished to see by inviting them to her own house.

I have found it a necessity of my London life to make the rule of *never* paying visits . . . and I am obliged to give up the *few* visits which would be really attractive and fruitful in order to avoid the *many* visits which would be the reverse. It is only by saying, 'I never pay visits', that I can escape being ungracious or unkind – only by renouncing all social intercourse but such as comes to my own fireside, that I can escape sacrificing the chief objects of life.[35]

Emily Davies, on the other hand, though finding it in some ways uncongenial, recognised that it might be worthwhile to cultivate 'high society'.

> There are difficulties . . . the talk is apt to run on people that one does not know, and things . . . that are quite out of one's way . . . I felt directly that if I went to Lady Stanley's again I must get a new bonnet. And is it well to spend one's money on bonnets and flys instead of on instructive books? But on the whole I think the advantages preponderate.[36]

The demands of society were more insistent and more tempting for women from wealthy families who commonly spent several months of the year in London. Elizabeth Gurney, Beatrice Potter and Florence Nightingale all had the entrée to the metropolitan society of their time and all, though with some hesitation and regret, rejected it. For Elizabeth Gurney this was a renouncing of worldly pleasure that attended her gradual acceptance of the tenets of the plain Quakers. Even music and dancing within her father's household became a source of distress to Miss Gurney and she gradually withdrew from such pursuits. After her marriage, although a great deal of entertaining took place, particularly of relatives and visiting Quakers, the atmosphere was more sober and family prayers and Bible reading, instituted by Mrs Fry, replaced the more frivolous domestic amusements of the Gurney family.

Miss Nightingale and Miss Potter were more exposed, through family custom, to the distractions of London and indeed European society. Both women delighted in theatres, balls and other entertainments and in the admiration aroused by their own personal elegance and cultivated minds. Both too were troubled by their susceptibility to what they increasingly defined as vain and trivial pastimes which conflicted with the anxious search for a serious purpose in their lives. In 1839, following eighteen months of foreign travel attended by admiration and success in the intellectual, political and literary society of Geneva and Paris, Miss Nightingale wrote that before she could be free to interpret God's call she must first overcome 'the desire to shine' in society.[37]

Beatrice Potter's early determination not to 'come out' melted away in the face of the expectations and attractions of London society but she later attacked that same society with devastating ferocity:

Now the first and foremost characteristic of the London season and country house life . . . was the fact that some of the men and practically all the women made the pursuit of pleasure their main occupation in life . . . How well I recollect those first days of my early London seasons: the pleasurable but somewhat feverish anticipation of endless distraction, a dissipation of mental and physical energy which filled up all the hours of the day and lasted far into the night; the ritual to be observed; the presentation at Court, the riding in the Row, the calls, the lunches and dinners, the dances and crushes, Hurlingham, and Ascot, not to mention amateur theatricals and other sham philanthropic excrescences. There was of course a purpose in all this apparently futile activity, the business of getting married . . . by the end of the season, indigestion and insomnia had undermined physical health; a distressing mental nausea, taking the form of cynicism about one's own and other people's character, had destroyed all faith in and capacity for steady work.[38]

The qualification for membership, Mrs Webb goes on, was some form of power over other people and the most obvious kind of power was wealth.

Hence any family of outstanding riches, if its members were not actually mentally deficient or legally disreputable, could hope to rise to the top, marry its daughters to Cabinet Ministers and noblemen and even become in time itself ennobled.[39]

In her own time, Mrs Webb remarks, men with broad culture and great experience of public affairs were beginning to be overshadowed by millionaire newspaper proprietors, distinguished neither by wit, wisdom, technical skill nor professional good manners.

What was even more demoralising than this degraded and coarsening scale of values, because it bred a poisonous cynicism about human relations, was the making and breaking of personal friendships according to temporary and accidental circumstances in no way connected with personal merit: gracious appreciation and insistent intimacy being succeeded, when failure according to worldly standards occurred, by harsh criticism and cold avoidance . . . It was this continuous uncertainty as to social status that led to all the ugly methods of entertaining practised by the crowd who wanted 'to get into society'; the variety or 'menagerie' element in many entertainments so often caricatured by *Punch*; the competition in conspicuous expenditure on clothes, food, wine and flowers; above all, the practice of inviting persons with whom you have nothing in common because they would attract desired guests to your house.[40]

Unlike their families, social life had no moral claims upon young women; quite the contrary. But to give it up might be painful enough. 'I do not wish to forego the society of my own class', wrote Beatrice Potter in 1887, 'and yet to enjoy means wasted energy.'[41]

Many of the ladies of this study were protected from the demands and expectations at any rate of London social life by more modest family circumstances or a provincial background. Octavia Hill seems to have lived in London within a congenial circle of Christian Socialists, family and fellow workers, untroubled by the lure of any more glittering society. Miss Carpenter apparently dismissed the claims of social intercourse in Bristol relatively easily:

and some time must, I know, be sacrificed to what are called the claims of Society; but it is not my intention to conform to them in the waste of time and energy usually passing under that name. There is no reason why one should be robbed of one's time and thoughts any more than of one's money.[42]

These remarks were made when Mary Carpenter was nearly 40. Earlier in her life she too had struggled with self-doubt, self-reproach and a sense of unworthiness, with vanity and a desire for admiration.[43]

Nor did social ambitions appear to trouble Agnes Jones who, according to her sister, early put aside worldly pleasures to devote herself to what she conceived to be God's will. Louisa Twining found her greatest interest in her visits and acquaintance among the poor and was little tempted by the more usual social exchanges.

The interest of these visits and these acquaintances was extreme, and I used to prefer them to the conventional and other profitless society of the classes far above them, for with the best of these humble people there was no artificiality and none of the unreality which so often repels friendship and admiration for others of higher rank.[44]

Miss Cobbe, eager to start educating herself at 18 after two years at a smart and inferior girls' school, persuaded her parents to allow her to withdraw from Dublin social life which she found boring; and when she was older and living in London with a large circle of literary and intellectual friends she continued to disclaim any wish to enter society.

Josephine Butler's experiences of social life were unusual in that she moved on marriage into the male dominated society of Oxford where she found women's opinions discounted and a double standard of sexual morality taken for granted. She reacted with shock and indignation, later expressed in her interest in and work for greater equality for women in education and in employment. But the Butlers fitted no more easily into the local society of Cheltenham or Liverpool. In Cheltenham they found themselves socially isolated by their opposition to the South in the American Civil War, and in Liverpool personal sadness over the death of her daughter and lack of interest in the conventional social lives of middle-class women led Mrs Butler to workhouse visiting and her activities with and on behalf of prostitutes.

WOMEN AND WOMEN'S RIGHTS

The ten ladies in this study overwhelmingly subscribed to the view that a woman's most important responsibilities and most enduring rewards lay within the network of family relationships. Even those most bitterly aware of personal conflict between domestic duties and their own ambitions still submitted to the claims of their families. The minority who married chose men who sympathised with their personal aspirations and from whom, with the exception of Annie Besant, they drew strength and support in their public endeavours. The minority who remained single, with the exception of Miss Nightingale, retained their respect for family life and for a woman's place within it.

What the early pioneers insisted, however, was that women should be able to choose alternatives to marriage if they so wished, and without any indignity or loss of public esteem. As Mrs Butler urged against those who maintained that a woman's place was in the home, many women had no home and unmarried women could be a great blessing to the community when they ceased to be 'soured by disappointment or driven to destitution by despair'.[45] Spinsterhood should be regarded as an honourable estate; women should be equipped by education and training to maintain their independence, and employment in government service and the professions should be open to them.

This was not to deny that women had peculiarly feminine attributes that fitted them for particular sorts of work. Indeed, the jobs canvassed for women tended to be those involved with the care or supervision of their own sex, or of children, the old or the sick. In other words, as Parsons later remarked, acceptable public roles for women tended to reflect their family responsibilities. The early female medical students insisted that far from medicine being an unsuitable profession for their sex it was especially important; delicacy required that women doctors be available to deal with women's ailments.[46]

In this sense the early reformers were pragmatists, aiming to remedy particular injustices rather than to elaborate a 'new female image'[47] or to question women's place within the family. Mary Carpenter is a good example of this kind of attitude in her refusal to take part in the discussions at a conference of workers supporting the reformatory school movement which she organised in 1851. 'To have lifted up her voice in an assembly of gentlemen would have been, as she then felt, tantamount to unsexing herself.'[48] The following year she refused an invitation to a meeting of a committee, appointed by the conference to forward its aims, to draft a bill to be submitted to Sir George Grey. 'She knows how jealous the Lords of Creation are of the interference of women, and thought it best to be of real use by . . . corresponding with the leading members of the committee.'[49]

Less than ten years later, however, Miss Carpenter read a paper to the Scientific Association, afterwards remarking on the progress made since 1836 when ladies were not even permitted to be present at the Association's meeting in Bristol.[50] By 1873 the position of women seemed to afford her nothing but satisfaction.

It is quite striking to observe how much the useful power and influence of women has developed of late years. Unattached ladies, such as widows and unmarried women, have quite ample work to do in the world for the good of others, to absorb all their powers.

Wives and mothers have a *very* noble work given them by God, and want no more.[51]

Nevertheless in 1877, encouraged by John Stuart Mill, Miss Carpenter shared the same platform with Miss Cobbe at a meeting in support of female suffrage.

The readiness to accept women's traditional place was also characteristic of Octavia Hill. When she was 21 she wrote to her sister describing Lord Shaftesbury's address to the first public meeting of the Ladies' Association for Sanitary Reform. He had 'urged ladies to attend to all the details of the question, as men could not. The legislative and theoretical work was to be done only by them; the minute and much of the practical by ladies.'[52] Miss Hill accepted this division of labour without comment, nor did she ever support women's suffrage though she was enthusiastic in the cause of higher education.

Higher education, however, could be seen as fitting women for the work especially suitable for them either inside or outside their families. Home life would be strengthened by acknowledging women's rights, Mrs Butler claimed, and to refuse them would 'hasten the day of disorganisation and uprooting of sacred traditions'.[53] Although women's sphere was said to be in the home, many women had no home. 'I trust that such mocking words as these will cease to be spoken.' Education and the possibility of a free and independent life for women with their entry into more important jobs would diffuse 'home influences' among the masses; it would also tend to an increase in marriage as the worth, attractiveness and dignity of women would be restored.

What dignity can there be in the attitude of women . . . when marriage is held to be the one end of a woman's life . . . when those who are soliciting a place in this profession resemble those flaccid Brazilian creepers which cannot exist without support and which sprawl out their tendrils in every direction to find something – no matter what – to hang upon; when the insipidity or material necessities of so many women's lives make them accept almost any man who may offer himself?[54]

Attitudes to female suffrage were far more cautious. This was not a reform that would in itself equip women any better for family life or for independent employment. Nor was it directed at the most glaring social evils. The demand for votes for women claimed a degree of equality between the sexes in abilities and faculties and public activity that challenged the traditional social divisions between men and women and the ideologies and interests which supported them. Nevertheless, while few of the ten ladies actively supported the suffragists only Octavia Hill consistently opposed them. Perhaps, as Harrison has suggested, female philanthropists and political hostesses represented the anti-suffragist ideal for women.[55] But the women in this study were not themselves among the 'Antis'. Even though many believed in 'separate spheres', none wished to restrict women to a child-bearing or domestic role or regarded them as unfitted for public life. The reserve about female suffrage among the group of ten arose partly because they themselves were protected by their class and families from the difficulties many women suffered, partly because they saw other matters as more urgent and endangered by the unpopular agitation for the vote and sometimes because, like Miss Nightingale, they doubted the commitment of other women to public causes. Miss Nightingale and Miss Potter both expressed these various attitudes. In the 1860s Miss Nightingale was impatient about the ambitions of women to train as doctors when there was a great shortage of women coming forward to train as nurses. Why should they want to emulate men? There were plenty of doctors already. 'Dear sisters, there is a better thing for women to be than "medical men", that is "medical women".'[56] In her introduction to *Memorials of Agnes Jones*, she wrote:

> Oh, fellow country-women, why do you hang back? Why are there so few of you? We hear so much of 'idle hands and unsatisfied hearts' . . . All England is ringing with the cry for 'Women's Work' and 'Women's Mission'. Why are there so few to *do* the 'work'? We used to hear of people giving their blood for their country. Since when is it that they only give their ink?[57]

People deplored the want of remunerative employment for women, she continued, but the true want was the other way. Remunerative employment was there in plenty. The want was the women fit to take it. Indeed, Miss Nightingale's views of other women sometimes bordered on contempt. There was no lack of opportunity, she argued, for those prepared to work, as she herself had done. The difficulty lay in lack of serious purpose, or perhaps in readiness to follow her own example.

My doctrines have taken no hold among women . . . I have lived with a sister 30 years, with an aunt four or five, with a cousin two or three. Not one has altered one hour of her existence for me. Not one has read one of my books.

It makes me mad the 'Woman's Rights' talk about the 'want of a field' for them – when I know that I would gladly give £500 a year for a Woman Secretary. And two English Superintendents have told me the same. And we can't get *one*.

As for my own family, their want of the commonest knowledge of contemporary history makes them quite useless as secretaries. They don't know the names of the Cabinet Ministers. They don't know the offices at the Horse Guards. They don't know who of the men of today is dead and who is alive. They don't know which of the Churches has Bishops and which not.[58]

Her irritation that women should confine themselves or be confined by others to conventional domestic lives extended to George Eliot's handling of Dorothea Brooke. 'This author now can find no better outlet for the heroine . . . than to marry an elderly sort of literary imposter and, quick after him, his relation . . . Yet close at hand in actual life, was a woman – an idealist too – . . . who has managed to make her ideal very real indeed.'[59] The idealist to whom Miss Nightingale was referring was Octavia Hill.

The movement for the vote caused Miss Nightingale peculiar irritation. Approached by Mill, she refused to join the committee of the London National Society for Women's Suffrage saying that while she believed women should have the vote, there were more urgent problems, such as the denial of property rights to married women, that could be far more easily remedied by legislation and that would be little affected by the female vote. In any case she had no time. 'It is fourteen years to this very day that I entered upon work which has never left me ten minutes leisure, not even to be ill. And I am obliged not to give my name where I cannot give my work.'[60] Furthermore, she added, she thought she could work better even for other women 'off the stage than on it'. The greater part of female misery was due to the economic situation of the whole nation, she asserted in a letter to Jowett, instancing the frightful burden of pauperism and the overflowing workhouses. 'The wives and daughters of all these people are starving, does Mr Mill really believe that the giving of any woman a vote will lead to the removal of even the least of these evils?'[61] In the 11 years she had passed in government offices, she claimed, she had never felt the want of a vote.

Mrs Webb was more tolerant of her sex. She explains her initial opposition to female suffrage partly as reaction against her father's over-valuation of women though also as a response to the 'narrow outlook and exasperated tone' of some of the suffragists. She nevertheless approved of women in public life, even of their taking on work earlier regarded as suitable only for men.

> I admire and reverence women most who are content to be among the 'unknown saints'. But it is no use shutting one's eyes to the fact that there is an increasing number of women to whom a matrimonial career is shut, and who seek a masculine reward for masculine qualities . . . I would do anything to open careers to them in which their somewhat abnormal but useful qualities would get their own reward . . . I think these strong women have a great future before them in the solution of social questions. They are not just inferior men; they may have masculine faculty, but they have a woman's temperament . . . I only hope that, instead of trying to ape men and take up men's pursuits, they will carve out their own careers . . . in which their particular form of power will achieve most.[62]

The root of her anti-feminism, Mrs Webb later wrote, lay in the fact that she never suffered the disabilities assumed to arise from her sex. As a woman she had no need to take up a 'money-making' profession, and could devote herself to disinterested social research. Here a woman was privileged, arousing less suspicion than a man and gaining more inside information. Moreover a capable female writer on economic questions had a scarcity value, was more able to secure rapid publication and, in Miss Potter's own experience, was paid a higher rate than male competitors.[63]

It is strange that Mrs Webb should disclaim any difficulties arising from her sex when her own early diaries reflect so clearly the conflict between social and family expectations and her commitment to her own work. Perhaps the advantages of her class position, of which she was very aware, seemed more important than the disadvantages arising from the duties attaching to her position in her family, which she seems to have considered perfectly legitimate and which in any case did not in the end hinder her independent life. For successful women, obstacles overcome may tend to lose their significance.

In 1906, Mrs Webb wrote to Millicent Garrett Fawcett to admit her change of mind about women's suffrage. Her earlier objections arose, she said, out of her disbelief in any abstract rights and her preference to see life in terms of obligation. She had not thought women under any obligation to take part in government, rather that they should concentrate their energies on their own peculiar duty of bearing children, advancing learning and promoting the spiritual life. But these obligations, Mrs Webb averred, had increasingly become the preoccupation of the community as a whole and women might thus feel a duty to take part in directing this new communal activity. 'This is in my view, not a claim to rights, or an abandonment of women's particular obligations, but a desire more effectually to fulfil their functions by sharing the control of state action in those directions'.[64]

This ingenious sophistry was Mrs Webb's justification for her altered opinions. But however convincing her argument, her letter underlines her conception of a woman's place and responsibilities which she herself had conscientiously observed within the Potter family. When she married she and Sidney chose not to have children in order to devote themselves to work. But, according to Caine, Mrs Webb remained uneasy with the decision;[65] bearing children as she pointed out to Mrs Fawcett was part of a woman's particular social obligation.

For the most part then, the women of this study all subscribed in their behaviour and in their writing to the traditional view of feminine duties and responsibilities. Their place was in their families, or in certain kinds of outside work where a woman's special qualities were particularly desirable. Not all women had the opportunity of marriage, so they should have the chance of independent work and be educated to do it. The cultivation of 'home values', of kindliness, religion and education in the wider society was conceived, as we shall see in Chapter 7, as an important way of resolving social problems, particularly by Octavia Hill, Mrs Butler and Mary Carpenter. Miss Nightingale was especially forthright in her insistence that it was perfectly proper for a woman to choose her own work rather than marriage, but in general the claim to freedom was implicit in the lives and behaviour of the ten women rather than explicit in their writing.

It meant a variety of compromises with family ties and duties. The readiness to contemplate public work derived from relatively liberal upbringing, but family support varied. At best it permitted rather than determined the move into public life. The insistence on women's rights was as much a justification of the desire for independence as an attitude that encouraged that desire. The drive to outside work in prisons or hospitals or social investigation came from elsewhere. It sprang from deep personal anxiety to understand the purpose and duties of life and determination to discover and to do what was right. For the nineteenth-century women of this study this was expressed in religious language as the search for a creed, or for faith, or to know the will of God. It is this quest that we shall now discuss.

6 Religious Experience

Of all the experiences of class, status, political and intellectual culture that the ten women in this study shared, none is so marked and so universal as the intensity of their religious lives. For some, such as Mrs Fry and Miss Nightingale, this meant years of anxious search for faith, of anguished examination of their own thoughts and actions to cast out doubt, pride and vanity, to achieve grace and to become worthy of God's service. For others, like Agnes Jones, Octavia Hill or Josephine Butler it was a matter of profound religious convictions which seem to have developed in early childhood, remained relatively undisturbed and which inspired and sustained their public activities. For yet others, Annie Besant and Frances Power Cobbe, the unremitting seeking after truth led in the end to the rejection of religion or at any rate of the evangelical Christianity in which they were both brought up. Miss Cobbe became an agnostic; as she remarked there was no Broad Church available in 1840 that might have offered an alternative more acceptable creed. The development of the Broad Church movement by the 1870s, however, did not prevent Mrs Besant from becoming an atheist.

The character of the religious experience of this group of women was thus very varied. But whatever form it took it expressed an unrelenting determination to discover a faith or a set of principles or values to enable them to interpret the world, and find a place and purpose for themselves within it; a quest that took them beyond the conventional and restricted lives of middle-class women of the time.

For the devout who wished to dedicate themselves entirely to service to God there were the sisterhoods, generally linked to the Catholic church and generally involving retirement from the world into some kind of institution. The women who joined them devoted themselves to nursing the sick and to looking after orphans, old and destitute people. It was to such institutions that Mrs Fry, Miss Nightingale and Miss Jones all looked for training and all of them visited the hospital, penitentiary and orphanage at Kaiserswerth, the early Protestant establishment from which deaconesses went out to work in communities all over Europe.

The ladies who were active in public social service did not, by definition, withdraw from the world. What then was the connection between their religious beliefs and the work they chose to do? We

118

have already suggested that the women in this study fall into roughly three groups in terms of their religious lives; we can now examine each in turn and consider how their experiences affected their public activities.

THE SEARCHERS AFTER RELIGIOUS TRUTH[1]

The first group comprises Elizabeth Fry, Florence Nightingale and, less certainly, Beatrice Webb. In some ways they present obvious contrasts: Mrs Fry belonging to the strict plain Quakers, recognised as minister among them, respecting the special conventions of speech, dress and behaviour; Florence Nightingale and Beatrice Webb with only very tenuous connections with any organised church and paying little regard to customary religious observances. When Miss Nightingale took up her appointment as superintendent of the nursing home for sick gentlewomen she moved into rooms away from the institution (as well as away from her family) where she could spend her free Sundays and so that patients should not be 'scandalised' by discovering that she did not go to church.[2] Beatrice Webb's faith was eventually expressed not so much in Christianity or even in the belief in a spiritual power, 'but in an intuitive use of prayer as . . . essential to the right conduct of life'.[3]

The shared characteristic was the intensity of their search as young women for a faith or a purpose to give direction to their lives and to justify their existence. For Elizabeth Fry this meant anxious deliberations over several years as to whether she should join the plain Quakers; for Florence Nightingale it was a prolonged and agonised effort, exacerbated by family opposition, to discover the work that God wished her to do. For Beatrice Webb it was a 'search after a creed by which to live'. But however expressed, the resolute seeking for truth, for personal salvation, and for the opportunity for service both inspired and guided the choice of work to be done.

Mrs Fry traced her Quaker ancestry back through both parents, but the Gurney household did not belong to the stricter sect of Friends. Mrs Gurney was, according to her granddaughters, a woman of 'excellent abilities and of considerable attainments as well as much personal beauty'. She preferred 'literary society' to that available locally but her intellectual and scientific interests brought her and her husband into association with people who doubted or were indifferent to 'the great truths of Christianity' at a time when 'talent was frequently allied to scepticism'. Such free association with people whose religious beliefs were at variance with their own must, the grand-daughters feared, have had an injurious effect upon the Gurney family life, especially after the death of Mrs Gurney who had watched carefully over her children, 'urging upon them the necessity of prayer and personal piety'. When she died she left her seven daughters appreciative of the 'beauty and excellence of religion' but with uncertain faith and wavering principles.

Unlike some stricter Quakers, Mr Gurney permitted music and dancing in his household. The family attended the Friends' meeting, though delicate health meant Elizabeth was frequently absent. She was persuaded by an uncle that it was her duty to attempt to go whenever possible and after the age of 16 or 17 the search for a right way of life assumed overwhelming importance. It led her away from the social entertainments of Norwich and London and eventually away from the musical evenings and dancing within her own household. Gradually such social activities were renounced as worldly, frivolous and vain; excitements that distracted her from her serious purpose of self-improvement. Her journals are a record of self-criticism, self-doubt and determination to do better. At the age of 17 having made her confession, she drew up for herself nine commandments.

I have seen several things in myself and others, I never before remarked; but I have not tried to improve myself, I have given way to my passions, and let them have command over me. I have known my faults, and not corrected them, and now I am determined I will once more try, with redoubled ardour, to overcome my wicked inclinations; I must not flirt; I must not ever be out of temper with the children; I must not contradict without a cause; I must not mump when my sisters are *liked* and I am not; I must not allow myself to be angry; I must not exaggerate, which I am inclined to do. I must not give way to luxury; I must not be idle in mind, I must try to give way to every good feeling, and overcome every bad; I will see what I can do, if I had but perseverance, I could do all that I wish, I will try.[4]

The good intentions did not have immediate effect. Later diary entries record her self-reproach: 'I am so very idle . . . my inclinations lead me to be an idle, flirting, worldly girl . . . I have neither activity nor persistence in what I think right',[5] tempered by an awakening interest in religion as a possible guide and consolation: 'I do not know if I shall not soon be rather religious, because I have thought lately, what a support, it is through life; . . . I think anybody who had real faith could never be unhappy.'[6] Habits of idleness and frivolity, however, were hard to resist. Four months later she wrote that she was more cross, more proud, more vain and more extravagant and that these faults arose from her great love of gaiety and the world. What a comfort, she thought, real faith in religion would be, 'but I am sorry to say I have no faith'.

A turning point seemed to come with a visit to Norwich of William Savery, the American Quaker, who greatly impressed Elizabeth Gurney with his teaching. 'I wish the state of enthusiasm I am now in may last for today I have felt *that there is a God*.'[7] From this time Miss Gurney's resolve to withdraw from worldly pleasures became firmer, sustained by friendship with Savery, new acquaintance with Quaker relatives and an increasing interest in local philanthropic work. 'There is nothing gives me so much satisfaction as instructing the lower class of people' she wrote of a Bible class she started for children at Earlham. By the summer of 1798 she had begun to think she would become a plain Quaker, 'a sort of protection to the principles of Christianity in the present state of the world' and from this time forward she began to abandon bright clothes, singing and dancing, and to adopt Quaker dress and speech. Her faith became increasingly important to her. When she married two years later it was only after serious consideration of whether the duties she might be called upon to perform in the church were compatible with those of wife and mother:

> I have had many doubts, many rises and fallings about the affair. My most amxious wish is, that I may not hinder my spiritual welfare, which I have so much feared, as to make me often doubt if marriage were a desirable thing for me at this time, or even the thoughts of it; but as I wish (at least I think I wish), in this as in other things, beyond everything else to do the will of God, I hope that I shall be shown the path right for me to walk in.[8]

This was a dilemma that many pious women had to face, as Davidoff and Hall point out in their discussion of religion and the middle class.[9] For Mrs Fry her marriage was followed by a period of domestic responsibilities, child-bearing, entertaining, nursing sick relatives, visiting friends and continuing doubts about faith. Eight years later, and with five children she wrote: 'My course has been very different to what I had expected; instead of being as I had hoped, a useful instrument in the Church Militant, here I am a care-worn wife and mother, outwardly nearly devoted to the things of this life.'[10] Four years earlier, however, she had come to believe that God wished her to be a minister, and eventually in 1811 the Friends acknowledged her as such.

The major part of Mrs Fry's work, as a Quaker minister, among prisoners in Newgate and on the female convict ships, visiting prisons and agitating for prison reform in England and in Europe, developed after this time. Conflicts between domestic and public responsibilities were often acute but in face of family troubles and outside problems her faith remained her fundamental strength. In fact it was virtually invulnerable because earthly events were an expression of God's will and purpose, ultimately benevolent if not immediately comprehensible. 'How much do I desire that above all things, I may have a life in doing the will of my creator',[11] she had written in 1806. Three years later anxiety over the illness of one of her daughters was softened by her piety:

> My dearest little Rachel has been seriously unwell for some time past, so as to make me very low at times; but I have not suffered much from painful anxiety . . . I desire with regard to my dear lambs to be ready to give them up if called for at my hand; for we know not what is best for them: and I believe we should seek to look upon them, as charges committed to our stewardship, and not as our property.[12]

And in 1823, referring to disappointments in her prison work, she again indicates the crucial important of her religious beliefs:

> There are times of encouragement and building up, and of discouragement and treading down. I remarkably experienced the latter state yesterday, as it respects the prison cause; I met with ingratitude amongst the prisoners such as I never remember before . . . Some reflections also that I found had been cast upon it, by one who understood the subject, tried me much. Still, on the prison subject, I have this secret feeling which wonderfully upholds me under the difficulties that may arise; in the first place, I believe I have been providentially brought into it, not of my own seeking; and secondly, that if He, who in a remarkable manner, has hitherto appeared to bless the work, should be pleased for a season to

permit a cloud to pass over it, that is nothing to me. I have always considered the work not mine, and have desired that self may have no reputation in it; if trials of this kind come they may be for our good who are engaged in it, and for our humiliation.[13]

For Mrs Fry the way to faith lay through deliberate acceptance of the practices of plain Quakers and later in her ministry among them. So far as her public activities were concerned she assumed a sort of partnership with God. If she were successful this was an expression of divine power, but if she were unsuccessful this too might be attributed to God's will, working for ultimate good though in a way she might not understand. Thus any reverses and disappointments could be tolerated without either the loss of belief in her own earthly work or loss of faith in her Creator. Two years before her death she avowed to one of her daughters that since her heart had been touched at 17 years old she had never awakened from sleep, in sickness or in health, by day or by night, without her first waking thought being how best she might serve the Lord.[14]

The religious experiences of Florence Nightingale were more turbulent, as were her attachments to friends and relations. Mr Nightingale was a Unitarian, and outward religious observances do not appear to have been marked in the household. For Miss Nightingale her faith was a private matter, not supported by formal attachment to any church, nor by dogma nor doctrine. It was evident, rather, in a belief in a God who spoke directly to her. The sense of a 'calling' was very strong in Miss Nightingale and continually recurs in her writing. 'On 7 February, 1837, God spoke to me and called me to his Service.'[15] This was the earliest experience but in 1874 Miss Nightingale noted three other similar occasions during her life.

The years between 1837 and 1853 witnessed an increasing intensity of religious feeling and a protracted struggle to free herself, often against her own inclinations, from the frivolities and trivialities of social and domestic life in order to prepare herself for her public work. Diaries and letters show the same self-criticism and self-doubt as those of Elizabeth Gurney. Travelling in Europe in 1838, Miss Nightingale reproached herself for being too fond of opera, balls and society. Back in England she endeavoured to improve herself and make herself worthy of God's service by working at mathematics, philosophy and Greek but social life also continued, followed by remorse for her love of social success and admiration. By 1845 she had decided her vocation lay in nursing but hopes of training at

Salisbury Infirmary were defeated by the opposition of her family. Again travelling abroad in 1848 after a period of ill-health, her resolution to pursue her vocation was strengthened after meeting Sidney Herbert, Manning and Shaftesbury and others concerned with hospital reform. Society with its associated hypocrisy and vanity became more distasteful to her. She entered a convent for ten days, an experience that confirmed her desire to carry out God's work. Later in the year plans to go to Kaiserswerth for nursing training were disappointed. This, coupled with growing dislike of the social round of her class, distrust of her own worthiness and unhappy personal relationships led to the verge of mental breakdown, more travel abroad and renewed determination to devote herself to God's service expressed in anguished private notes:

> To-day I am 30 – the age Christ began his mission. Now no more childish things. No more love. No more marriage. Now Lord let me think only of Thy Will, what Thou willest me to do. Oh Lord, Thy will, Thy will.
>
> Tomorrow is Sacrament Sunday; I have read over all my history, a history of miserable woe, mistake and blinding vanity, of seeking great things for myself.[16]

At this point she was able to go to Kaiserswerth for a short visit of inspection and her nursing resolve was again strengthened but she returned home to renewed family opposition. Her struggle for effective nursing training continued. She considered but rejected the idea of joining the Catholic church for the sake of the training available to women as nuns. As her religious sense of dedication developed, tolerant of any faith that emphasised good works, so did her dissatisfaction with the Anglican church for failing to provide any work or serious instruction for women:

> The Church of England has for men Bishoprics, Archbishoprics and a little work . . . For women she has – what? . . . I would have given her my head, my heart, my hand. She would not have them . . . She told me to go back and do crochet in my mother's drawing room; or, if I were tired of that, to marry and look well at the head of my husband's table. You may go to the Sunday School, if you like it, she said. But she gave me no training even for that. She gave me neither work to do for her nor education for it.[17]

In 1851 she had spent three months at Kaiserswerth but returned once again to the resentment of her mother and sister. Later attempts to enter Catholic hospitals in Paris and Dublin failed in face of the claims of family duties, but eventually she won her independence as superintendent of the London benevolent institution. Here, disputes with the ladies' committee as to whether patients of all denominations should be admitted did nothing to increase Miss Nightingale's respect either for women or for committees or for the Anglican church: 'From Committees, charity, and schism – from the Church of England and all other deadly sin – from philanthropy and all the deceits of the Devil, good Lord deliver us.'[18]

Nor in later years did Miss Nightingale join any established church. Periods of illness became more frequent alternating with periods of desperately hard work, self-reproach, despair and efforts to reconcile herself to what she conceived to be God's will. Her religion remained a private matter between herself and God and she developed a keen interest in philosophical and theological speculation. In 1859 she arranged for the private printing of a volume entitled *Suggestions for Thought*, an attempt to provide a new religion for 'intelligent artisans'. The book received the approval of John Stuart Mill but adverse criticism from Jowett and Froude. Later, on Jowett's suggestion, she wrote a series of essays on the idea of God and made a selection of bible stories for a Children's Bible, though not of a conventional kind. She wrote to Jowett with scorn about the familiar biblical tales: 'There are some things in Homer we might better call "Holy Writ" – many, many in Sophocles and Aeschylus. The stories about Andromache and Antigone are worth all the women in the Old Testament put together, nay almost all the women in the Bible.'[19]

By the 1870s Miss Nightingale had turned to mysticism, but of an active not a contemplative kind. Her public work and her religion remained tightly bound together. The struggle to understand God's will was the struggle to know what her work should be and the belief that she was doing God's work was the faith that sustained her in the periods of greatest difficulty:

Oh Father I submit, I resign myself . . . Deal with me as thou seest meet. Oh how vain it is, the vanity of vanities to live in men's thoughts instead of God's . . . O my Creator, thou knowest that through all these twenty horrible years I have been supported by the belief (I must believe it still or I am sure I could not work) that I was working with thee who wert bringing everyone, even our poor nurses, to perfection.[20]

The faith that Mrs Webb eventually fashioned for herself was perhaps even further removed from conventional religion than that of Miss Nightingale. She grew up in a family where both parents were communicants, but where there was little pressure for the children to attend church services. When in London Mr Potter would take his daughters on Sunday mornings to hear the most exciting speakers on metaphysical or religious issues, and Manning and the Bishop of Gloucester were family visitors. Mrs Webb looks back on the last decades of the nineteenth century as the period when agnosticism, coloured by scientific materialism, was challenging Christianity. The first 15 years of her thinking life were spent 'in seeking a creed by the light of which I could live the life I had to lead!'[21]

As with Florence Nightingale and Elizabeth Fry the process was a painful one of self-examination, doubt, self-criticism and self-reproach for vanity and folly. Beatrice Potter began to record such feelings at the age of 14:

But one thing I have learnt is, that I am exceedingly vain, to say the truth I am very disgusted with myself; whenever I am in the company of any gentleman, I cannot help wishing and doing all I possibly can to attract his attention and admiration; . . . and contriving everything to make myself more liked and admired than my sisters. The question is, how can I conquer it . . . Meanwhile I feel my faith slipping away from me, Christ seems to have been separated from me by [a] huge mass of worldliness and vanity. I can no more pray to Him with the same earnest faith that I used to, my prayers seem mockeries . . . And intellectual difficulties of faith make it impossible to believe. I am very wicked . . . I feel that if I continue I shall become a frivolous, silly, unbelieving woman, and yet every morning when I awake I have the same giddy confident feeling and every night I am miserable. The only thing is to give up any pleasure rather [than] go into society; it may be hard, in fact I know it will, but it must be done else I shall lose all the remaining sparks of faith, and with those all the chances of my becoming a good and useful woman in this world, and a companion of our Lord in the next.[22]

The search for faith, the self-recrimination and the doubt continued, interspersed with periods of ill-health:

And above all I must guard against that self-satisfaction which I consider is one of my worst faults. If I give in to it, it will prevent my ever improving myself. And the only way to cure myself of it is to go heart and soul into religion. It is a pity I ever went off the path of orthodox religion; it was a misfortune that I was not brought up to believe that to doubt was a crime. But since I cannot accept the belief of my Church without inward questioning, let me try to find a firm belief of my own, and let me act up to it. That is the most important thing. God help me to do it![23]

Shortly afterwards Miss Potter went to a fashionable girls' school and was there confirmed, but religious doubts and doctrinal scruples persisted.

Oh that I had more charity, true charity, so that I might see and reverence and not sneer at and despise what I do not understand! God only can give me help. I am so weak, so vain, so liable to fall into self-confidence.[24]

So did her vanity and her desire for admiration. She wrote in her diary that she must work harder, become more truthful, be less vain and admiration-seeking. She also wrote that she wished her main aim in life to be understanding and acting up to religion, but two years later she had dismissed not only Christianity but all traditional belief. Agnosticism however satisfied only the rational part of her nature and something more was needed. Rejecting Christianity, she yet retained a faith,

that it is by prayer, by communion with an all-pervading spiritual force, that the soul of man discovers the purpose or goal of human endeavour, as distinguished from the means or process by which human beings may attain their end.[25]

It was a faith that Mrs Webb herself found difficult to express. In 1926 she wrote that she was 'perpetually brooding' over her inability to make clear to herself, let alone to others, why she believed in religious mysticism and why she hankered after a church 'with its communion of the faithful, with its religious rites, and its religious discipline, and above all with its definite code of conduct.'[26] But whatever her perplexities, her peculiar form of belief was one of the things that upheld her. She was able to get through the exhausting work as Poor Law Commissioner, she wrote, by will power induced by prayer.[27] And she related an awkward dinner with R. B. Haldane when her assertion that prayer was an important part of her own life was greeted with mocking disbelief.[28] Her sense of the fundamental importance of religion was so strong that she considered that modern authors, particularly Shaw and H. G. Wells failed in realism because they completely ignored it.[29]

THE FOLLOWERS OF CHRIST

Distinct from Mrs Fry, Miss Nightingale and Mrs Webb, whose search for faith was attended by anguish and conflict, were those women whose religion was a more tranquil experience, arousing neither doubt nor any sense of personal sin. Agnes Jones, Louisa Twining, Josephine Butler, Mary Carpenter and Octavia Hill do not seem to have suffered from the feelings of unworthiness that tormented the first three women. This may reflect the more modest family circumstances and style of living which offered fewer opportunities for the social activities that threatened to ensnare Miss Nightingale and Miss Potter. But also, apart from Miss Twining who is unusually reserved about personal relationships, there is more evidence of close family affection among this second group of women which may have contributed to more confident feelings of self-worth. Finally, all grew up in families where religious belief was strong, where doubt, if not regarded as a crime, was not seriously entertained and where religious practices were outwardly observed. Miss Twining remarks that the custom of family prayers was begun in her family in the 1830s and that it was not common before that time,[30] but it was normal in the households of the other four women.

Religious observance, however, did not mean acceptance of the doctrines or attitudes of the established church. Dr Carpenter was a Unitarian minister and the radical politics of many of the families of the philanthropic women led to an uneasy relationship with the Anglican church. John Grey was angered that only two bishops should support the Reform Bill, and George Butler, an ordained Anglican and eventually Canon of Winchester, came into conflict with the Archbishop of York over his support for the repeal of the

Contagious Diseases Acts. Mrs Butler herself held to no particular set of doctrines and did not regard herself as a member of any particular church but retained complete faith in the power and authority of God. Referring to what she interpreted as a slight on her belief she wrote:

> Now the things which I believe I had learned direct from God. I never sat at the feet of any man; I never sought light or guidance even from any saint, man or woman, though I dearly loved some such whom I had known, and learned much from their example; nor on churches and creeds had I ever leaned. I had already for years earnestly sought to know the truth which has sustained me through life; and, therefore, at that moment it seemed to me that the smile of contempt was directed at Him, my sole authority, in whom I believed all truth centred.[31]

The sense of a 'calling' is explicit in the writings of this group of women. Sometimes, as with Agnes Jones, the religious impulse seems to be of paramount importance, the recognition of the kind of work to be done developing only after many years. In other cases, as with Octavia Hill or Mary Carpenter it was more a matter of social problems existing around them that became evident to them in their work with Sunday school or ragged school children, and which, in the light of existing religious commitment, they defined as offering opportunities for God's service. Whether the awareness of social problems or the sense of vocation was the more important is hard to say. Often they were intermingled. Whatever the case their faith was a continuing support and consolation for all these women in their public work.

Agnes Jones lived for only 34 years. Growing up in a family with keen interests in missionary work and Bible reading and to whom she was closely attached, she herself developed an intense religious life. Before she was 20 she was visiting the sick and the poor near the family house in Ireland. Before she was 30 she had been to Kaiserswerth in search of training. Admiring Florence Nightingale, she became convinced that her own vocation lay in nursing, though she worked as a Bible missioner for a time before her mother gave her consent for her to train as a nurse. She wished, she wrote, to devote what gifts God had given her to his service. She had no sympathy with the High Church party so would not have entered a sisterhood even had she been free from home ties. Otherwise, the decision about what she should do she left, as she saw it, to God. 'My aim . . . is . . . How can I work best for God? . . . Trustfully and prayerfully have I left it in the hands of my heavenly Father.'[32]

When she was asked to go to Liverpool to supervise an experiment to introduce trained nurses into the poor law infirmary her fears were calmed by her faith. 'From no one point can I see any fitness in myself; I can only say it is God's work, and He must do it. He can work by my inefficiency for success or failure, whichever He intends as the result.'[33]

After two years a favourable report from the workhouse committee led to a proposal to extend and make permanent the arrangements for using trained nurses. Miss Jones again invoked the assistance of God. 'Much is hoped from me, and I feel so incapable, I can only cast all on God, and tell Him as He has chosen, so He must fit me for the work.'[34]

In 1866, her health damaged by overwork, Miss Jones died of typhus and her sister has provided one of the few tributes, which bears witness to her character.

> For those who would seek ease and pleasure and enjoyment, this is indeed no path; – it needs what Agnes had, the single eye to God's glory, the steadfast will to follow His leading, the yearning desire to use every talent He had given in His service. The battle was indeed a hard one – painful to flesh and blood – every nerve quivered, every tender feeling was wrung, – mother, sister, home, these had all to be renounced, and for what! To live among the lowest and most degraded of human beings, to seek to do them good, physically and morally, and then to die . . . never to see success . . . on earth.[35]

The religious life of Louisa Twining seems to have been similarly straightforward, though her autobiography reveals little about her attitudes and emotions and suggests a self-contained and somewhat prosaic personality. As a young woman, however, she was a regular listener to the lectures and sermons of Maurice and Kingsley, Wilberforce and Manning, and in the 1850s she attended Bible classes conducted by Maurice so she was presumably liberal in her beliefs. In her memoirs she recalls her habit of attending daily services. 'It was a great refreshment, when depressed and disheartened by the sight of so much misery, sickness and vice, to be able to turn to a higher help, and feel that there was help and comfort for all who

could be brought to look for it.'[36] She also looks back to the year
1860 when she read the prayers at the opening ceremony of a home
that she had set up for girls who would otherwise have been consigned
to the workhouse. 'In the Psalms for that evening was the verse,
"commit thy way unto the Lord and he shall bring it to pass". That
was my motto in work from that day forward.'[37]

If Miss Twining remains a somewhat shadowy figure, Mrs Butler
emerges from her writings as a colourful and volatile personality, 'very
excitable and emotional, and of an over-sympathetic temperament',
though also 'touched with genius', according to Jowett in a letter to
Florence Nightingale who had asked his advice as to whether she
should support the Ladies' Protest against the Contagious Diseases
Acts.[38]

In her biography of her father Mrs Butler tells how serious illness
from typhus as a young man marked a change from conventional
Christianity to a more fervent evangelicalism. Mrs Grey was descen-
ded from Huguenots driven from France by the revocation of
the edict of Nantes and remembered that when a small child in
Northumberland her family, who welcomed religious teachers of any
kind who passed their way, was visited by John Wesley. Though
refusing to accept any particular creed or sect, the Greys were
committed to their faith. Family lessons and Bible reading for their
children were complemented by attendance at church services,
Anglican and Methodist, and on one occasion they received into the
household one of Wesley's followers who was holding revivalist
meetings in the border country.[39]

The faith of the Grey family was in a God who created the world
and revealed himself through Christ, who was accessible through
prayer and contemplation, in whose sight all men and women were
equal and who was the source of a moral law that called for action
against injustice and oppression. The close association between faith
and action seems to have been evident to Mrs Butler as a young girl.
Her grandson quotes a letter she wrote shortly before her death,
referring to a note she had sent to a few friends:

I don't know that I have ever before recorded what I have recorded
in that – to show how a long *incubation* and a painful one is often
required for a person whom God appoints to sow a little mustard
seed of truth, which is to grow to a large tree. I told them that this
preparation and all its *travail* of soul began with me when I was
only seventeen! In the virtuous and beautiful country home of my

father, that is . . . so great was the burden on my soul about the inequalities, injustices and cruelties in the world, that I used to run away into these woods where no-one followed me; and kneeling on the ground, I used to *shriek* to God to come and deliver! This is awfully true. My sisters thought I was a little mad. Perhaps I was; but God turned the madness to a purpose he had.[40]

The unsectarian character of the family religion remained a feature of Josephine Butler's faith. As she grew older she numbered Cardinal Manning and Catherine Booth among her friends. When her husband became a Canon of Winchester she 'attended unobtrusively' some of the Cathedral services, liking them, her grandson claims, for the opportunity they afforded for uninterrupted contemplation but uninterested in the tenets of the Church of England.[41] What she could not tolerate was the scepticism about the central beliefs of Christianity that she encountered in Oxford.[42]

The direct turning to God in times of trouble was characteristic of Mrs Butler throughout her life. When she was asked to lead the campaign for the repeal of the Contagious Diseases Acts in 1869 it took her three months to reach her decision.

The toils and conflicts of the years that followed were light in comparison with the anguish of that first plunge . . . I worked hard at other things . . . with a kind of half-conscious hope that God would accept that work . . . But the hand of the Lord was upon me: night and day the pressure increased . . . This is perhaps, after all, the very work, the very mission, I longed for years ago, and saw coming, afar off, like a bright star. But seen near, as it approaches, it is so dreadful, so difficult, so disgusting, that I tremble to look at it; and it is hard to see and know whether or not God is indeed calling me concerning it. If doubt were gone and I felt sure that He means me to rise in revolt and rebellion (for that it must be) against men, even against our rulers, then I would do it with zeal, however repulsive to others may seem the task.[43]

In the end Mrs Butler decided that God was indeed calling her. After a meeting to launch the campaign addressed by her husband and Charles Birrell, a Baptist cousin, she wrote:

And now it is revolt and rebellion, a consecrated rebellion against those in authority who have established this 'accursed thing' among us. We are rebels for God's holy laws . . . It is war to the knife. In a battle of flesh and blood, mercy may intervene and life may be spared; but principles know not the name of mercy.[44]

Later, in 1871, she was asked to give evidence to the Royal Commission enquiring into the working of the Contagious Diseases Acts and described her experience in a letter to her husband.

It was even a severer ordeal than I expected. It was distressing to me, owing to the hard harsh view which some of these men take of poor women, and of the lives of the poor generally . . . But there was one who stood before me. I almost felt as if I heard Christ's voice bidding me not to fear.[45]

The peculiar power of her personality was noted by at least one member of the Royal Commission to whom she was presenting her evidence: 'I am not accustomed to religious phraseology but I cannot give you any idea of the effect produced except by saying that the influence of the spirit of God was there.'[46]

In 1883, before the crucial Repeal debate, Mrs Butler again demonstrated her belief in the efficacy of prayer. In the weeks before the debate she organised public prayer meetings all over the country. In London intercessionary meetings were addressed by High Church men and Salvationists and also by George Butler, who asked that his friend Mr Gladstone, then Prime Minister, be brought to realise his great responsibility. A band of women supporters hired a hall in the Westminster Palace hotel on the morning of the debate and held continuing intercession for more than twelve hours. Victory for the abolitionists followed after a crusade that Mrs Butler saw as 'one of the most vital moments of Christian times'. Only 20 years later, however, she was questioning whether such public expressions of faith could ever occur again. 'I long to tell the story properly; for it is so urgently neeeded now, where human science is so to the fore and prayer is in the background. I wonder if such a thing would be possible today. I fear not.'[47]

But if the second part of the nineteenth century witnessed increasing belief in the power of science to remove human misery, a period, according to Mrs Webb, when the 'impulse of self-subordinating service' was transferred from God to man, this did nothing to disturb

Mrs Butler's faith in a God who could intervene in the world. Those who sought His help must have a clear purpose, concentration of energy upon it and self-mastery.

> By union with the Divine, and concentration on something that you will, you create an atmosphere, a circle, round you, unseen but real. In holding to God, you and He together hold and weald (if you will it) a vast creating energy and power.[48]

In a more personal sense also, her own belief in a benevolent God remained unshaken. Writing about a dangerous illness in Rome in 1894 she said:

> I was busy with my Master's work, doing what I could, quietly with faith and prayer, when suddenly – in a moment – I was struck down by this sickness. I had no power or sense to protest and lay hold of the power of God, so as to conquer the thing; and there was no-one near who was in the spiritual position to do it for me . . . I had five weeks of torment. The spiritual darkness was even greater than the physical suffering. Why the God of love *allows* a child of his to be so knocked down and stamped upon, I *cannot* understand. He will explain it some day. I continue to affirm that He *is* love.[49]

On a later occasion, ill again in Switzerland, the help she demanded was forthcoming.

> I appealed to His honour to fulfill His promise of help to those who really believed in Him. I said, 'now listen, Lord, in pity. I *do* desire something – that I may get home to England safely, and that I may see all my dear children again before I die, if I have to die'. Then, in the silence in which I sat, a great peace *came to me*. I did not urge myself to be peaceful but peace *came*; and I felt that Christ is so *honourable*; he could not give that promise and not keep it.
> I fell asleep; and, in the morning I felt a good deal stronger, without taking any remedy.[50]

As Josephine Grey, so Mary Carpenter grew up in a family where religious faith was beyond doubt. Dr Carpenter was a teacher as well as a Unitarian minister, and his daughter received an education far beyond that usual for girls at the time, but it left her without any taint of the scepticism common among the friends of Mr and Mrs Gurney, that affronted Mrs Butler in Oxford and with which Beatrice Potter had to contend. James Martineau, writing after her death, pointed to her 'absorbing veneration for the person of Christ as supernatural' which 'excluded the finer perceptions of the historical sense'. This early set of her religious affections made the newer Biblical criticism unwelcome to Miss Carpenter, her nephew comments, but her reforming instincts were readily turned in practical directions.[51] A few years before she died when her interests had extended to the position of women in India and to prison reform in America and Europe, she wrote of the inspiration of her work. 'I do not often like to allude to religion in public . . . but you will gather from each of my books . . . that this has been the moving spring of my life. The spark was kindled by my beloved father.'[52]

But although her faith may have been as constant, Miss Carpenter was more troubled by the vanities and attractions of the world than Mrs Butler. Her diaries, particularly before 1840, reflect the depression, self-doubt and sense of unworthiness, self-reproach for the desire for admiration, for irritability and vanity that are so characteristic of Elizabeth Gurney, Florence Nightingale and Beatrice Potter. Like Miss Nightingale remaining unmarried, a certain loneliness pervaded Mary Carpenter's life, though it found only muted expression. If God had wished her to have a companion in her pilgrimage, he would not have withheld the blessing, she had written in 1846. After her mother's death in 1856 she made several attempts to relieve her solitude, taking in an orphan girl, sharing her house for a time with Frances Power Cobbe and later bringing two Indian boys to be educated in England under her direction. As an old woman, according to her nephew, her loneliness was very great. Absorption in her work had meant that she had avoided ordinary society; she had 'sacrificed much of what she might have *been*, in order to accomplish the work which she felt it was given her to *do*'.[53]

The desire to find work to do was stimulated by the cholera epidemics of the 1830s. On the Fast Day appointed on the appearance of the disease she wrote:

I wish on this day appointed for public humiliation before God to record my earnest desire to become more useful to my fellow-creatures, and my prayer to our Heavenly Father to guide me by his light into the way of discovering the means and of rightly employing them.[54]

And later, on the day appointed for thanksgiving:

This day has been set apart for public thanksgiving to our Heavenly Preserver during the dreadful scourge . . . But this day has been one of renewed resolutions of benefiting my fellow creatures. I have never forgotten the resolution I made on the day of public humiliation, nor has it at all weakened, but I have not yet had the means of putting it into action. God grant that I soon may have them.[55]

By 1835 Miss Carpenter had established a society for visiting the homes of the Sunday school children, herself visiting the poorest district. This first knowledge of the 'perishing and dangerous classes' seems to have presented the opportunity she had been waiting for.

In the year 1832 . . . I made a solemn determination to devote myself in any way that lay in my power to the good of my fellow creatures. A means appears to be now open to me . . . and I feel much gratitude to my Father for it.[56]

A period of depression and poor health followed but in 1837 she recorded in verses which included the following stanzas a profound religious experience.

> I felt as ne'er I had before,
> I knew that I should sin no more;
> And straight within my soul
> There was a calm and holy peace
> A joy so true it ne'er could cease,
> A gentle sweet control.
>
> I knew that I was with my God,
> Yet feared I not his chastening rod,
> Fear dwelleth not with love;
> I felt his presence ever nigh,
> 'Twas bliss to live beneath his eye,
> It was in Heaven above.[57]

The complete faith in a benevolent God, working in ways she might not understand, her strength in the face of the poverty and misery she met in her work is something she shared with women like Elizabeth Fry and Agnes Jones. It is expressed in a letter to a friend in 1845.

> But I feel the most supporting view to take to be a firm conviction of the parental character of the Deity, and of His infinite wisdom, love and power. He would not permit all these evils but for His own benevolent purposes.[58]

If this sounds somewhat bland and submissive it should be remembered that any submission was to God, not to men. Apart from the hard physical labour in the Bristol slums and in the institutions she established, Miss Carpenter, like most of the other women in this study, worked unremittingly and in ways often very uncongenial to herself, to persuade other people to organise more humane and effective services for destitute and delinquent children. Writing about the need for reformatory schools in 1851 she said:

> I wish that I could pursue the work I love so much without anyone seeing me . . . It is a *great pain* to me to be brought into any degree of notoriety; but yet I must speak for I have to tell a solemn truth which has not yet been clearly told.[59]

This particular part of her campaigning required lobbying MPs, jail chaplains, magistrates and many others. It also involved arranging a conference of workers for reform – the occasion when Mary Carpenter herself took no part in the discussions as she had no taste for raising her voice in an assembly of gentlemen. A year later, giving evidence to a committee of the House of Commons on Juvenile Delinquency she thanked God for supporting her in her ordeal.

> Father of my spirit I would here record the overflowing homage of my heart that thou hast permitted me in some small degree to bear a testimony to the cause of those forsaken young immortals whom I love with my heart's love . . . I have still another day of testimony. May the words of my Saviour and the spirit of my Heavenly Father sustain me.[60]

It was also on God's work that Miss Carpenter went to India to strive for the 'elevation' of women in 1866 and after a visit to America in 1873, devoted to lectures and meetings in the cause of prison reform, she reviewed the past year in words which could describe her whole life:

> The year has passed away! Its trials, its efforts to do the Father's work, its grief, its pain, its desolation, its struggles, its weakness. I wonder at times how I have been borne through it. Yet it has had its joys . . . its treasures of work and of sympathy; some *very* glorious scenes of nature . . . Still more, the certainty that I have been permitted to sow some seeds which may bear fruit . . . My Father, may I consecrate all to thee.[61]

Octavia Hill is the fifth of the women who found religion a steady and continuing force in their lives. For her, however, it was a relatively quiet experience. There is little sign in Miss Hill's writing of the fervent evangelicalism, the sense of sin, the guilt and self-criticism that appear in the letters and journals of some of the other women. The atmosphere in which she grew up was not markedly religious and the interests of her grandfather, father and mother in social questions, in education and in the arts seem to have left the deepest impression on her personality. It was perhaps the socialism of the Christian Socialists, rather than their Christianity, that most influenced her, though it was F. D. Maurice, she claims, who led her to the church:

> who had shown me a life in the creeds, the services and the Bible; who had interpreted for me much that was dark and puzzling in life; how the belief in a Father, a Son and a Holy Ghost might be the most real faith, not a dead notion; that I might believe, not only that God was manifesting himself to each man in the inward consciousness of light and beauty in himself and all around . . . that those had led to infinite perplexities and doubts, but that a real person had come amongst us, who had known the Father, whose will had been brought into harmony with His; that He was stronger than doubts and sorrow and had overcome them; that He had declared that we might have life, that life was knowledge of God.[62]

Certainly Miss Hill's work seems to have been inspired by an unshakeable sense of duty. Writing to a friend she ponders the source of 'that imperative must' which compels the opening of 'some terrible vista of difficulty or pain'. 'Why is the soul accustomed to obey that voice of duty? Why are its commands so clear, coming in the hushed hours? Why does self-indulgence, why does love and peace never gain victory?'[63] In fact the strong sense of social obligation was bound up with religious belief. The nature of Miss Hill's commitment appears in her account of a conversation with a friend urging her to take more rest – especially on Sundays. She explained that she thought that work was a duty and that she dared not claim any time as her own. Occasionally she had thought she had earned some rest, but had then recollected 'that all time was God's and to be used for Him'.[64]

For Miss Hill faith was not only a spur to greater effort, it was also the source of her own strength and the necessary foundation on which the children she was trying to teach must build their lives:

There must be many a cloud, and many a storm, and many an earthquake; and yet we must rise victorious, to lead these children to love truth . . . to teach them that in the principle of sacrifice lies all strength; to open their hearts and eyes to all beauty; to bring out the principle of obedience and sacrifice, as opposed to selfishness and lawlessness. This is not a small work, and they must learn to do that which lies before them, to look upon the fulfilment of the duties which God has given them, in whatever position they may be, as that which will open to them the kingdom of heaven. This is a work which we must ask to be able to undertake in all humility, all energy, all earnestness, all faith; feeling that our *only* strength, our *sufficient* strength is that God is working with us.[65]

But in spite of the driving sense of social duty, Miss Hill's life was free of the bitterness that attended Miss Nightingale's battle for independence. There were few constraints on Miss Hill's ambitions. Her growing interest in social affairs and social action was shared and supported by her family and her circle of distinguished friends. She was able to rest confident that she was doing God's work without the desperate appeals for strength and guidance to which some of the other women were driven by family opposition and public hostility or indifference.

THE UNBELIEVERS

Frances Power Cobbe and Annie Besant are the two eccentrics of this study. Like the other women they had a religious upbringing and for both the faith they absorbed as children had a marked evangelical character which emphasised family prayers and Bible reading, good works and social duty. Both finished their formal education before they were 17, both became very interested in Christian literature and theology and both in the end rejected Christianity. Miss Cobbe had become an agnostic by the time she was 20 and later moved through Deism to Theism. Annie Besant had her first doubts about the infallibility of the Bible when she was 19 but it was six years before she finally became an atheist. When she was 42 she joined the Theosophists and it was at this point, as she relates, that Bradlaugh lost his faith in her reason.

It is the rejection of Christian belief that distinguishes Miss Cobbe and Mrs Besant from the other women. Mrs Webb and Miss Nightingale were perhaps nearest to them in their scepticism and questioning of Christianity but both grew up in families where the religious atmosphere was more tolerant and more liberal. Less constrained to accept dogma and doctrine, their reaction against it was less violent. The mysticism towards which both inclined did not lead them out of the Christian church to join an alternative movement or institution, though in later life Mrs Webb's reverence for Soviet Communism may have had something of the flavour of a new creed.

That Mrs Besant and Miss Cobbe should formally reject Christianity may reflect the strongly evangelical character of their earlier religious education. Brought up to believe in the infallibility of the Bible, both became incredulous about the literal truth of the scriptures and neither could reconcile the existence of an all-powerful and benevolent Deity with the pain and injustice that they saw around them. Mrs Besant relates her atheism to her sense of her own personal degradation and bondage within her marriage; to the spectacle of her mother defrauded and in debt; to the misery and patience of the poor whom she visited; to the grave illness and suffering of her own child. In face of all this the belief in Christ's 'constant direction of affairs' could not survive. The presence of pain and evil in a world created by a good God, she found incomprehensible. Her atheism, she claimed, was 'not a desire for moral licence . . . it was the sense of outraged justice and insulted right'.[66]

The acceptance of a purpose they could not understand, evident in the writing of Mrs Fry and Mrs Butler, was not possible for Mrs Besant nor for Miss Cobbe. A more liberal interpretation of the meaning of Christianity was not readily available in 1840. But loss of faith was a bitter and painful experience. Mrs Besant speaks of a struggle of three years and two months that nearly cost her her life and of the 'fearful anguish' inflicted by doubt on the truly religious soil. 'No life in the empty sky; no gleam in the blackness of the night; no voice to break the deadly silence; no hand outstretched to save.'[67] From her husband she received no help. As a woman it was her duty to attend to her home, not to distract her brain with questions that had puzzled the greatest thinkers and still remained unsolved. Dr Pusey, to whom she appealed in Oxford, offered nothing better. 'It is not your duty to ascertain truth . . . It is your duty to accept and believe the truths as laid down by the Church.'[68]

Mrs Besant refused to observe this injunction. She persisted in questioning not only religious doctrine, but the social beliefs and political arrangements that she found around her. She became an ardent teacher, speaker and writer, in the first instance a free thinker and propagandist for atheism and later notorious for her support for birth control. Her defiance of public opinion, her militancy in the pursuit of unpopular causes, were characteristics she shared with Mrs Butler, but she was not sustained by Christian faith nor by a devoted circle of family and friends. Rather she was driven by her experience of and indignation over personal and social injustice. The sense of duty and service and of personal submission to God that lent some calm to the lives of women like Josephine Butler and Mary Carpenter were not a part of Mrs Besant's personality. She was a life-long rebel or 'protestant'. As with Hannah Mitchell, her reformist zeal sprang from the unhappiness of her own life. It was nonetheless powerful for that, though the bitter personal experiences may help to explain the direction of her later interests towards political action and propaganda and away from day-to-day social work with prisoners or destitute children which called for different qualities of self-sacrifice and acquiescence.

Any attempt to generalise an association between personal misfortune, rejection of religious faith and a form of social service that leans to reform rather than to social work, immediately founders however on the person of Frances Power Cobbe. Miss Cobbe's autobiography, written when she was over 70, exudes a cheerful contentment. Mere natural existence she says was always a positive pleasure. Happy in her family and her home life, her later interest in women's rights did not stem, she says, from her ever having felt in her own person a 'woman's wrongs'. Nevertheless as with Mrs Besant, the loss of belief was a terrible experience. She grew up in an evangelical household with family Bible reading, where Sunday was strictly observed and where great emphasis was placed on duty and the practice of devotion. The search for religious truth started when her formal education finished and she found herself at home in Ireland where Dublin society offered little to interest her. It led, through great anguish, to the rejection of evangelical Christianity: 'I saw all that had made to me the supreme glory and joy of life fade out of it, while that motive which had been presented to me as the mainspring of duty and curb of passion, namely the hope of Heaven, vanished as a dream.'[69]

But although her faith in what she termed the 'apocalyptic' side of Christianity had faded, Miss Cobbe retained a belief in a 'God of conscience' and in immortality. Although her later activities tended towards writing and reform – she supported various women's rights movements as well as the anti-vivisectionists – she retained her interest in social work. As a young women she had observed the conventional charitable duties attaching to her social position, visiting the poor and the sick on her father's Irish estate and teaching in the village school. After her father died, however, she left the comfortable existence in Ireland to join Mary Carpenter in her ragged school work and in the hope, as she explains, of religious sympathy for her own unconventional views. She had wished for a country life but decided that work among the ragged school children wanted doing and that by devoting herself to it she could best do God's will. After a year, however, Miss Cobbe left the austerity of Mary Carpenter's house and 'hideous Bristol' to live independently on the edge of the town. She continued to work in the ragged schools but also started workhouse visiting, Miss Carpenter declaring that workhouses sadly wanted voluntary inspection. This later work was to begin with repellent to Miss Cobbe:

> the very name conveyed to me such an impression of dreary hopelessness that I shrank from the thought. To lift up the criminal and perishing classes of the community and cut off the root of crime and vice by training children in morality and religion, this was a soul inspiring idea. But to bring a small modicum of cheer to the aged and miserable paupers, who may be supposed to be

generally undergoing the inevitable penalties of idle or drunken lives, was far from equally uplifting.[70]

Having started, however, Miss Cobbe felt she must continue and workhouse conditions and workhouse visiting became a major interest. She worked for better arrangements for supervising children, for more trained matrons, to establish aftercare for girls leaving the institutions, and for more women guardians. She wrote pamphlets and papers and addressed meetings. She joined Miss Twining in the national movement to encourage workhouse visiting and establish the workhouse visiting society. She won Jowett's support for her objectives but a warning about the means of reaching them.

But don't go to war with Political Economy. 1st. Because the PEs are a powerful and dangerous class. 2nd. Because it is impossible for ladies and gentlemen to fill up the interstices of legislation if they run counter to the common motives of self-interest. 3rd. (You wont agree to this) Because the PEs have really done more for the labouring classes by their advocacy of free trade, etc., than all the philanthropists put together.

I wish it were possible as a matter of taste to get rid of all philanthropic expressions, 'missions, etc.', which are distasteful to the educated.[71]

Gradually, through the 1860s and 1870s, Miss Cobbe stopped 'practical work among poor folk' and her interests shifted to writing on religious matters and propaganda in support of women's rights and anti-vivisection.

It is perhaps no accident that the women with the most unorthodox religious views should be at the reformist end of social service activity. This is as true of Miss Nightingale and Mrs Webb as it is of Mrs Besant and Miss Cobbe. Their instincts were to challenge the injustice, inefficiency and inhumanity in the world as much as to attend to the victims. Mrs Butler also shared the reformist approach, though her religious faith remained undisturbed. She too, however, was somewhat unconventional in her beliefs. Moreover, it was a keen sense of the many man-made injustices in social arrangements derived from her radical family upbringing that inspired her public work and made political agitation a natural means to her ends.

The distinction between social reform and social work must, of course, remain imprecise. It is a matter of degree. Elizabeth Fry,

Octavia Hill and Mary Carpenter all worked for reform as well as in the prisons and the homes of the London poor and the Bristol ragged schools. But Octavia Hill in particular also believed that social improvement was essentially a matter of moral regeneration through personal relationships without which large scale schemes of national reform would be useless and damaging. It is to the different conceptions of the nature of social problems and how they might be tackled to which we turn in the next chapter.

7 Social Problems and their Remedies

The most remarkable thing about the way in which the women in this study conceived and approached social problems was their overwhelming pragmatism. Beatrice Potter was an exception, and so perhaps was Annie Besant. But for the rest the squalor, poverty and ignorance common and especially evident among the urban working class after the 1830s, and the casual brutality so often a feature of the institutions for the sick and the poor, were the result of personal accident or vice or of administrative failure. There was little conception of an arbitrary political and economic system that concentrated wealth and power among a tiny group of people and left one third of the population in poverty.

This understanding of social problems as a consequence of individual misfortune or faulty public arrangements carried with it the assumption that they were best tackled by the personal intervention of educated charitable people who would visit and befriend the poor in their homes, in the hospitals and in the workhouses. In some cases government measures might be required; to regulate insanitary housing, to permit magistrates to send young children to reformatory and industrial schools rather than to prison, to encourage boards of guardians to admit lady visitors to their institutions or to appoint women as inspectors within the central poor law administration to oversee the local treatment of female paupers and of children in the workhouse schools. But within the legislative framework, the essential work of dealing with social distress or, as it was often seen, of reclaiming the poor was a matter for voluntary effort. Mary Carpenter, Octavia Hill and Louisa Twining were all untiring advocates of parliamentary action, though they were also among those most committed to the view that the problems of the poor reflected personal failure or inadequacy that could only be remedied by education and religion.

Thus, for most of the ladies, government measures were needed to clear the way for voluntary action, not to provide or manage state run services or institutions. And legislation was an *ad hoc* response to particular evils, rather than involving any comprehensive re-ordering of social institutions or the social distribution of income and

145

opportunities. Beatrice Webb was exceptional in her desire to alter the structure of local government services in such a way as to *prevent* poverty and so pauperism, rather than to arrange a more effective private or public response when they arose.

It was the youngest of the ladies, the two born around the middle of the century, who were most inclined to compare the bare subsistence of the poor with the affluence of the rich and conclude that some radical redistribution of resources was called for. For Beatrice Potter, her own easy circumstances made her sufficiently uncomfortable to require justification, and the justification was that material comfort enabled her and Sidney to devote themselves more effectively to a life of social research. Annie Besant was never wealthy so the sense of personal guilt lay less heavily upon her.

The other women all belonged to an earlier period. Mrs Fry to the late eighteenth century, Miss Nightingale, Miss Twining, Miss Cobbe and Mrs Butler all born in the 1820s and Octavia Hill and Agnes Jones in the following decade. But they were mostly very long-lived; all except Agnes Jones, Mary Carpenter and Elizabeth Fry survived into the twentieth century. It is therefore interesting that none of them were much influenced by Marxist or native socialist writing which interpreted social distress as emanating from the class structure and which postulated very different methods of reform.

No doubt their very membership of the bourgeois class was an important factor in predisposing many charitable women against the view that history is the history of class struggles. Indeed the conventions of social behaviour and social responsibility that they inherited could be seen as a contradiction of any such proposition. The gulf between the classes was bridged within the well-to-do households by the characteristic lifelong attachment to family servants, particularly the children's nurse who might also act as confidante to the parents and who might spend her life in the family's service, sometimes moving on to bring up a second generation of children and to die nursed by those she had attended when they were young. Outside the household more flimsy bridges of social obligation led into the village schools and the homes of the poor and the sick and provided some semblance of harmonious class relations.

Perhaps such social exchanges were easier to maintain in the country and during times of reasonable prosperity. It remains surprising that the political and social unrest of the middle of the century, the emerging Marxist analysis of it and the accumulating statistics detailing the living and working conditions of the poor made only a limited impact on this group of women who dedicated themselves to social improvement. Miss Nightingale and Miss Cobbe were relatively protected in their country houses, as Miss Nightingale recognised.

Ought not one's externals to be as nearly as possible an incarnation of what life really is? Life is *not* a green pasture and a still water, as our homes make it . . . life is seen in a much truer form in London than in the country . . . You cannot get out of a carriage at a party without seeing what is in the faces making the lines on either side, and without feeling tempted to rush back and say, 'Those are my brothers and sisters.'[1]

But Mrs Butler, Octavia Hill, Louisa Twining and Mary Carpenter all lived and worked among the urban poor.

Beatrice Webb attributed the increasing interest in the life and labour of the people that developed through the nineteenth century neither to philanthropy nor intellectual curiosity but to 'panic fear of the newly enfranchised democracy'.[2] Her own scepticism about democratic theory, 'that by multiplying ignorant opinions indefinitely you produce wisdom',[3] remained with her and hardened throughout her life. That England did not produce even the mildest of revolutions was remarked with some surprise by Miss Nightingale.

In London there have been the usual amount of Charity Balls, Charity Concerts, Charity Bazaars whereby people bamboozle their consciences and shut their eyes. Nevertheless there does not seem the slightest prospect of a revolution here. Why, would be hard to say, as England is surely the country where luxury has reached its height and poverty its depths.[4]

It is not surprising that revolutionary socialism received little support. It was associated with the violence and class hatred of revolutionary movements in France and with the kind of reforms which could invest the poor and uneducated in Britain with power that they might abuse. Mary Carpenter elaborates this view:

I have found that only the least respectable, the most ignorant of the labouring classes join them [the Chartists] . . . There are great abuses existing in England, but it needs the highest wisdom and knowledge to rectify them; the awful example of Paris shows that a mobocracy is the worst of all governments, and that it is not sufficient to have the best intentions if one has not knowledge.[5]

Moreover, the Marxist predictions of social polarisation and revolution were not borne out by events in Britain and perhaps the failure of this element of socialist thought cast doubt on any suggestion that the genesis of social problems lay in the class structure. Certainly the last few decades of the century witnessed widespread optimism about the combined power of science and the benevolence of the rich to conquer and alleviate the poverty and distress of an industrial society. The documentation and measurement of the full extent of urban poverty by Booth and Rowntree came only at the end of the century, too late to disturb the belief in the possibility of social progress through personal service, carefully organised voluntary effort and occasional government intervention.

If their class background was some protection against socialist doctrine, so too was the associated definition of social problems which was the inheritance of a particular family tradition and social background. The issues that aroused the enthusiasm of the radical and liberal families from which most of the ladies came were the great international questions of liberty and equality, of the emancipation of slaves, of free trade, of parliamentary reform and of the struggles for independence of small nations. Miss Carpenter and Mrs Butler were especially committed to the abolition of slavery. Mrs Butler and Miss Nightingale were fired by the cause of Italian nationalism. Conflicts tended to be seen as conflicts between races or between nations rather than between classes within nations. Few of the philanthropic ladies of this study paid much attention to inequalities within their own country either between the classes or between the sexes, as opposed to the most obvious injustices or the most acute poverty. India was another matter. Towards the end of her life Miss Carpenter was very active in support of the education and emancipation of Indian women and Miss Nightingale laboured to improve the sanitary conditions and public health of the civilian population. But at home, as we have seen, many of the early social workers were half-hearted in their support for votes for women; for instance. And the movement for women's education in which Mrs Butler played a prominent part was essentially a movement to make higher education accessible to middle-class women rather than to spread opportunities to women or men of the working class.

Religious conviction may also help to explain the resistance to a structural explanation of social problems. For many, especially for Octavia Hill, Mary Carpenter, Josephine Butler and Elizabeth Fry, this meant belief in a benevolent God who ordered earthly life for the best, and trust that apparent injustice and pain would be resolved in the future or served some purpose not immediately evident. Thus, faith was the answer to the problems of the world and even the most sadly afflicted could find consolation in Christian doctrine and Christian belief. 'To anyone who knows the way in which a thought of God transcends all sorrow and subdues all fear, the idea of there being *any* life which need be forlorn sounds strange.'[6] Such trust in providence did not deter the early social workers and social reformers from determined efforts to alter the world in the ways they saw fit. Belief in divine power did not imply submissive acceptance of circumstances they saw as unjust or wrong. But choices were made about the kinds of problems to be tackled and about the best ways of resolving them.

The choices arose out of particular views of the world and how it might be changed; and three broad approaches emerge among the women in this study. On the one hand is the majority whose conception of social problems rested on their own experiences of the poverty and sickness and delinquency that they found around them. They tended to see such conditions as the outcome of ignorance, or misfortune or some defect of character. And they looked for a remedy to Christianity and education and the spreading among the poor of what Mrs Butler called 'home influences'. Their immediate response was personal visiting to offer sympathy and help, friendship and moral instruction to people in trouble. This was essentially an individualistic approach; social problems were to be resolved by fostering independence and strengthening individual character through private charity and benevolence. Public action and universal provision should be avoided as dangerous and demoralising. Such views are forcefully expressed in a report from a district committee of the Charity Organisation Society in 1876.

> The principle is, that it is good for the poor that they should meet all the ordinary contingencies of life, relying not upon private or public charity, but upon their own industry and thrift, and upon the powers of self help that are to be developed by individual and collective effort . . . The working man does not require to be told that temporary sickness is likely now and then to visit his household; that times of slackness will occasionally come; that if he marries

early and has a large family, his resources will be taxed to the uttermost; that if he lives long enough, old age will render him more or less incapable of toil – all these are contingencies of a labourer's life, and if he is taught that as they arise they will be met by State relief or private charity he will assuredly make no effort to meet them himself. A spirit of dependence, fatal to all progress, will be engendered in him, he will not concern himself with the causes of his distress, or consider at all how the condition of his class may be improved; the road to idleness and drunkenness will be made easy to him, and it involves no prophesying to say that the last state of a population influenced after such a fashion will certainly be worse than the first. One thing there is which true charity does require the working man to be told, and it is the aim of this society to tell him, not in words merely, but in acts that cannot be confuted. We desire to tell him that those who are born to easier circumstances sympathise with the severe toil and self denial which his lot imposes upon him; that many are standing beside him ready and even eager to help if proper occasion should arise; and that if he, or wife, or child should be stricken with *protracted* sickness, or with some special infirmity, such as we all hope to escape, there are those at hand who will gladly minister to his necessities, and do their best at least to mitigate the suffering which it may be beyond their power to remove.[7]

A different approach is represented by Beatrice Webb and Florence Nightingale whose formulation of social problems depended more on their private efforts to educate themselves, on the laborious study of government reports and Blue Books, than on first-hand knowledge of ragged school children and their families, or prostitutes, or the squalid slums of East London. For all the women the driving force that led into social service was similar; an anxious search for a purpose in life that was linked often to religious commitment, sometimes to some personal grief. But for Miss Nightingale and Miss Potter the way to their special interests was through contemplation of social statistics and social enquiries. Both women worked for some time among the sick or the London poor but for both this was a short prelude to a life of documentary research and investigation. The emphasis of their reforming activities was in their writing and in the political influence they attempted to exercise on government policy of the day.

The third and more direct political response to what are perceived as social problems involves organising national campaigns and pressure groups. Social work, social research and social reform may all be different means to the same end of social improvement. But efforts to influence government and public opinion through memorials to members of parliament, letters to newspapers and public meetings are a more immediate attempt to alter things. These were the strategies of the suffragists, but they were also important elements in the work of some of the women of this study. Mrs Webb turned to public campaigning in support of her proposals for reforming the poor law, and Mrs Butler led the national campaign against the Contagious Diseases Acts in public meetings all over the country. Mrs Besant was above all else a journalist and public speaker who used her vivid pen and oratorical gifts to attack the injustices she found in the world.

Both the researchers and the campaigners placed more emphasis on legislation than on charity. We can now turn to elaborate the distinction between those who put their faith in private philanthropy as the way to social progress and those who preferred some kind of collective action.

THE PHILANTHROPISTS

For the majority of the early social workers, concern about poverty, sickness and crime stemmed not from an intellectual appraisal of the state of the nation nor from contemplating Chadwick's statistics which showed that the labouring classes could expect to live only half as long as people in the professional classes,[8] but from the miserable living conditions of the men and women and children dwelling immediately around them. Not that the contrast between evident poverty and their own relatively luxurious lives seemed to arouse great discomfort. The acceptance of gross social inequalities no doubt reflected the belief that God ordered all things, including men's material circumstances, for the best. Miss Carpenter put her trust in a Deity who would only permit evil for His own benevolent purposes.[9] And even at the age of 17 Octavia Hill was invoking similar sentiments in dealing with the more rebellious ragged school children.

> I told her that there was in all positions some work to be done for which the world would be nobler . . . that I was sure we never could do any work well, until we were content to do our own well

. . . that no change of circumstances, before death or after it, could ever make us conscientious, zealous or gentle; and that I was quite sure that, if any one of them could have done more good in any other position, they would have been there.[10]

But if the stark inequalities aroused little consciousness of collective sin, to use Beatrice Potter's phrase, they did stimulate a keen sense of social obligation. The immediate response to human misery and distress was the visiting of the poor, in their own homes, in the workhouses and in the hospitals, and it was rooted in the charitable traditions of family and class.

Mary Carpenter, growing up in a household which was 'a centre of intellectual culture', taught in the Sunday school attached to her father's ministry, but also helped in the instruction of the school boys whom Dr and Mrs Carpenter received into their family. When ill health obliged Dr Carpenter to give up his own school, his wife and daughters started one for girls and by the time she was 24 Miss Carpenter was superintendent of the afternoon Sunday school. Visits to the homes of Sunday school children, the Bristol riots over reform and the advent of cholera all impressed upon her the poverty and ignorance that existed in the city. By 1835 she had established a society for visiting the homes of Sunday school children and members of the congregation. Visitors were allotted districts, records were instituted and relief only given if sanctioned by the committee. Miss Carpenter herself worked in the poorest district of all and it was this experience that determined her to devote herself, as she put it, 'to the good of my fellow creatures'.

The religious and pedagogical influences that surrounded Mary Carpenter as a child and young woman transformed her work with destitute children into something of a crusade.

We are to free that divine nature from the still more than heathenish darkness in which it is growing to become a fiend, a worse than American slave. I feel this work inexpressibly glorious, nor have I ever felt the inextinguishable greatness of the human soul so much as I have at seeing it rise superior to such very degrading circumstances as it does in many of these children.[11]

The fortitude of the human soul was assisted by improvement schemes for dwellings, the provision of wash houses, baths, water and playgrounds, but it was the need for enlightenment that was the fundamental issue.

> I shall attempt to show first that 'the people perisheth for lack of knowledge', that the appalling increase of juvenile depravity can *only* be checked by real education – intellectual, moral and religious: that this cannot be given by the parents and will not be sought by them; that for mere self-defence, if for no higher motive, we must give it them.[12]

Writing about her own book, *The Neglected Child*, she comments that it gives but a faint idea of the cruel wrong inflicted on the children. 'The sufferings of the Negroes seem to me of even secondary importance to the wrong done to the immortal souls of these young creatures.'[13] With some insight she notes the power of richer families to shelter and protect their children from experiences which would be their inevitable ruin. By contrast, among the poor, children almost from infancy, immature, inexperienced and untaught, faced the dangers and shared the treatment of a man.[14]

The crimes of the young delinquents, however, Miss Carpenter insists, are a matter not of poverty but of drunkenness and vice. They must be rescued through education and religion. Christian men and women must become the fathers and mothers of those 'moral orphans', who must be placed in families. This was not to imply that children should be taken from the streets into the homes of the well-to-do, though Josephine Butler did favour the spreading of 'home influences' in precisely that way. For Miss Carpenter it meant that children should be kept out of prisons, 'the only infirmary provided by the parental care of the state for the care of her erring children's souls',[15] which were centres of depravity, useless as reformatory institutions and which boys preferred to the workhouse because the food was better. Instead, reformatory shcools should be available, run as far as possible on family principles. This meant the schools or homes should be small, but above all the teachers' minds must be 'imbued by the spirit of love and actuated by a principle of religious duty'.[16] Natural parents should not be relieved of responsibility for their offspring. If their inability to provide for their children were their own fault they must be punished, if not they should be helped by the state, 'the parent of all'.

The idea of family-type homes is familiar enough in contemporary discussion of arrangements for children in public care. But for the early social workers the familial ideal was inextricably entwined with fervent religious belief in a way which would be less usual among their professional descendants.

> First, and above all, there must be in the minds of those who plan, and of those who carry out the work, a strong faith in the immortality of the human soul, the universal and parental government of God, and the equal value in His sight of each one of these poor perishing young creatures with the most exalted of our race. We must feel even a reverence . . . for these children . . . and be able to discern under the most degraded exterior the impress of God's creative spirit, one of those for whom Christ died.[17]

Some 30 years after Miss Carpenter found her way into the homes of the poor through Sunday school and ragged school teaching, Octavia Hill was following her along a similar path. It was through the sickness and frailty of the toy workers she supervised and of the women who gathered for sewing classes in the Hills' kitchen in Nottingham Place, that Miss Hill discovered the damp and unhealthy dwellings of the poor. Her own experiences and, according to her sister Emily, recollections of the work of her grandfather, Dr Southwood Smith, in East London convinced her of the desperate need for decent working-class houses. With Ruskin's money she bought her first tenement in 1865. But the people's homes were bad, she was to write ten years later, only partly because they were badly built and arranged. They were ten times worse because the tenants' habits and lives were what they were.[18] So it was the habits and lives that Miss Hill set herself to alter. First she would collect rent at regular times and tenants would clean to receive her and have the pleasure of seeing her satisfaction; then she would go at unexpected times 'to raise them to the power of having it always clean'.[19]

Success, she said, depended on duly arranging the inmates; not too many children so as to overcrowd a house, not too few so as to overcrowd another; not too many bad people side by side as they would drink together; not a very bad person beside a very respectable one. The importance of supervision was crucial. People and their houses could not be dealt with separately. Inhabitants and their surroundings must be improved together.[20]

For Miss Twining, too, character was a major determinant of poverty and misfortune. In 1860 she set up a home for workhouse girls, and writing about it 30 years later her language is unusually vivid.

> I could fill a volume with the history of this Home during nearly twenty years, in which time I learnt much as to character and the amount of depravity in our midst of which I knew little before. The great fact and power of heredity was also for the first time fully impressed upon me; and I found to my grief and disappointment how little we were able to do in combating the inherited wickedness, vice and drunkenness of generations. I also came to learn that the fearful tempers with which we had occasionally to deal, were, without doubt, forms of insanity, owing to the same causes.[21]

The insistence that social improvement depended on moral regeneration and that this could only occur through the influence of educated and sympathetic people, was a fundamental belief of the men and women associated with the COS. But Miss Hill at any rate demanded very high standards. The same delicacy and courtesy were required in helping the poor as in helping the better off. Help might differ in amount because needs were greater; it should not differ in kind. Nor should it take the form of indiscriminate doles which would demoralise those who received them.

> Restraining yourselves from alms giving . . . is the only true mercy to the poor . . . I think small doles unkind to them . . . First of all I think they may make them really poorer. Then I think they degrade them and make them less independent. Thirdly, I think they destroy the possibility of really good relations between you and them. Surely . . . you have better things to do for them than to give them half crowns. You want to know them . . . to make their lives a little fuller, a little gladder. You who know so much more than they might help them so much at important crises of their lives; you might gladden their homes by bringing them flowers, or, better still, by teaching them how to grow plants; you might meet them face to face as friends; you might teach them, you might collect their savings, you might take them into the parks, or out for quiet days in the country in small companies, or to your own or your friends' grounds or to exhibitions or picture galleries . . . the gift you have to make to the poor, depend upon it, is the

greatest of all gifts you can make – that of yourselves, following in the great Master's steps, whose life is the foundation of all charity.[22]

Here is an eloquent statement of the tradition of social thought that sees social progress as founded not on the dictates of governments but on individual personality. And in two senses; the poor must be educated and encouraged in better habits, but that would only be effected through the individual influence and friendship of the rich.

Transplant them tomorrow to healthy and commodious homes, and they would pollute and destroy them. There needs and will need for some time, a reformatory work which will demand that loving zeal of individuals which cannot be had for money and cannot be legislated for by parliament.[23]

The belief in a kind of equality that transcended the most glaring material differences and permitted the development of friendship and mutual respect between rich and poor was an essential element in this same tradition. It was rooted in the idea of the equality of all men in the sight of God and linked with the keen sense of self denying moral obligation to help the wretched and the destitute which was characteristic of many of the early social workers. The desire to develop the personal association between rich and poor was expressed in a more organised fashion in the settlement movement but it was also a spur to conduct for many individual charitable people and it was seen not only as a way of resolving particular evils but also as a step towards bridging the gulf between the classes. Mary Carpenter comments on the importance of the reformatory school movement in opening the way for the rich to serve the poor. 'It has tended to establish the practical conviction that we are all of one human family, and that, as such, the strong ought to try to help the weak.'[24]

The conviction that the salvation of the poor and the delinquent could only come through individual effort, by both the poor and the rich, was an assertion that the good society must be founded on good people; it was not to be won through the arbitrary fiat of government. The feckless and the wicked must strive for self-improvement and the better-off must support and assist them with moral instruction, acting as teachers and parents where natural parents could not fulfil this vital role.

The emphasis on family principles and home influences as a way of leading people to better lives pervades the writing of Mary

Carpenter and Octavia Hill. But Louisa Twining, too, used the family as a model for public administration in pointing to the need for women's influence to be brought to bear on the poor law treatment of women and girls. Her own workhouse visits began in 1853 and she records the unsatisfactory quality of the workhouse superintendents for both adults and children – 'persons from a low and uneducated middle-class'.[25] In 1873 she was party, with Lord Stansfield, President of the Local Government Board, to the appointment of Mrs Nassau Senior as Inspector of Workhouse Schools whose first report supported Miss Twining's own convictions, shared by many charitable ladies, of the need for more female influence in the institutions. 'The enquiries I have made on all sides have convinced me that what is wanted in the education of girls is more *mothering*.'[26]

The election of women to serve as guardians to the poor was another way of influencing the administration of the poor laws. Miss Twining herself joined the Kensington guardians in 1884, less than ten years after the first woman to be elected. But she remained disturbed by there being so few people ready to serve. At the end of the 1890s there were still 300 out of 648 local poor law boards without any women members and Miss Twining expressed both surprise and regret that in country districts so few residents came forward to fill such posts. She noted particularly the difficulty of finding a suitable woman to succeed her when she retired, even 'in so large and wealthy and leisurely a place as Tunbridge Wells'.[27]

The problems of reconciling even the minimal provision of the poor law with individual responsibility remained however. Miss Twining quotes with approval a 'long and interesting' letter with 'valuable remarks on the Poor Law' that she received in the 1850s from Lord Lyttleton: 'it is quite essential that a legal system of relief . . . should be such as to repel rather than attract the poor; – pauperism is essentially and ineradically, [sic] an evil state to be in, and one morally injurious to the character';[28] and she adds that among the greatest evils was the tendency to relax filial ties and the sense of duty to parents.

Such arguments must have presented a dilemma to those who wished to make the administration of the poor laws more humane. But it was left to Mrs Webb and the Poor Law Commissioners signing the Minority Report of 1909 to propose the development of a comprehensive set of public services outside the poor law to prevent pauperism. Miss Twining represented those who preferred to rely on better organised charitable effort to remove the deserving from the harsh influences of the Local Government Board. Hence her work to develop voluntary after-care schemes and residential provision for people who would otherwise have been left to the workhouse. One home for old women was extended to take thirty incurables; 'they were a happy family, and the three floors were fitly named "Harmony", "Concord" and "Peace".'[29]

Perhaps the strongest supporter of the family was Mrs Butler, for whom it represented 'the nursery of all virtue, the fountainhead of all true affection and the main source of the strength of our nation', sustaining not only those who dwelt within it, but acting as an elevating influence for anyone in trouble. But Mrs Butler had to reconcile respect for the almost sacred character of the family with a similar respect for women's rights. The social issues debated in the Grey household in which she grew up were the great questions of liberty and equality; of national independence, free trade, the emancipation of slaves and parliamentary reform. But also within the family was a tradition of support for women's rights and for sexual equality, expressed by Mr Grey himself, but more especially by his sister Margaretta.

The double standard applied to sexual morality that Mrs Butler encountered at Oxford, and the offence against civil liberties and discrimination against women that she later discovered in the Contagious Diseases Acts, aroused her implacable opposition.[30] But the 'woman question', she insisted, was no more to do with women than with men. The Contagious Diseases Acts secured the enslavement of women and increased the immorality of men and history showed that these two results were never separated. The legislation offended against the principle of just law and encroached upon individual liberty.[31] The movement for repeal was not so much a woman's war against man's injustice. For her own part, 'it was as a citizen of a free country first, and as a woman secondly, that I felt impelled to come forward in defence of the right'.[32]

The ultimate remedy lay in changed social attitudes and the withdrawal of the offending laws, and towards these ends Mrs Butler worked through writing, public speaking and the Ladies' National Association for Repeal. In this sense she was a political activist, but her immediate response to the plight of exploited and oppressed women was to take the victims into her own home – first, in Oxford, the girl imprisoned for killing her illegitimate child, and later, in Liverpool, the sick and destitute women from the streets and the workhouse.

Mrs Butler was awakened to the 'double standard' in Oxford by discussions in her own drawing room, where Mrs Gaskell's *Ruth* was denounced as an immoral book and a moral lapse in a woman condemned as 'immensely worse' than in a man. But in Liverpool it was sorrow for the death of her only daughter that drove her to the oakum sheds of the workhouse.

> Music, art, reading, all failed as resources to alleviate or interest. I became possessed with an irresistible desire to go forth and find some pain keener than my own . . . the only solace possible would seem to be to find other hearts that ached night and day, and with more reason than mine.[33]

Again, however, the response to sickness and poverty was to bring the women into the cellars and garrets of her own home and, as the numbers grew, into a separate House of Rest and Industrial Home with a widowed sister to help her and her husband acting as chaplain, friend and adviser to the inmates.

Before she became the leader of the Ladies' National Association for the Repeal of the Contagious Diseases Acts, Mrs Butler had been active in the movement for better employment and educational opportunities for women generally. Again, the problem was one of freedom, equality and opportunity. She pointed to the three million unmarried women revealed in the 1861 census to be working for subsistence wages, shut out from decent employment, from apprenticeships and from education. And this was reference not to those 'forced downwards to the paths of hell' (a subject too painful to be included in a book for general reading) but to 'the wholesale destitution which goes on from year to year among women' and which had no parallel among men.[34] Mrs Butler went on to emphasise the urgency of preventive measures, especially the development of technical and industrial education, 'to avert this terrible destruction of human beings', noting that prostitutes were drawn from the lower middle as well as from the working class.

> It is not in their case a positive lack of a meal for today that drives them into this, but it is their generally exposed condition, the presence of temptation to frivolity, the absence of all mental resource, empty-headedness, love of dress and the craving for some little affair of the heart to enliven the insipidity of their lives.

And what, save a good education, can tend to the correction of all this?[35]

Nor, as we have seen, would Mrs Butler allow that more educational opportunities for women would weaken family relationships. Acknowledging women's rights to education, she argued, could only have beneficial effects. Granting the demands of women would tend to the restoration of 'true home ideals'; their denial would hasten the day of 'disorganisation and uprooting of sacred traditions'. And a freer life for women would tend to an increase in marriage as a result of their increased worth and attractiveness.[36]

Thus were radical demands for women's education reconciled with the traditional reverence for family life. The interest in Mrs Butler's approach is her attempt to fuse individualism with state welfare. Insistent always on the importance of family influences she mistrusted large-scale private philanthropy as much as statutory organisations for the tendency to 'centralisation of rule, to vast combinations, large institutions and uniformity of system', which would leave the poor worse than they had found them. A large infusion of 'home elements' into workhouses, schools, hospitals, orphanages, reformatories and prisons was required to avoid the danger. Home life was better than the costliest institution – more women died in lying-in hospitals than in their own homes. Workhouse girls brought up in masses never turned out well. Lunatics were more apt to recover when boarded out.

Everything . . . thrives better where there is the principle of play and freedom which home affords . . . the wholesale system tends to turn human beings into machines instead of training them to be self-depending responsible beings . . . the large and magnificently ordered Institution is in danger of becoming as fatally a pauperising influence as the Lady Bountiful, but the home develops freedom and energy.[37]

Thus not only must 'home elements' be infused into institutions. The beneficial effects of family life on the wider society could also be encouraged in other ways. There is often, Mrs Butler claims, a conservation of family comfort which approaches to selfishness. Family life was weakened by the private enjoyment of comforts 'while the homeless are wailing outside'. Many people visit the poor but they then return to very different worlds. 'I think means might be found . . . to break down . . . such a separation, and to give forth more freely of the strength and comfort and sweetness of family life to the homeless and solitary and sinful.'[38] It would be good, she suggests, for servants and children if families were to take in the outcast or the lunatics.

Mrs Butler distinguished between feminine and masculine phil-anthropy. The first, involving individual ministering to the poor, had failed. The second, involving comprehensive measures planned by men and sanctioned by parliament, was also in danger of failing unless the two principles could be united.[39] Thus male and female roles are properly complementary in public arrangements as they should be in marriage. In expressing these sentiments Mrs Butler is voicing with peculiar force the New Liberalism of the end of the nineteenth century. It was an assertion that the state must intervene to control and remedy social evils, that it could indeed be a liberator of the oppressed, but equally that social progress could only be built on personal character and respect for the freedom and independence of individuals.

The importance of freedom for people to develop the means to lead a civilised life appears in the writing of many of the social service ladies. Mary Carpenter spoke of freeing the divine nature of the children of the 'perishing and dangerous classes' from heathenish darkness. Annie Besant proclaimed her desire to spread liberty and truer thought among men and make the world freer and better than she found it. Octavia Hill wanted to free poor people from the tyranny of bad landlords, from the corrupting effects of degraded fellow lodgers, from the weight of accumulated dirt. 'That so the never dying hope which I find characteristic of the poor might have leave to spring and with it such energy as might help them to help themselves.'[40]

The generous desire for freedom and independence for the poor had its harsher side, however, as Miss Hill's words suggest, in the doctrine of self-help, for the price of respectability was sometimes very high. The most popular remedy for dependency was some kind of voluntary or compulsory saving scheme, and Louisa Twining was especially severe.

It is evident that the classes who spend thousands, or even millions, a year in drink, to say nothing of the luxuries of tobacco, and 'sweets' for their children, could, if they desired, provide for the inevitable evils of sickness in themselves and their families, by small monthly or weekly payments either in clubs or dispensaries; and now that the latter, under the Poor Law, are so improved and efficiently served, all who are not classed as 'destitute' could surely afford the weekly pence which would enable them to be free of pauperising dependence.[41]

Octavia Hill took a similar view when arguing that doles of money should not be given without thorough investigation of circumstances and that instant payments would destroy forethought and thrift.

The smaller the earnings the more need of providence; and there is no man so poor that he might, by effort, at least have a few shillings in hand for emergency, if he really felt it important . . . that is all that is wanted to do away with this clamour about urgency. That every man should at some time of his life put aside five or ten shillings which should be ready for need.[42]

There should be some kind of 'forced' independent sick club she concluded, for there is no way in which the better off could help the people so thoroughly and well as by helping them to help themselves.

Abstinence as well as thrift was considered a vital element in the independence and self reliance of the working class. Heavy drinking was frequently associated with destitution, sickness and crime. Many of the men and women working among the poor formally took the pledge, not because it made any difference to their own habits, but because they saw drunkenness as a vicious social evil. Miss Twining during her time as poor law guardian in Kensington between 1884 and 1890 met considerable opposition in her insistence that officers be dismissed for being drunk and incapable. She managed, however, to put a stop to the occasional issue of drink to workhouse inmates – 'in 1889 we gained the glorious victory against beer on Christmas Day, by a majority of two'.[43]

The demand for austerity on the part of the poor was not inconsistent with the ladies' own lives. For them, too, earnest efforts at self improvement were the norm and personal self indulgence scorned, albeit within a way of life supplying solid material comforts and extensive cultural opportunities. Miss Twining insisted the Kensington guardians travel third class rather than first when they visited poor law homes. Miss Carpenter's ascetic domestic habits were remarked by Miss Cobbe who described her as a stoic both by temperament and by principle. Octavia Hill was indifferent to her own dress, and the disciplined family life is illustrated by Mrs Hill's description of a day's activities during a family holiday.

> We are all very happy here. A and Octa bathe every day and read Virgil together after breakfast . . . After early dinner we all sit out of doors, and the others work while I read Spencer . . . Octa paints the sunset every night from the field above the house . . . at 9.30 we sing a hymn and read prayers and then separate, some to bed. F. and I perhaps walk by starlight; – some read in their own room till bedtime. They all go out at low tide to find things which have 'suffered a sea change into something rich and strange' on the rocks; and have been very successful, to F.'s great delight . . . We are very merry.[44]

A rather different picture of the same holiday is given by one of the sisters.

> Mama, A. and O. all seem to me gloomy; they declare they are not. Ockey is rather like a *man* taking a holiday; she thinks it is her duty to be idle, and does not quite know what to do with herself; but I am going to worry her down to the rocks to hunt for zoophites; and she has promised to read 'Modern Painters'.[45]

Thus, if self discipline, hard work and piety were required of the working class, these were also the ideals that the ladies strove after themselves. That the achievement of such virtues might be peculiarly difficult for people in poor, crowded and unhealthy homes, oppressed by long hours of work and with little opportunity for education or leisure was only partially recognised by many charitable people. Miss Hill, as we have seen, believed that God and family ties were the two greatest blessings in life. No life need be forlorn for the thought of God transcends all sorrow and family ties exist in all classes.[46] The secondary gifts, however, of music, art, nature, space and quiet were *very* unequally divided. The answer was to clear and preserve open spaces amidst the courts and tenements of East London, to create playgrounds, parks and gardens and to take the people from the crowded dwellings to concerts and to galleries, to the spacious homes of rich friends and to the countryside. Such expeditions might be undertaken with some trepidation.

I took the B Court people to Woodford. I feared to leave them a
minute. They were all of a class so low as to be quite amazed and
delighted, at the end of the day, to find that they had not got
drunk. Our thankfulness was extreme, but that theirs should be so
was curious.[47]

The effort to bring art and music to the homes of the people and
to preserve open spaces led eventually to the formation of the Kyrle
Society in the 1870s and to the National Trust in the 1890s. But the
movement initially attracted mockery and derision, and its growth
was slow as Octavia Hill remarked to her sister.

When I first began the work, people would say, 'I will give money
for necessaries for the poor; but I do not see what they want with
recreation.' Then after a few years, they said, 'I can understand
the poor people needing amusement; but what good will open
spaces do them?' And now everybody recognises the importance
of open spaces.[48]

For Miss Hill, however, the whole movement was essential for what
she called 'good citizenship'. The idea of citizenship as a principle
ordering social relationships was crucial in the battle against poverty
of the late nineteenth-century philanthropists. It was a concept that
involved duties, rights and responsibilities, though not equality. Poor
people had a duty to be thrifty and clean and struggle for independence
and self-improvement. Rich people had a responsibility to help them
in their efforts, not through impersonal and indiscriminate charity
or doles of money but through individual friendship informed by
compassion and respect. 'You want to know them, . . . to make their
lives a little fuller, a little gladder,' as Octavia Hill told her volunteer
visitors among the poor.
     Citizenship was not just a matter of visits, however. It required a
more total commitment. Mrs Butler remarked that many people gave
part of their day to visiting the poor but then returned to very
different worlds. A way should be found to break down such
separation and extend the 'strength and comfort and sweetness of
family life' to the homeless and solitary and sinful. Miss Hill argued
the same cause, 'all good gifts for which we are bound to lift our
hearts in praise to God, seem to retain their sanctity only when they
are shared', and luxury and ease and splendour became almost ghastly
when they were enjoyed by those who never considered the poor.

The geographical separation of the social classes was regarded by Octavia Hill as we have seen as a special problem.

It is our withdrawal from the less pleasant neighbourhood . . . which has left these tracts what they are . . . I would urge you all . . . as citizens of a city fearfully so divided, to weigh well your duties; and, never forgetting the near ones to home and neighbourhood, to remember also that when Europe is sacrificed to England, England to your own town, your own town to your parish, your parish to your own family, the step is easy to sacrifice your family to yourself.[49]

The logical development of this strand of thought was the settlement movement, the attempt to bridge the physical distance between rich and poor by establishing centres in the large cities where young men and women from the professional classes would live among the poor, the better to befriend, teach and work with them and where they could pursue their interests in social research among like-minded people. Toynbee Hall was one of the earliest and most famous of the London settlements,[50] conceived by the Barnetts as the University of East London. It grew out of Samuel Barnett's vicarage at St Jude's in Whitechapel, owing much to the energy and devotion of Henrietta Rowland, 'one of Octavia's best workers', who married Barnett in 1873,[51] and to the young men from the older establishment in Oxford who followed Dr Jowett's advice to 'find their friends among the poor'.[52]

The definition of social problems as matters primarily of character to be resolved first and foremost through civilised social intercourse, friendship and shared cultural interests between the social classes, gradually gave way to an analysis that placed more emphasis on structural and environmental causes of poverty. To some extent the re-definition sprang from the settlement movement and the fact-finding social enquiries often associated with it, which were a mark of the later years of the nineteenth century. Booth's investigation in London led him to change his views about the need for state old-age pensions. Beveridge's work on unemployment caused him to analyse it in 1909 as a problem of industry,[53] and the development of Fabian Socialism, represented in this study by Beatrice Webb, put great emphasis on the need for government action to redress social injustice and distress.

The earlier social workers and social reformers, as we have seen, were not blind to the necessity for state intervention. In some circumstances it might be imperative. But it could never be sufficient, and it was potentially dangerous in the threat it posed to liberty and fraternity, a problem to which Titmuss returned in his discussion of altruism nearly a century later,[54] and after publishing a collection of essays under the title *Commitment to Welfare*. For the charitable men and women of the end of the nineteenth century, legislation was a means of establishing the conditions in which private benevolence could flourish; a way of encouraging voluntary action and directing it to where it was most needed. Faith in the strength of charitable effort, in the increasing awareness of social distress and the growing commitment to dealing with it, is a notable characteristic of most of the women in this study. After the turn of the century and in the hands of the Fabians such optimism tended to be directed to the efficacy of state action to resolve social ills, a belief strong in some sections of the Labour Party in the 1930s and which Crossman retrospectively denounced as one source of later troubles in the welfare state.[55]

For the earlier philanthropic ladies, however, hope for social progress and a better society lay in the mounting evidence of the compassion and sympathy of the better off. In the 1840s Mary Carpenter had been impressed both by the extent of and necessity for voluntary action.

> There is a *very* large amount of individual exertion in our country to do good to others . . . never more than at the present moment has the public mind been called to direct its energies to the removal of the heavy burdens which oppress our nation, and which . . . are so enwrought in our social fabric that no Government measure, however good, can produce more than a very partial and inadequate effect.[56]

And a few years later she repeated her view that the public was more awakened than it had ever been to the duty of man to care for his fellow men, 'so I thank God and take courage'.[57]

Mrs Butler was one of the strongest supporters of personal intervention, particularly of the extension of 'home influences' to encourage people to be 'self-depending responsible beings' and of the need to combine 'feminine philanthropy' with parliamentary measures to avoid the 'wholesale manipulation of the poor'.[58] Writing at the same time, Octavia Hill was insisting that the 'disciplining of our immense poor population' must be affected through individual influence which could change it from a 'mob of paupers' into a body of self-dependent workers.[59] Ten years later in a paper read to a Charity Organisation Society meeting she remarked that 'tender pity' for the poor had been a growing characteristic of the age.[60]

Even Miss Hill, however, had some misgivings about the power of charity to match the need for help.

> What a good thing it might be if each of your congregation here would undertake to help with money and with work in some poor district. . . . Only remember, though you may send your money . . . the gift is a very poor one compared with that of your love and knowledge, your sympathy, your resolution – above all, your knowledge; for if you saw you could not leave things as they are . . . on a summer evening sultry as this, there are thousands of families who have no place to sit in but one close room, in which the whole family have eaten, slept, washed, cooked. It is stifling . . . they go to the public house; do you wonder?
>
> I know how people are coming forward year by year to do more of their duty to the poor. The interest deepens and spreads and that rapidly. Haven't I myself such a body of fellow workers as makes me hardly know how to be thankful enough? . . . But forgive me if the sight of all that is needed sometimes makes me a little impatient.[61]

The value of voluntary effort, though, lay not only in its being the best way of effectively helping the poor. It was also important that the rich have the opportunity to express their philanthropic instincts.

> After all, even if Government did give it, that only means all being taxed; and surely, so long as riches exist, there is need to call upon those who have them to give of their abundance freely and heartily . . . even without *asking* them, to make it possible for those who *want* to give to give helpfully, and, so long as there are quite poor people with any surplus, it is a pity they should not have the joy of giving freely. Is it to be all compulsory taxes and no free-will offering?[62]

This 'freedom to give' is again a notion discussed by Titmuss in his study of altruism in 1970. For him too the 'gift relationship' lies at the heart of a decent and civilised society.

The insistence on private philanthropy as the most effective

response to poverty, and the insistence also on help through personal
relationships, friendship and moral instruction, evident in the teaching
of the Charity Organisation Society and the writing of Octavia Hill
was, however, qualified in a crucial respect in regard to unemployment. Octavia Hill managed her property on a firm economic basis.
She had agreed with Ruskin that capital invested should yield a five
per cent return which might then be used for improvements; tenants
who persistently failed to pay their rent were evicted. For the poorest
families she recommended smaller dwellings with 'less elaborate
appliances', in fact single rooms. But even among the better paid
artisans sickness and irregular work might lead to arrears. Miss Hill
recognised such hazards by setting aside work on her buildings to be
offered to tenants in difficulties; but she displayed some ambivalence
about unemployment and decided severity to those who experienced
its effects, which must be more or less pernicious, 'and which the
childishness of the poor makes doubly so. They have strangely little
power of looking forward . . . This is very curious to me.'[63]

There is little appreciation here of the way in which personality
may be moulded by social environment. Rather an insistence on the
power of individuals over their lives however precariously balanced
on the edge of disaster. But Miss Hill came to modify her views in
the increasing importance she attached to the public provision of
employment. Writing to her sister in 1867 she spoke of the 'frightful
confusion of chances' governing men's lives. Underpaid work was
supplemented by erratic and inadequate doles of charity. There was
no 'certainty, quiet or order' in such a way of existing. And as a man
has 'an innate sense' that his natural wants should be supplied if he
worked, he took gifts resentfully. The solution seemed to lie in some
kind of organisation of the labour market: 'but please God one day
we shall arrange to be ready with work for every man, and give him
nothing if he will not work; we cannot do the latter without the
former I believe.'[64]

Such views were no doubt influenced by Ruskin, who expressed
his own opinions a few years later in a forthright letter commenting
on a paper written by Miss Hill and criticising some of her doctrines.
Ruskin begins by acknowledging the necessity of more sympathy and
personal intercourse with the poor. But the closest intercourse and
kindest feeling would be useless without what he called 'right methods
of action'; and right methods of action would always be useful,
however narrow or unsympathetic the feeling.

'Raising the Poor without gifts'. You mean without gifts given to maintain them in habits of idleness and base dependence. But your subscription list at the end of your report is a list of gifts – spent in procuring for your poor the best gift that Heaven sends Man – Employment. . .

Again, when you speak of raising the poor without gifts you do not mean I suppose to stop the current of charity but to direct that current to the giving of employment. There has been an almost unanimous shriek from the good clergymen of London lately – against alms-giving . . . if that church has ceased to consider alms-giving as much a duty as prayer-making, it is certainly no longer a Christian one. What they mean, I presume, is . . . that the first duty of charity is to collect a wages fund, and to employ, compulsorily if needful, all idle persons at a fixed rate of wages, adequate to the maintenance of themselves and their families . . . and to do this in direct contradiction of the modern stupidity, ineffable as abominable, of leaving wages to be depressed by competition – and filling up the gap to something like level of life maintaining with alms as indiscriminate as the wage paying . . . But that is not 'raising the poor without gifts'. It is raising them by direct and continual gifts, granted to them on condition of their doing daily a certain quantity of useful work to the systematising of which you give further the richest gift, your own care, discipline and personal sympathy . . .

Remember I entirely concur in all you say and illustrate of the harm of giving assistance to people who might get work if they chose. But this Gospel of refusing help to the idle is vain or deadly, unless coupled with the far more necessary one of the necessity of making that idleness cease by clearly defined direction of labour.[65]

Perhaps state intervention to organise work was a form of collective action least threatening to those who believed so firmly in the duty of self-help. Creating employment could hardly destroy independence or demoralise the worker. In this sense it was more acceptable than General Booth's 'huge scheme of centralised despotically-managed relief'[66] which disquieted Miss Hill and others like her in the 1890s. But if more acceptable in theory, employment policies have proved difficult to maintain. In the 1940s Beveridge was arguing the government's responsibility for maintaining full employment as part of his plan for social reconstruction. Moreover the only test of men's willingness to work was that jobs be available for them. It is ironic that in the years after the Second World War, in a society increasingly committed to all forms of state welfare, governments have signally failed to secure full employment and we have a 'huge scheme of despotically-managed relief' that is larger and more centralised than ever before.

THE COLLECTIVISTS

The approach to social problems that placed more faith in the activities of government and of public bodies is represented in this study especially by Beatrice Webb, but also in a rather different way by Florence Nightingale. Josephine Butler and Annie Besant can also be regarded as women whose major work was to challenge existing practice and conventions through parliament and the law courts. Mrs Butler campaigned against the Contagious Diseases Acts, though her object was the withdrawal of legislation rather than more public intervention in people's lives. Mrs Besant fought in the courts for the publication of the Knowlton pamphlet to establish the right of free discussion of birth control and, after joining the Fabians in 1885, delivered lectures on socialism all over the country.

This alternative conception of social evils and how they might be tackled had two distinguishing characteristics. First, the appreciation of sickness or poverty or maladministration depended more on the growing number of social surveys and the accumulation of social statistics relating to living conditions both in England and abroad than on first-hand experience of the circumstances of the poor. Second, there was far greater confidence in the power of parliamentary action to put things right. The vision was not so much of a good society founded on good people – independent, responsible, educated, enjoying music and art and open spaces and mindful of the common good and the well being of their neighbours. Rather, and particularly for Mrs Webb, it was of a somewhat unruly, self-regarding, ignorant mob, protected from the consequences of their own folly and restrained from anti-social behaviour by state regulation and supervision and a reformed public administration.

Beatrice Potter's early ambition, when she was 25, was for training for research into the constitution and working of social organisation in order to better the life and labour of the people. To this end she got up at five in the morning to read for four hours so that the rest of her day could be given to social duties. Her reading was supplemented by 'friendly intercourse with those most concerned', at dinner parties in London and weekend parties in country houses, not only with politicians and business men but also with 'men of science and with the leaders of thought in Philosophy and Religion'. Out of all this came faith in scientific method, a conception of service to man replacing service to God and the desire of Miss Potter to become a social investigator.

The interest in social conditions and the circumstances that shaped people's lives led to a period as a rent collector with Octavia Hill, several visits to working-class relations in Bacup, work with Charles Booth on his London survey and a month living in the East End investigating dock life and sweated labour. But for Miss Potter these experiences were means to a further end. Social intercourse with the poor to elevate and enlighten them and as an expression of citizenship was not her object as it was for Miss Hill who spoke of dwellings nearly purified from very gross forms of evil merely by the constant presence of those who abhorred them: 'dirt disappears gradually in places that cleanly people go in and out of frequently. Mere intercourse between rich and poor, if we can secure it without corrupting gifts, would civilise the poor more than anything.'[67]

Miss Potter, on the contrary, saw the visits of the lady collectors as an 'altogether superficial thing'. She was led into the homes of the poor, she claimed, not by the spirit of charity, but by questions about economic and social organisation; as to whether poverty was a necessary condition of wealth and whether political and industrial democracy should be extended. 'I delight in this slow stepping towards truth. Search after truth by the careful measurement of facts is the enthusiasm of my life.'[68]

Her preoccupation with painstaking research, with the gathering and analysis of information, brought her into disagreement with Octavia Hill who insisted that the greater need was for more action. But it was not only Miss Hill with whom Beatrice Potter was at odds but with the doctrines of the Charity Organisation Society that she represented and had helped found. Some of the principles of the COS might be admirable – the insistence on personal service to the poor, the accepting of responsibility for the consequences of their charitable actions and the careful enquiry into individual cases. But the great fault lay in what Mrs Webb later described as the belief – almost an obsession – that the 'mass-misery of great cities' was caused mainly by indiscriminate and unconditional doles, either of charity or poor relief, that undermined the desire to work and encouraged

deceit and greed, and the unwillingness to countenance any universal
system of relief. Behind the array of argument about the disastrous
effects of doles on wage-earners lay the subconscious bias of 'the
Haves' against taxing themselves for 'the Have Nots', Mrs Webb
continued. And added to the sectarian creed as to the need to restrict
the impulse of charity was an equal resistance to any extension of
state or municipal action,

> whether in the way of the physical care of children at school,
> housing accommodation, medical attendance, or old-age pensions,
> however plausibly it might be argued, in the spirit of Chalmers and
> Chadwick, that only by such collective action could there be any
> effective prevention of the perennial recruiting of the army of
> destitutes. Hence Octavia Hill, C. S. Loch and their immediate
> followers concentrated their activities on schooling the poor in
> industry, honesty, thrift and filial piety; whilst advocating, in
> occasional asides, or by parenthetical phrases, the moralisation of
> the existing governing class, and its spontaneous conversion to a
> benevolent use of its necessarily dominant wealth and power.[69]

It was this judgement of Mrs Webb that led her to conclude that
however aware the leaders of the COS may have been of personal
short-comings they had not the faintest glimmer of 'the consciousness
of collective sin'. They took for granted that modern capitalism was
the best form of industrial organisation and that, barring accidents,
any poor family could maintain its independence if its members were
industrious, thrifty, honest, sober and dutiful. They assumed that
public or private interference to ease the 'natural' struggle for
existence would undermine those vital qualities of personality and
make things worse than before. But for Beatrice Potter in the 1880s
these were the very questions at issue. 'Were we or were we not to
assume the continuance of the capitalist system as it then existed;
and if not, could we, by taking thought, mend or end it?'[70]

Mrs Webb offered her own answer much later when she removed
the question mark from the title page of her study, with Sidney, of
Soviet communism. But her opposition to the non-interventionist
approach of the COS became clear in the views she developed as a
Poor Law Commissioner between 1905 and 1909. Public authorities
should extend health and welfare services without any taint or stigma
of the poor law to paupers and non-paupers alike in an effort to
prevent destitution and provide a national minimum standard of

living. The campaign mounted by Mr and Mrs Webb to win support for the proposals of the Minority Report of the Poor Law Commission was first organised through a National Committee for the Promotion of the Break-up of the Poor Law but after a year its name was changed to the National Committee for the Prevention of Destitution. And destitution, Mrs Webb maintained, was not merely a physical state; it destroyed the soul.

> Destitution in the desert may have been consistent with a high level of spiritual refinement. But destitution in a densely-crowded modern city means, as all experience shows, not only oncoming disease and premature death from continued privation, but also, in the great majority of cases, the degradation of the soul. Massed in mean streets, working in the sweating dens, or picking up a precarious livelihood by casual jobs, living by day and by night in over-crowded one-room tenements, through months of chronic unemployment or persistent under-employment; infants and children, boys and girls, men and women, together found themselves subjected – in an atmosphere of drinking, begging, cringing and lying – to unspeakable temptations to which it is practically inevitable that they should in different degrees succumb, and in which strength and purity of character are irretrievably lost. Anyone acquainted with the sights and sounds and smells of the quarters of great cities, in which destitution is widely prevalent . . . learns to recognise a sort of moral malaria, which undermines the spiritual vitality of those subjected to its baleful influence and, whilst here and there a moral genius may survive, saddened but otherwise unscathed, gradually submerges a mass of each generation as it grows up, in coarseness and bestiality, apathy and cynical scepticism of every kind. When considerable numbers of people in such condition are found together – still more when they are practically segregated in cities of the poor – this means that the community of which they form part is, to that extent, diseased. It is in this sense that we are entitled to say that destitution is a disease of society itself.[71]

If destitution is defined as a disease of society, arising out of a particular set of social circumstances which could be prevented by properly organised public services, then the remedy becomes obvious. Governments must be persuaded to institute the necessary measures and public opinion must be aroused to urge the politicians to act.

Mrs Webb is famous for her entertaining of powerful men. During the campaign for the Minority proposals she tirelessly offered and accepted breakfast, lunch and dinner with leading members of the Cabinet and of the Opposition and with the heads and senior civil servants of the relevant government departments. She also delivered lectures – at Fabian summer schools and throughout the country and this latter activity she considered a vital part of her work. Churchill, at one of her dinner parties, advised her to leave the job of converting the country to the politicians and concentrate on converting the Cabinet. 'That would be all right if we wanted merely a change in the law', Mrs Webb replied, 'but we want to *really change* the mind of the people with regard to the facts of destitution, to make them feel the infamy of it and the possibility of avoiding it.'[72]

Mrs Webb, then, stands firmly among the researchers and reformers rather than the social workers in this study. Political agitation and campaigning were things she enjoyed.

> Since we took up this propaganda we have had a straightforward job, with no problems of conduct, but with a great variety of active work; organising office work, public speaking and personal persuasion of individuals, work which absorbs all one's time without any severe strain on one's nerves. I enjoy it because I have the gift of personal intercourse and it is a gift I have never, until now, made full use of. I genuinely *like* my fellow-mortals whether as individuals, or as crowds; I like to interest them, and inspire them, and even to order them in a motherly sort of way. Also, I enjoy leadership. Everyone has been kind and appreciative; and money has come in when I asked for it, and volunteers have flocked round us.[73]

This was a comment written on New Year's Eve 1909 at the beginning of the campaign for the Minority plan to end destitution, but Mrs Webb's enthusiastic optimism was to end in disappointment as it was the more conservative proposals of the Majority that won greater official approval. Men and women of all parties, classes and creeds were ready and anxious to combine in a serious campaign against destitution, Mrs Webb asserted. The real opponents were the party of the *status quo* which although 'as weak in controversy as we could wish', she acidly remarked, had behind them all the forces of political inertia. These were not only the Commissioners who had signed the main report but also members of the existing boards of guardians, the political and civil servant heads of the Local Government Board and the local government inspectors, all, according to Mrs Webb, opposed to any changes in the structure and working of the existing poor law.

Hostility to the Minority proposals also stemmed from ideology, a fear of any extension of collective social responsibility. The universal organisation of preventive services, with the different departments of local authorities attending to different needs of their populations, ignored the distinction between paupers and independent workers, essential for those who believed that poverty was linked to personality defects. The specialised form of administration could also be represented as undermining the family, as different family members would be the responsibility of different departments. 'We propose to deal with the family as a whole; the Minority propose to disintegrate it by sending each item of it to a separate committee.'[74]

The details of the disagreement of the Commissioners over the reform of the poor laws, the opposition of ideologies and of principles of administration and of interests have been discussed elsewhere. The importance of the battle for this study of women in social service is the way in which it illustrates Mrs Webb's particular form of public activity, her conception of the nature of social problems, of the character of destitution and of how it should be tackled. Essentially the remedy lay in parliamentary action and changes in local government structure. And it was this that Mrs Webb set out to effect, through research, writing and lecturing and through the carefully contrived social entertaining of men and women important to her cause. These activities frequently brought her, as did Octavia Hill's social work among the London poor, to the verge of physical and mental exhaustion. She was sustained, as she reveals in her diaries, by the companionship of her husband and by prayer.

As for Mrs Webb, so for Miss Nightingale, social evils tended to be defined as problems of social organisation rather than of human wickedness. And the remedies therefore lay in government measures to establish and maintain high standards of service and of public administration, especially within the War Office, in the organisation of army supplies, and in medical and sanitary reforms. No doubt the character of the problems with which Miss Nightingale was most concerned – unskilled nursing and insanitary institutions – themselves dictated, to some extent, the appropriate remedy. Little in the way of self-help could be expected from individual patients and much might be gained from clean and orderly hospitals, from professional nursing, appropriate diets and adequate provisions and medical supplies for sick people. Nevertheless, for many charitable women of the nineteenth century amateur nursing of the poor was in fact their response to this particular evil. The religious orders, which offered nursing training, tended to confine their activities to the care of the sick poor immediately around them, either in their own homes or in the retreats and refuges established to receive them. Miss Nightingale's distinction rests on her rejection of the conventional charitable practices of the time, on the widening of her interests beyond concern for the local poor to national and international matters. Her great contribution lay in the development of strategies for tackling the abysmal level of medical care in the army and among the civilian population both in India and in Britain.

As we have seen, and as with Beatrice Potter, Miss Nightingale's desire to devote herself to some public cause seems to have reflected her frustration and impatience with the usual social and family preoccupations of upper middle-class women. She records in her diaries that God first called her to his service when she was 17 and this led first to attempts to gain nursing experience among the villagers near the Nightingale's country homes and later to efforts – often vain – to obtain training in local hospitals and in Protestant and Catholic institutions abroad. It soon became apparent, however, that Miss Nightingale's conception of the problems of nursing the sick would take her beyond the cottages around Embley and Lea Hurst and even beyond the hospitals in the Crimea. Ultimately it led to attempts to set up professional training for nurses, efforts to reform the administration of the War Office, work to establish an army medical service, pressure to introduce sanitary measures into the Indian Army and later for the civilian population and eventually to urging the adoption of irrigation schemes for the Indian sub-continent. 'What is the good of trying to keep people in health if you can't keep them in life?', she wrote to Lord Houghton.[75]

For Miss Nightingale, then, as for Beatrice Potter, problems of sickness and destitution were to be tackled not so much through careful attention to individual cases, necessary though this might be, but through re-defining public responsibilities and overhauling public administration. The nursing of sick people was a step to further ends, a revelation of the need for wider action. A woman from one of the cottages in Embley died, she noted 'because there was nothing but fools to sit up with her'. This was in 1845 and it was another eight years before Miss Nightingale eventually started on her nursing career, but during that time she acquired some nursing training, absorbed available medical and sanitary statistics and became acquainted with doctors and politicians interested in hospital and health reforms – especially Sidney Herbert. As we have seen, the direction of Miss Nightingale's interests was noted by her sister: 'I believe she has a little or none of what is called charity or philanthropy . . . she . . . would like well enough to regenerate the world with a grand *coup de main* or some fine institution . . . it is the intellectual part which interests her not the manual. . . .'[76] And Mrs Gaskell, too, had remarked Miss Nightingale's preoccupations: 'she will not go among the villagers now because her heart and soul are absorbed by her hospital plans' she wrote in 1854, adding in extenuation,' but then this want of love for individuals becomes a gift and a very rare one, if one takes it in conjunction with her intense love for the *race* her utter unselfishness in serving and ministering. . . .'[77]

Suspicion of amateur philanthropy appears in Miss Nightingale's own denunciation of the ladies' and gentlemen's committees overseeing the benevolent institution of which she became superintendent in 1853: '. . . from philanthropy and all the deceits of the devil, good Lord deliver us.'[78] Like Beatrice Potter, she was suspicious of the vagaries of charitable effort and too aware of the social injustice and collective ineptitude lurking behind individual misfortune to rest satisfied with the care of individual hard cases. But lack of sympathy for personal suffering is hardly borne out by contemporary accounts of her unceasing attention to sick soldiers in the Crimea.

I have known her spend hours over men dying of cholera or fever. The more awful to every sense, any particular case, especially if it was that of a dying man, the more certainly might her slight form be seen bending over him administering to his ease by every means in her power, and seldom quitting his side till death released him.[79]

However, the soldiers needed more than nurses. 'The state of the troops who return here . . . is frost-bitten, demi-nude, starved, ragged', Miss Nightingale wrote to Sidney Herbert and such conditions led her on to a comprehensive and highly critical review of the organisation of supplies for the army in the Crimea. So far as medical services were concerned the needs were for clean hospitals and bedding, for proper diets for sick men, for trained nurses and well paid ward orderlies, for a medical school at Scutari, for the collection

of data and keeping of records. Where public money was not
forthcoming Miss Nightingale used her own and her attention quickly
shifted from the medical care to other aspects of the treatment of
the soldiers.

> What the horrors of war are no one can imagine. They are not
> wounds, and blood, and fever . . . and dysentery . . . and cold
> and heat and famine. They are intoxication, drunken brutality,
> demoralisation and disorder on the part of the inferior; jealousies,
> meanness, indifference, selfish brutality on the part of the
> superior.[80]

Accordingly Miss Nightingale turned to setting up schools and
recreation rooms, arranging lectures and closing drink shops. Her
allegations of indifference and neglect among senior officers were
confirmed by the Commission into the Supply of the British Army in
the Crimea in 1856, but her efforts to intervene to lessen the damage
aroused opposition among some of the army officers at Scutari and
Balaclava, only suppressed by an official statement of her powers
and responsibilities from Sidney Herbert.

Miss Nightingale was supported not only by the confidence of
ministers but also by the sympathy of the Court. Her long descriptions
of conditions in the Crimea, usually addressed to Sidney Herbert,
were passed to ministers and to the Queen, who in return sent gifts
of clothing for Miss Nightingale to distribute to the troops. In England
a Nightingale fund was opened and public meetings were organised
in recognition and appreciation of her work, addressed by Sidney
Herbert, Monckton Milnes and Lord Stanley. It was not easy, said
Lord Stanley, to do what no one had done before. Many would face
great hardship and danger if they had popular sympathy and approval.
'But in this case custom was to be violated, precedent broken through,
the surprise, sometimes the censure of the world to be braved. And
do not under-rate that obstacle for we hardly know the strength of
the social ties that bind us until we attempt to break them.'[81]

Lord Stanley went on to point to the significance of Miss Nightingale's work for the position of women. She had opened up a new
profession. The claim for more extended freedom of action, based
on approved public usefulness in the highest sense of the word, with
the whole nation looking on and bearing witness, was one which
must be listened to and could not be easily refused.

The years in the Crimea however were only the beginning of efforts towards more far-reaching reforms. At Scutari and Balaclava Miss Nightingale had seen the ravages of disease and neglect. 'I stand at the altar of the murdered men', she wrote in a private note of 1856, 'and, while I live, I fight their cause.'[82] The fight led her to parliament and royal commissions – not of course in person but in collaboration with doctors, statisticians and ministers and with the sympathy of the Queen. 'We have made Miss Nightingale's acquaintance, and are delighted and very much struck by her great gentleness and simplicity, and wonderful, clear, and comprehensive head. I wish we had her at the War Office.'[83] ·

Miss Nightingale's first concern was to establish a royal commission to examine the health of the army. Reforms were imperative to avoid the disasters of the Crimea: 'the blood of such men [who died at Sebastopol] is calling to us from the ground not to avenge them but to have mercy on their survivors.'[84] The Royal Sanitary Commission on the Health of the Army was set up with Sidney Herbert as chairman. Working closely with him and with many others – William Farr, Edwin Chadwick, Lord Stanley and Dr John Sutherland – Miss Nightingale prepared material, briefed members, and herself gave written evidence to the Commission. She contributed to the writing of the final report and received due acknowledgement from the chairman. 'I never intend to tell you how much I owe you for all your help during the last three months, for I should never be able to make you understand how hopeless my ignorance would have been among the Medical Philistines. God bless you.'[85]

Unremitting work brought serious illness. In 1857 Miss Nightingale wrote a letter to Sidney Herbert to be delivered after her death, which she thought imminent, made a will leaving the Nightingale Fund to St Thomas's Hospital in London and instructed her sister to arrange for her burial in the Crimea. She survived, however, to submit a paper on hospital construction to the Social Science Association and to be elected a member of the Statistical Society in 1858. The publication of the Report of the Royal Commission on the Health of the Army in that year was very restricted, so Miss Nightingale set out to arouse popular interest in reform by privately printing and circulating her own *Notes on the Army*, Harriet Martineau providing extra publicity and support in the columns of the *Daily News*. In 1859 Sidney Herbert came back into government as Secretary for War under Palmerston and the labours for the reform of the War Office continued, though Florence Nightingale's interests were now extending from military to civilian nursing and hospitals.

The collection and analysis of mortality statistics to demonstrate the extent of preventable mortality were the foundation of her efforts for sanitary improvement, though her attempt to extend the 1861 Census to enumerate the sick and infirm and to note housing conditions was unsuccessful.

With the death of Sidney Herbert in 1861 Miss Nightingale's power to influence military reform diminished. 'These three years', she wrote in 1864, 'have been nothing but a slow undermining of all he has done [at the War Office]. This is the bitterest grief. The mere personal craving after a beloved presence I feel as nothing. . . .'[86] The following year the death of Lord Palmerston meant the loss of another powerful friend.

> Lord Palmerston is a great loss. I speak for the country and for myself. He was a powerful protector to me . . . I never asked him to do anything – you may be sure I would not ask him often – but he did it – for the last nine years. He did not do himself justice. If the right thing was to be done, he made a joke, but he did it.[87]

By this time, however, she had become closely involved in Indian affairs urging the setting-up of a sanitary commission and then working closely with Lord Stanley, its chairman, preparing evidence, drafting questions to military stations in India, writing her own observations and having them privately printed to supplement the meagre official summary of the Commission's report. Once more she won the gratitude and appreciation of the chairman.

> Every day convinces me more of two things: first, the vast influence on the public mind of the Sanitary Commission of the last few years – I mean in the way of speeding ideas which otherwise would have been confined to a few persons; and next, that all this has been due to you, and to you almost alone.[88]

Through the 1860s, though more or less bed-ridden, Miss Nightingale was in constant communication with ministers, politicians and civil servants; writing letters, holding interviews, drafting minutes and proposals and providing briefs for parliamentary debates. Her biographer suggests she acted as a sort of advisory council to the War Office, though with a relationship closer than any council would normally have.[89] Even so, Indian affairs did not exhaust her energies. She was also active in the reform of workhouse nursing and medical services and in establishing nursing as a proper occupation for women of all classes and one that required training and payment.

The personal costs of the formidable intellectual and physical effort was very high. The combination of continuous work and ill-health obliged Miss Nightingale to deny herself ordinary social intercourse, even the companionship of old friends, and it was a self-denial that aroused bitterness and resentment. 'I cannot live to work unless I give up all that makes life pleasant' she told Mme Mohl. 'No-one ever did give up so much to live who longed so much to die.'[90]

Miss Nightingale's public work depended on allies in high places and on her own freedom of action. During the 1870s her influence on Indian affairs declined and her efforts to introduce irrigation schemes into the sub-continent were of no avail, partly because she lacked friends both at the India Office and in India itself. But during these years she was also distracted by family duties, being called to act as companion and nurse to her ageing parents. It was the only time for 22 years, she wrote to Mme Mohl, that her work had not been the first reason for deciding where she should live. Now it was the last reason. It was the caricature of a life.[91] By 1882, however, both parents having died and with Lord de Grey appointed as Viceroy she resumed her active interest in Indian politics and continued to receive Indian sanitary papers until she was 86.

In popular memory Miss Nightingale's distinctive place is in the wards of the military hospitals at Scutari and Balaclava. But although her compassion for wounded soldiers won her the acclaim and admiration of the Queen and the nation, the personal nursing of sick men was a small part of her work. She stayed in the Crimea for less than two years. But her experiences there led to the enduring commitment to medical and administrative reforms, both army and civil, to which she devoted the rest of her life. She fought the cause of the men who died in the Crimea at the War Office, at the India Office, on royal commissions and in her own privately printed and circulated notes and memoranda. Her weapons were her exhaustive knowledge of army administration and medical matters and her remorseless determination that the work must be done. Her allies were her powerful friends among ministers, doctors and statisticians, and family wealth and companionship which sustained her as a semi-invalid, relieved her of household cares and guaranteed the privacy and personal affection which enabled her to carry on her public labours. A note from Jowett captures the essential nature of her work: 'There are those who respect and love you, not for the halo of glory that surrounded your name in the Crimea, but for the patient toil which you have endured since on behalf of everyone who is suffering or wretched.'[92]

Conclusions

We can now return to the questions posed in the early part of this study. The middle-class women who moved out of private family lives into public work in the later part of the nineteenth century were challenging the conventions of their class and time, and they were also exchanging a life of cultivated ease for one not only of laborious days but also of considerable discomfort and danger. Florence Nightingale survived near fatal fever in the Crimea, but Agnes Jones died of typhus in the Liverpool workhouse. The questions to be answered are how they came to choose their particular destinies and what were the circumstances that made their way more or less smooth.

In earlier chapters we have examined a number of facets of the lives of the ten women selected for special study; their family background, their religious beliefs, their sense of the privileges or handicaps of their sex, their conception of social problems and of how they might be resolved. Out of these biographies there emerges a social portrait of a particular kind of feminine personality rooted in the peculiar circumstances of Victorian England. But it is also a picture with a more universal reference; a recognisable combination of plain living and high thinking, of courage, determination and self-discipline which may be found in every age and either sex though the aim in view and the penalties and hazards of the effort to reach it may vary. So a further question is how far the experiences of women who made their way into public life more than a hundred years ago may be relevant in considering the position of women in England at the end of the twentieth century.

It is tempting to see the movement out of domestic into public life as depending above all on a particular kind of personality. But personalities are socially constructed. They grow out of a special set of social constraints and opportunities, reflecting both the distribution of economic and cultural resources and the character of prevailing ideologies. Material circumstances and social and family expectations about behaviour were both highly significant in the life histories of the women in this study. It is important to avoid allotting too much weight to personality in offering explanations of women's public work. This book is largely based on the lives of ten people who are, by definition, the ones who succeeded. A wider study, were records available, would no doubt discover more who might in similar circumstances have followed in the footsteps of Florence Nightingale or made their own way into the prisons and workhouses and the homes of the poor. The unwritten lives of working-class women might well testify to personal qualities of courage and dedication which, however, in their different circumstances, were directed to family and neighbourhood matters rather than to national concerns.

But nor must too much weight be accorded to circumstance. For there were also many women born into middle-class families who chose very different lives than those of Octavia Hill or Louisa Twining. Beatrice Potter was the only one of nine Potter sisters whose interest in the working of capitalism led her into a life of social research. Only one other sister was at all unconventional in insisting on an independent life before her marriage in order to work with Octavia Hill in East London. Nor is it a simple dichotomy of character and circumstance. The varying conjunction of class, religion, family and region created an almost infinitely complicated range of opportunities and aspirations.

The movement from private life into public social service has to be explained by a mixture of pre-disposing circumstances and individual character traits. This study does not offer any detailed comparisons with women who followed other possible paths into the outside world – as writers, for example, or as leaders of fashionable society, or as active suffragists or suffragettes, or through work in the movement for higher education for women. So we cannot be sure how far the experiences of the ten women we discuss were peculiar to those who entered some form of social service. It seems very likely that those whose interests led them to work with the sick and the delinquent and the destitute might have particular characteristics and special experiences that marked them off from other women. But we have restricted ourselves to the significant events in the lives of the women who did move into social service. How far such events were common among women moving into other kinds of public activity can only emerge from further enquiries.

The most important aspect of the family background of the ten women of this study was not so much the level of material wealth which in any case was very variable, though all were middle class. It was rather a characteristic family culture that combined an interest in social and religious questions, political issues and intellectual debate with belief in the possibility of social progress and the power of science and knowledge and the goodwill of educated people to bring it about. They belonged to a confident and optimistic age. For Beatrice Potter the great question of her time was whether capitalism could, or should, survive. But through the century the economic effects of the Napoleonic Wars and the ideological excitement of the European movements for national independence and the American Civil War stimulated the British movements for parliamentary democracy and the extension of the franchise and fired the debates about the condition of the native poor and about questions of liberty and equality that extended beyond slavery and the freedom of nations to relations between the sexes and the rights of children. At the same time the religious revival among the Nonconformists and the Evangelicals, and the High Church as well as the Broad Church movement, both reflected and opened the way to the questioning of religious doctrine and belief, offering in the process a link between faith and social action. In Beatrice Potter's words, it was a time when the 'impulse of self-subordinating service' was transferred from God to man.

In one way or another all the women in this study were linked to the wider intellectual and political movements of their time. For such as Beatrice Potter and Florence Nightingale it was through wealth and status and the associated social connections. Others, such as Mary Carpenter, Agnes Jones and Frances Power Cobbe, grew up in families where religious belief was especially strong and associated with a stern sense of duty and social obligation. Josephine Grey came from a political and professional family where her father, renowned for his agricultural work, was prominent in the movements for parliamentary reform and the abolition of slavery. Octavia Hill was the grand-daughter of the sanitary reformer and her mother was a keen supporter of women's education. But whatever the connection with the affairs of the world, the important point was the interest in public issues and the assumption that it was normal for women as well as for men to take an active part in public affairs.

Family links with politics and social reform and a devout upbringing that tended to be unsectarian, but placed heavy emphasis on social responsibility, provided clear encouragement to social service. But the women of this study also grew up in families where they were protected from the grosser forms of sexual discrimination. On the contrary, girls were, on the whole, carefully educated and encouraged to interest themselves in political and social questions. Such experiences in their families denied the more conservative prejudices of the time about the position of women, and were calculated to encourage a challenging of conventional feminine roles. Challenges might also come, of course, from those subject to more oppressive family upbringing. Emily Davies writes bitterly about her restricted life as a cleryman's daughter, expected to fill her time with parish visiting and Sunday school teaching.

> Probably only women who have laboured under it can understand the weight of discouragement produced by being perpetually told that, as women, nothing much is ever to be expected of them, and it is not worth their while to exert themselves . . . that whatever they do they must not interest themselves, except in a secondhand and shallow way, in the pursuits of men, for in such pursuits they must always expect to fail.[1]

Beatrice Webb, by contrast, says that she and her sisters, though lacking university education, associated on terms of educational equality with men of affairs in business and politics and with the leaders of thought in science, philosophy and religion. She claimed her father was the only man she knew who believed women were superior to men and acted as though he did. Josephine Butler grew up in a religious and liberal household that received visitors from all over the world. Her father was an active and practised public speaker and his liberality extended to support for women's education, while his sister Margaretta Grey was a strong proponent of the need and right for women to have the chance of useful occupation. Mrs Butler, accustomed to an atmosphere of free and earnest debate on social and moral issues, records her shock on moving to Oxford to find a male society where women's opinions counted for very little.

Among the less wealthy families there were fewer opportunities for social intercourse with distinguished men and women. But home values emphasised education and cultural interests and social obligation. Mary Carpenter grew up in a household which, according to James Martineau, was a centre of intellectual activity, of scientific enquiry and of political debate. Annie Besant and Octavia Hill both came from relatively poor families and Mr Wood and Mr Hill had both died when their daughters were young. But this did not seem to involve any narrowing of intellectual or cultural interests.

The strong and affectionate bonds of family relationships are what is noticeable among the ten women rather than the problems they caused. Only two of them found family attachments or duties a serious impediment in their lives. Florence Nightingale and Beatrice Potter both had to delay their independent work until they were over 30 and, for Florence Nightingale especially, the conflicts of interests were very severe. Miss Cobbe, who acted as housekeeper for her father until a similar age, appears to have felt no resentment. When she became a woman's rights woman, she said, it was not because she had ever in her own person felt a woman's wrongs. Rather it was the wrongs of other women that came to weigh heavily upon her. Even Florence Nightingale, who wrote at length about the oppressive and restrictive character of family life for women, and especially for herself, was ambivalent about her family attachments and depended heavily upon them as she grew older. When she was receiving public acclaim for her work in the Crimea, she wrote to her parents that if they were pleased that was the greatest reward she could have. Mr Nightingale took a house for his daughter in London a few doors away from her sister, as Sir Harry and Lady Verney thought she should be near them and did much of her entertaining for her. When her sister died Sir Harry wrote of her intense devotion to Miss Nightingale – who later made the Verney house at Claydon her own home.

Even though some aspects of family relationships might be difficult, the possibility of choosing independent work was yet fostered by the special character of family upbringing. Although the conventional division of roles between the sexes might be assumed, there was little idea of the inferiority of women. The combination of educational opportunity and a highly articulate family culture involving the discussion of public and social issues encouraged a measure of confidence on the part of the women in their right and duty to take part in public affairs, which was more important than any disabilities perceived as attaching to their sex. The difficulties in the way of their public work were not so much deterrents as problems to be overcome. Thus Mary Carpenter accepted that ladies should not 'raise their voices in assemblies of gentlemen' and sent written evidence to conferences and committees of enquiry rather than appearing in person. Some found their sex a positive advantage. Beatrice Potter remarked that had she been a man she would have had to devote herself to some money-making profession rather than work as a social investigator. Florence Nightingale discovered that a woman might obtain from 'military courtesy' what a man effectually hindered. For

Josephine Butler the status of a married woman and with children was an essential qualification for leading the movement for the repeal of the Contagious Diseases Acts.

The very close emotional attachments that this group of women had with several members of their families is evident. Not only, however, were there emotional bonds. There was also active co-operation in work. The Hill family worked together. In 1878 Octavia Hill had written to her mother from abroad:

> My thoughts of you all make me realise how you are all doing, and have done so much . . . How I think of you all, of dear Andy bearing the burden of all management; of dear Florence keeping to work with her frail health; of dear Gertrude so marvellously carrying on my work; and of dear Minnie doing all so perfectly, and thinking of everyone.[2]

One of Josephine Butler's sisters came to help her in Liverpool with the homes and refuges for prostitutes. Elizabeth Fry used family money to advance prison work and so did Miss Nightingale to buy supplies in the Crimea. Mary Carpenter worked with her mother and sisters in the school for girls that they established in their home.

Out of this mixture of early experiences there emerged women who were talented, self-confident, curious about the problems of the world, optimistic about the possibility of solving them, and with a keen sense of their own personal responsibility for doing so. It is not surprising that such women should assume both a duty and a right to take part in public affairs, nor that those who contemplated marriage should consider most carefully how far it might interfere with their opportunities for independent work.

Both Florence Nightingale and Beatrice Potter rejected proposals of marriage that they thought would destroy their freedom of thought and action. The marriages that did occur were very carefully planned. Just as their families of origin provided, for the most part, encouragement and support for women taking up public work, so did the families they entered on marriage, with the one exception of Annie Besant. Mrs Besant was unfortunate, marrying on slight acquaintance but in the expectation that as a clergyman's wife she would have opportunities for working with the poor, only to find herself robbed of any chance of independence. The three other women were luckier, or more careful, in contracting marriages that assured them affection and loyalty, shared values and common interests. Before Beatrice Potter married Sidney Webb she turned aside, with great distress, from a marriage that she believed would have absorbed her life into that of a man whose aims were not her aims and who would refuse her all freedom of thought in her intercourse with him.[3] The famous partnership with Sidney Webb, carefully planned to support her own life of research and investigation, deliberately childless, seems to have been crucial in providing intellectual companionship and emotional security.

The other two women who married were similarly prudent and similarly fortunate. George Butler was more than a helper to his wife in her work, she writes; he had had a part in the formation of the first impulse towards it. Elizabeth Fry relied on her 'beloved husband and children' to an extent that made her work away from the 'comforts of home' a great trial to her. She was only one of the women who left a comfortable and affectionate home for difficult and even dangerous outside work. She and others like her illustrate the great determination of those who chose to move into public life but also the crucial importance of a family who encouraged it.

Of those who remained single, one at least, Florence Nightingale, did so by choice. Nor among the others is there any evidence that spinsterhood caused great distress. Miss Cobbe says in her autobiography that life had been pleasant and interesting even without marriage. Agnes Jones devoted herself to service to God and to nursing. Mary Carpenter, Octavia Hill, Louisa Twining, and Florence Nightingale all achieved national recognition in their public work. All were dedicated to the pursuit of their causes. All had cultural and intellectual interests and a wide circle of friends and acquaintance. There is little suggestion of work being a second best to marriage.

On the other hand, while the women grew up in families where they were encouraged to interest themselves in political and social matters and to regard themselves as in crucial respects equal with men, they were also expected to observe the conventional division of responsibilities between the sexes. For the wealthy, this meant entering society and marriage. The women who went into public social service were exceptional among the daughters in their own families in either remaining single or in making unusual marriages that would safeguard their independence.

If family and social background can provide only partial explanation of the movement into public work we must turn to consider the distinctive personalities of the women concerned. The characteristic they all shared was a deep unease about how they should live their lives, and a relentless search for a purpose and an aim. For some this was vividly expressed in religious language. Josephine Butler, Florence Nightingale, Agnes Jones, Mary Carpenter and Elizabeth Fry all believed themselves called by God to his service and all earnestly sought to fit themselves for the work they might be required to do. Beatrice Potter as a child and young woman anxiously sought for a creed to live by – in her earlier years looking for religious faith, later pursuing her work in social research but retaining an insistent belief in the need to combine the quest for scientific proof with 'personal holiness'.

Of the remaining women, Octavia Hill and Louisa Twining seem to have led relatively tranquil religious lives, but Mrs Besant and Miss Cobbe both rejected the evangelical Christianity which they had learned from their families. But whether or not it took a religious form, common to all the women was the determination first to discover and then to pursue some objective that could justify their existence.

It may, of course, be argued that the restless search for something to lend meaning to their lives arose out of the boredom and dissatisfaction with the restrictions surrounding early Victorian women rather than from any especially strong religious commitment. But the argument is not convincing. The women in this study were exceptionally fortunate in the opportunities open to them and in the respect accorded to them, and thought themselves to be so. It was the sense of duty, of a 'calling' to do God's work, to use the contemporary language so disliked by Jowett, as much as the tedium of their daily existence that led them to renounce the distractions and vanities of social amusements, often with great regret, and drove them into public work. Florence Nightingale and Beatrice Potter, the only two who were expected to enter fashionable society as well as attend to home duties, found their lives particularly restricted. But most of the women saw the family as a source of security, of affection and of morality, and as a model for public arrangements for the care of the poor and the sick.

Whatever the mixture of motives that led them into social service, there is no doubt that the women themselves regarded their work as an expression of God's will. It was this belief that enabled them to defy opposition and to endure the disappointments and vicissitudes of their public lives whether supervising nurses in the Liverpool workhouse, giving evidence to parliamentary committees, struggling to persuade the Poor Law Commissioners to abolish the poor law or addressing public meetings for the repeal of the Contagious Diseases Acts. Not that the women were conventional in their religious beliefs. Many belonged to no organised church and attached little importance to the dogmas and doctrines of any sect. But the essential thing was the way in which faith in some form of divine inspiration, the conviction that they were working towards some goal that was more important than their own personal comfort or interest, gave them the courage and resolve to encounter the most formidable obstacles.

This is not to suggest, of course, that fervent religious belief necessarily led Victorian social workers and reformers in directions that would now be approved; only that it was both an incentive and a source of strength in whatever they decided to do. In fact, the acceptance of social inequalities and the easy assumption of the right and the duty to order other people's lives that was often linked with religious faith would offend modern notions of correct professional behaviour. It is ironic that Octavia Hill, one of the first to insist on principles and methods and discipline in charitable work that would turn it into a professional activity, should herself appear particularly vulnerable in this respect, as Mrs Barnett's account of one of the Hill gatherings demonstrates.

> I recall the guests coming in shyly by the back entrance, and the rather exaggerated cordiality of Miss Octavia's greeting in the effort to make them feel welcome; and Miss Miranda's bright tender way of speaking to everyone exactly alike, were they rich or poor; and old Mrs. Hill's curious voice with its rather rasping purr of pride and pleasure and large-heartedness, as she surveyed her motley group of friends; and the two Miss Harrisons (who presumably had entered the house by the front door), those beautiful and generous artistic souls, the one so fat and short and the other so tall and thin, and their duet, purposely wrongly rendered to provoke the communion of laughter, ending with the invitation to everyone to say 'Quack, Quack', as loudly as each was able, if only to prove that they were all 'ducks'. Miss F. Davenport-Hill was there, and Mr. C. E. Maurice, and Miss Emma Cons and Miss Emily Hill and Mr. Barnett.[4]

It is perhaps no accident that of the ten women in the study, the two who rejected Christianity were the least involved in social work. Both Annie Besant and Frances Power Cobbe were increasingly active in a variety of reform movements from women's suffrage and anti-vivisection to home rule for India. It seems that the emphasis on personal service and social obligation that was central to the lives of the more conventionally religious women was more likely to lead them to work directly with the poor and the delinquent. This is not to suggest that either kind of social intervention was the more valuable or efficacious, only that each tended to be linked to different conceptions of social responsibility. As Mrs Webb noted, the movement for votes for women was about rights rather than duties.

But if the different formulations of social responsibility reflected different religious beliefs they also reflect a different understanding of social problems. The women who devoted themselves to social service did so not only because of some kind of religious inspiration, but also because they believed that they knew how to solve those problems. Beatrice Potter and Octavia Hill had very different ideas on the reform of the poor law and the relief of distress; what they shared was an unshakeable conviction that each was right and the other wrong.

Few of the women took an active part in the movement for women's suffrage. This was an aspect of feminism which interested them rather little. As we have already seen, they took for granted their own right and capacity to intervene in public affairs. Sometimes their sex might make this awkward, sometime it might prove an advantage. But whatever the difficulties they were overcome. Their own success was built on solid foundations of material security and family affection and individual determination to discover what was right and to do it. Their achievements were a demonstration to themselves as well as to others that others might, if they chose, do the same. Any disabilities that women might suffer because of their sex appeared a much lesser evil than the neglect of soldiers in the Crimea, or of pauper girls and women in prisons and workhouses, or of the children of the 'perishing and dangerous classes' in the Bristol streets. Certainly, for Florence Nightingale, the sense of her own ceaseless efforts led to some impatience with women's demands for the vote which would, she thought, have little effect on more urgent problems. Only for Mrs Butler was the issue of equality between the sexes especially important, in her fight against the Contagious Diseases Acts and to establish higher education for women. For all the others, their preoccupations were with problems that appeared to them more pressing than the rights of women in general, or female suffrage in particular.

Finally, any study of the way in which women moved out of their families into different kinds of social service in Victorian England prompts the question as to how far their experiences may be relevant for the larger movement of women into outside work at the present time. It is now usual for married women to have some kind of paid employment, though for most it is part-time and generally women with young children stay at home to look after them. There is, however, some evidence of a novel kind of 'symmetrical family' emerging, perhaps less clearly than Young and Willmott suppose,[5] but where both professional employment and domestic responsibilities are shared between husband and wife. Perhaps Sidney and Beatrice Webb may be regarded as an early example of this sort of arrangement, though a private income, considered as vital by Mrs Webb, ruled out the need for much attention to domestic matters and children were reckoned to be incompatible with a life of writing and research.

The growing tendency for women to take on work outside their homes and families results from a complex mixture of demographic, economic and ideological trends. The drop in fertility over the last 150 years from five children to just under two in the average family at the present time gives women more freedom for outside employment. The continuing growth in the service sector of the economy, already beginning at the end of the nineteenth century, has provided semi-professional and clerical jobs and shop work. The increasing importance attached to sexual equality has been taken to mean that women should have similar chances to men to be educated and take paid employment and the notion that household management and child rearing are specifically woman's work is increasingly challenged. There is, indeed, considerable social pressure on women to take some form of outside employment to demonstrate their independence and equal status, while work within the household is held in low esteem. But the move towards greater equality is not always reciprocated. Many men remain as unequal as they ever were in taking only a small part in the domestic responsibilities traditionally preserved for women.[6]

Moreover, the greater independence and wider interests that public employment may bring still appear to leave the majority of women in families whose economic status and social class is determined by the male head of the household. Only for single women or those bringing up children on their own does their class position reflect their own attachment to the market. It is to be expected, perhaps, that the member of the family whose earnings are greater and whose employment is more permanent should influence more strongly not only the living standards but also the social behaviour and social attitudes of the household. The debate about women and class analysis that centres on the significance of women's work for defining the social class of their families, underlines the tendency of women to derive their class position from their husband's occupation in spite of attempts to emphasise the importance for class analysis of women's work.[7] This is not to deny that in two-earner families women's jobs may affect their material living standards and their social attitudes but they rarely lead to a radical change in class position. In this sense the emancipation and equality that women have achieved through work has been limited and they still remain to a large measure dependent for their social status on their fathers or the men whom they marry.

If we compare the circumstances of women moving out of domestic and family life in the last quarter of the twentieth century with those of the Victorian women discussed in this study, what is immediately striking is the vulnerability of the women of the present day. The Victorian ladies had three important strengths: adequate material resources, strong family networks and, whether or not religiously inspired, a commitment to work which they could see as crucially important in bringing about a more just and merciful society.

For contemporary women these assets are less certain. It is no longer only the privileged minority from the upper and middle classes who move into outside work, but women from all social groups. And for many of them the money they can earn is an important incentive and a significant part of the family income. Domestic comforts are less assured, despite the spread of labour-saving machinery and home entertainments. Moreover, as general prosperity has increased so have social expectations. It may well be that women of the present day are induced to enter the market to help to provide themselves and their families with the material paraphernalia of modern living. The Victorian women of this study were less vulnerable to such social pressures. They led lives that were personally ascetic, albeit within a culture that permitted extensive travel, usually for educational or health reasons, and assumed the comfort and support of family servants.

Second, the drop in fertility since the turn of the century and increased geographical mobility have weakened family networks for most people. The many close attachments and co-operation in work of the Gurney, Hill, Carpenter, Grey and even the Nightingale families are now less usual, and personal sympathy and support at critical events less reliable. Brown notes the lack of a close and intimate relationship with mother or spouse, or other person, as a factor in depression among working-class women with young children.[8] That outside employment also offered some protection emphasises the importance for modern women of a chance to escape from their particularly restricted and solitary lives.

Thus the solid base of material comfort and firm family attachments are less evident when women move into outside work from all social groups and when families are small and often scattered. The third source of determination, energy and consolation for the Victorian women was their profound sense that their work was divinely inspired, of moral and social obligation. Josephine Butler wrote of her work to repeal the Contagious Diseases Acts as 'the great crusade' but many of the other women considered themselves subject to a kind of moral imperative which they at any rate thought distinct from and often in conflict with their own interests or ambitions. The conception of their work as of supreme religious as well as social importance made it easier to respond to setbacks and conflicts with fortitude and equanimity.

But this last resource is also doubtfully available for the great majority of contemporary women in employment. Religious belief and religious observance have declined sharply and most of the jobs that women do are of a fairly routine character that cannot be seen to be of great social significance. They offer sociability and money rather than any high moral purpose or even much intrinsic interest. A few women in professional employment may draw great satisfaction from their work and may regard it as a vocation and retain the dedication to 'service' that is one of the marks of professional activity. But they are a small and fortunate minority, for whom the commitment to the professional ethic and to the common good may supply the encouragement and self-discipline that their Victorian forebears were more likely to find in religion. For many women, the lack of clear inspiration and the less obvious social value of their jobs may leave them more vulnerable to the difficulties of combining their family and public lives.

The tenor of these remarks is to suggest that for women in the 1980s the step from domestic into outside work remains a difficult one when family responsibilities are also retained. Social attitudes now tolerate and even encourage public employment for women, though the highly paid professional and managerial and civil service jobs remain largely the preserve of men – or of single women. At the same time women still carry the major responsibility of household work and child care. In the absence of personal wealth and extensive family support it can only be expected that choices will increasingly have to be made between outside employment and family life, particularly the bearing and rearing of children, and that attempts to combine the two will remain hazardous.

The Victorian social workers and reformers in this study all thought women had an important part to play in public life, particularly in social service. On the whole, however, they saw such activity as an alternative to marriage. Beatrice Webb thought it most important to open up careers for those unable to marry in which their 'somewhat abnormal but useful qualities would get their own reward'. Mrs Butler, too, wanted women to have wider opportunities, especially for education which she assumed would fit them better both for independent work and for marriage. She also, however, as much as Octavia Hill or Louisa Twining or Mary Carpenter believed that in the end the well-being of society depended on the strength and security of family relationships and on the dissemination of 'home elements' through the whole community.

It is somewhat paradoxical that, in spite of their profound commitment to the value of family life and in spite of their highly privileged circumstances, only two of the Victorian women of this study managed successfully to combine families of their own with their public work. At the same time, they were deeply sceptical about the capacity of the state to provide satisfactory alternatives for people in trouble and particularly for bringing up children. As more women have the choice of outside employment in circumstances in many ways more difficult than those of their Victorian ancestors, it remains to be seen how far this will be at the cost of those 'home values' and 'home influences' on which the Victorians founded their hopes of social progress.

Appendix:
Biographical Notes

Annie Besant (*née* Wood)   1847–1933

Family of origin: no. of children   3
Marital status   M/S
Own children   2

1866: marriage and subsequent birth of two children. 1873: separation. 1874: joined Secular Society – friendship with Charles Bradlaugh; mother died. 1877: re-publication of the 'Knowlton Pamphlet', *The Fruits of Philosophy*, on birth control and subsequent prosecution for obscenity; later associated with Edward Aveling, and G. B. Shaw; joined Fabians and SDF. 1888: organised the Match Girl strike. 1889: conversion to Theosophy; subsequent work in India to establish schools for girls and for Indian Home Rule; continuing support of women's movements in England and especially of female suffrage.

Josephine Butler (*née* Grey)   1828–1906

Family of origin: no. of children   9
Marital status   M
Own children   4

1852: marriage and move to Oxford; birth of 3 children. 1857: move to Cheltenham – George Butler appointed vice-principal of Cheltenham College; birth of only daughter, who died 1863. 1866: move to Liverpool; beginning of work with prostitutes and for women's education. 1867: President of North of England Council for Higher Education of Women. 1869: leadership of Ladies National Association for the Repeal of the Contagious Diseases Acts. 1874: campaigning in Europe. 1882: George Butler Canon of Winchester.

Mary Carpenter   1807–77

Family of origin: no. of children   6
Marital status   S
Own children   —

1829: ill health of father; joined sister and mother in running school for girls. 1839: father died. 1852: opened first Reformatory School for boys. 1856: mother died. 1864: travel to India and interest in problems of Indian women; increasing supporter of women's rights.

Frances P. Cobbe   1822–1904

Family of origin: no. of children   5
Marital status   S
Own children   —

1836–8: attended fashionable school for girls in Brighton. 1847: mother died;
sent away from home for 10 months for religious doubts; then returned to
run father's household; period of reading and writing on religious subjects.
1857: father died; foreign travel. 1858: joined Mary Carpenter in Bristol;
ragged school work and workhouse visiting. 1859–79: travelling in Europe;
set up house with Mary Lloyd; journalism and writing; work for women's
rights and anti-vivisection.

Elizabeth Fry (*née* Gurney)   1780–1845

Family of origin: no. of children   12
Marital status   M
Own children   11

1782: mother died. 1798: became aquainted with William Savery, visiting
American Quaker minister; started Sunday school; became plain Quaker.
1800: marriage. 1804: belief that God wished her to be a Quaker minister;
appointed visitor to Quaker school and workhouse. 1811: acknowledged by
Friends as a minister; beginning of prison visiting. 1815: young daughter
died. 1822: 11th and youngest child born. 1827: Irish tour visiting Quaker
asylums and prisons and holding meetings. Later travelling in Europe.

Octavia Hill   1838–1912

Family of origin: no. of children   5 (11)*
Marital status   S
Own children   —

1840: bankruptcy and physical breakdown of Mr Hill. 1851: Mrs Hill and 5
daughters move to London; becomes acquainted with Ruskin, F. D. Maurice
and Christian Socialists; work with ragged school children. 1861: setting up
Nottingham Place school. 1865: beginning of housing work. 1875: consulted
over planning of Artisan's Dwellings Act 1875; appointed to central committee of Charity Organisation Society; works for Kyrle Society and the National
Trust. 1905: appointed to the Royal Commission on the Poor Law and the
Relief of Distress from Unemployment.

Agnes Jones   1832–68

Family of origin: no. of children   3
Marital status   S
Own children   —

1837: family moves to Mauritius but returns to Ireland after a few years.

* Total number of children from Mr Hill's three marriages

1848: Agnes to school at Stratford. 1850: father dies. 1851: works in Ireland in ragged schools and visiting the poor. 1860: to Kaiserswerth to train as a Sister; to London to work as Bible missioner. 1862: to St Thomas's as a Nightingale probationer. 1864: Superintendent of nurses at Liverpool workhouse infirmary.

Florence Nightingale 1820–1910

Family of origin: no. of children   2
Marital status   S
Own children   —

1849: visits Kaiserswerth. 1853: appointed as Superintendent of London Sanatorium for Sick Gentlewomen – without pay. 1854: request from Sydney Herbert, Minister at War, that she take a party of nurses to the Crimea. 1856: works for sanitary reforms in army and India; to establish nursing training. 1880: mother dies.

Louisa Twining 1820–1911

Family of origin: no. of children   8
Marital status   S
Own children   —

1853: begins workhouse visiting. 1857: formation of Workhouse Visiting Society. 1860: sets up home for workhouse girls; work to improve workhouse nursing. 1879: establishing of Workhouse Infirmary Nursing Association. 1884: elected member of Kensington Board of Guardians.

Beatrice Webb (*née* Potter)   1858–1943

Family of origin: no. of children   10
Marital status   M
Own children   —

1882: mother dies. 1883: first visit to Bacup; work with Charles Booth; becomes acquainted with Joseph Chamberlain. 1892: father dies; marriage. 1905: appointed to the Royal Commission on the Poor Law and Relief of Distress.

Notes and References

Introduction
1. Davidoff and Hall (1987) ch. 6.
2. Letters 111, 474–5. Quoted in Strachey (1959) p. 182.
3. Banks, J. A. (1954) p. 3.
4. Brontë, A. (1979) p. 440.

1 Employment and Charity
1. Hollis (1979).
2. Hollis (1979) p. 33.
3. Queen Victoria to Mrs Martin, 1870. Quoted in Strachey (1959) p. 246.
4. Gaskell (1970) p. 254.
5. *Veblen* (1948) p. 208.
6. Neff (1966) p. 203.
7. Hollis (1979) p. 53.
8. Neff (1966) p. 153.
9. *Quarterly Review*, vol. 84 quoted in Neff (1966) p. 167.
10. Brontë, C. (1975) pp. 255–6.
11. Holcombe (1973); Morley (1915).
12. Abel-Smith (1960).
13. Vicinus (1985). This study contains a useful account of the various Sisterhood and Deaconesses' Houses in England in the latter part of the nineteenth century.
14. Prochaska (1980) p. 180. See also Holcombe (1973).
15. Morley (1915); Holcombe (1973).
16. Pinchbeck (1966).
17. Hewitt (1958).
18. Neff (1966).
19. Pinchbeck (1966) p. 30.
20. Quoted in Hewitt (1958) p. 171.
21. Hewitt (1958) Appendices II and III.
22. Rowntree (1901) p. 206.
23. Hewitt (1958) pp. 12–17.
24. Neff (1966) p. 63.
25. Hewitt (1958).
26. Michael Anderson notes that relatively high wages for young workers in part of Lancashire in the nineteenth century gave children more freedom from parental authority and allowed them to leave their families and live separately. Anderson (1971) pp. 125ff.
27. Prochaska (1980) p. 13.
28. Ibid., pp. 224–5. Prochaska notes that the 1891 census showed no other female employment apart from domestic service accounting for anything like 500 000 women. Hollis' figures however (1979) p. 53, suggest both clothing and textile workers numbered well over half a million. The discrepancies no doubt reflect different groupings of occupations.
29. Simey (1951) p. 58.

30. Roberts (1984) p. 187.
31. Rathbone (1927).
32. Diary of Lord Ashley, 17 December 1827. Quoted in Hodder (1886) p. 43.
33. Heaseman (1962) p. 292.
34. Memorandum of Catherine Gurney. Quoted in *Life of Elizabeth Fry*, vol. 1 (1847) p. 4.
35. Diary of Elizabeth Fry, First Month 24th, 1814. Ibid., pp. 215–16.
36. Simey (1951) p. 24.
37. Hill 'Effectual Charity' in *Our Common Land* (1877) pp. 171–2.
38. Prochaska (1980) pp. 50ff.
39. Mowat (1961).
40. MS. diary, July 1884. Quoted in Webb, *My Apprenticeship*, p. 166.
41. Simey (1951) p. 29.
42. Webb, *My Apprenticeship*, p. 123.
43. Ibid., pp. 112ff.
44. Flinn (1965). Professor Flinn discusses the significance of the collection of data and the development of sanitary and medical knowledge in relation to the public health movement in his introduction to Chadwick's report of 1842.
45. Carpenter, J. E. (1879) p. 29.
46. Prochaska (1980) p. 139.
47. Webb, S. & B. (1929) pp. 122ff.
48. Twining (1898) p. 55.
49. Prochaska (1980) p. 7.
50. Twining (1898) p. 179.
51. Carpenter, J. E. (1879) p. 158.

2   The Nature of Social Service

1. Hollis (1979) pp. 322–8.
2. Carpenter, J. E. (1879) p. 426.
3. Delamont and Duffin (1978).
4. Parsons, 'The Kinship System of the Contemporary United States', in *Essays in Sociological Theory* (1949).
5. Ruskin, 'Of Queens' Gardens' in *Sesame and Lilies* (1880) pp. 91–2.
6. Parsons (1964) pp. 51–67.
7. Simey (1951) p. 62.
8. Mowat (1961) p. 104.
9. Emily Davies to Elizabeth Garrett, 7 December 1870. Quoted in Stephen (1927) p. 124.
10. Elizabeth Garrett to M. J. G. S. Anderson, 15 December 1870. Ibid., p. 125.
11. Twining (1898).
12. Simey (1951) p. 62.
13. Woodham-Smith (1950) pp. 178ff.
14. Cook, vol. 1 (1913) p. 246.
15. Parsons, 'The Professions and Social Structure', in *Essays in Sociological Theory* (1949).
16. Florence Nightingale. Quoted in Cook, vol. 11 (1913) p. 271.

Part II   The Genesis of Social Service
1. Octavia Hill to M.H., 1869. Quoted in Maurice, E. S. (1928) pp. 202–4.
2. Webb, *My Apprenticeship*, p. 237.

3   Family and Social Background
1. *Life of Elizabeth Fry*, vol. 1 (1847) p. 7.
2. Memorandum by Catherine Gurney. Quoted in *Life of Elizabeth Fry*, vol. 1 (1847) pp. 5, 6.
3. *Memoir of the Life of Elizabeth Fry*, vol. 1 (1847) p. 8.
4. Journal of Elizabeth Gurney. Quoted in *Life of Elizabeth Fry*, vol. 1 (1847) p. 18.
5. Woodham-Smith (1950) p. 5.
6. Cook, vol. 1 (1913) p. 21.
7. Diary of Florence Nightingale, Cairo, 1849. Quoted in Cook, vol. 1 (1913) p. 93.
8. Webb, *My Apprenticeship*, p. 6.
9. Ibid., p. 37.
10. Ibid., p. 36.
11. Ibid., p. 116.
12. MS. diary, December 1903. Quoted in Webb, *My Apprenticeship*, p. 33.
13. Webb, *My Apprenticeship*, p. 124.
14. Ibid., p. 149.
15. John Grey, public address, 1831. Quoted in Butler (1874) p. 117.
16. Letter from the prime minister to John Grey, 20 April 1832. Quoted in Butler (1874) p. 122.
17. Butler (1874) p. 127.
18. Passages from the *Economist*, undated. Quoted in Butler (1874) pp. 132, 137.
19. Obituary of John Grey in the *Agricultural Gazette*, n.d. Quoted in Butler (1874) p. 133.
20. Butler (1892) pp. 108ff.
21. Johnson and Johnson (1911) p. 163.
22. Butler (1892) p. 95.
23. Later Mrs Butler took the girl, who had been sent to Newgate for killing the infant whose father had deserted her, into her own house as a servant, where she apparently remained happily for many years.
24. Butler (1892) p. 98.
25. The biographical information in the following paragraphs comes from Louisa Twining's autobiography, *Recollections of Life and Work*.
26. Twining (1893) p. 111.
27. Ibid., p. 134.
28. Carpenter, J. E. (1879) p. 7.
29. Letter from James Martineau to the author. Quoted in Carpenter, J. E. (1879) p. 9.
30. Diary of Mary Carpenter, 31 December 1846. Ibid., p. 100.
31. Mary Carpenter to Miss Follen, 17 February 1849. Ibid., p. 125.
32. Diary of Mary Carpenter, January 1866. Ibid., p. 293.
33. Cobbe, vol. 1 (1894) p. 285.

34. Ibid.
35. Ibid.
36. Ibid., p. 64.
37. Ibid., p. 170.
38. Miranda Hill, n.d. Quoted in Maurice, C. E. (1913) p. 4.
39. Octavia Hill to Miranda, 14 June 1852. Ibid., p. 23.
40. Octavia Hill to Miss Harrison, 16 July 1855. Ibid., p. 50.
41. Octavia Hill to Mary Harris, 19 March 1857. Ibid., pp. 95–6.
42. Besant (1893) p. 188.
43. Besant, *National Reformer*, May 1884. Quoted in Nethercot (1961) p. 218.
44. Besant (1893) p. 58.
45. Ibid., p. 78.
46. There is little published writing about or by Agnes Jones. I have relied on *Memorials of Elizabeth Agnes Jones*, by her sister (Strahan, 1871).
47. Agnes Jones, a paper on her reasons for electing for nursing training. Quoted in *Memorials of Elizabeth Agnes Jones* (1871) p. 243.

4 Family Relationships

1. Emily Davies to Barbara Bodichon, 14 November 1865. Quoted in Stephen (1927) p. 108.
2. Mitchell (1968) p. 42.
3. Ibid., p. 57.
4. Ibid., p. 88.
5. Ibid., p. 100.
6. Ibid., p. 149.
7. Ibid., p. 242.
8. Woodham-Smith (1950) p. 13.
9. Ibid., p. 8.
10. Ibid., p. 13.
11. Florence Nightingale to Hilary Bonham Carter, December 1845. Quoted in Woodham-Smith (1950) p. 56.
12. Florence Nightingale to Hilary Boham Carter, September 1846. Ibid., p. 62.
13. Ibid.
14. Ibid., p. 76.
15. Ibid., p. 77.
16. Florence Nightingale, private note, December 1850. Quoted in Woodham-Smith (1950) p. 86.
17. Florence Nightingale, private note January 1851. Ibid.
18. Florence Nightingale, private note June 1851. Ibid., p. 88.
19. Florence Nightingale, private note, *c.* 1852. Quoted in Cook, vol. 1 (1913) 122.
20. Florence Nightingale, private note 1862. Quoted in Woodham-Smith (1950) p. 103.
21. Florence Nightingale to Mme Mohl, August 1853. Quoted in Cook, vol. 1 (1913) p. 133.
22. Mrs Sam Smith to Florence Nightingale, n.d. Ibid., p. 123.

23. Parthenope Nightingale to Mme Mohl, January 1853. Quoted in Wood-ham-Smith (1950) p. 107.
24. Mrs Gaskell to Emily Shaen, 27 October 1854. Quoted in Chapple (1980) pp. *xi–xii*.
25. Florence Nightingale to her parents. Quoted in Cook, vol. 1 (1913) p. 270.
26. Sir Harry Verney to Florence Nightingale, 15 May 1890. Quoted in Cook, vol. 1 (1913) p. 382.
27. Webb, *My Apprenticeship*, pp. 8–9.
28. Caine (1986) pp. 18ff.
29. Webb, *My Apprenticeship*, p. 11.
30. Ibid., p. 10.
31. MS. diary, 1888. Quoted in Webb, *My Apprenticeship*, p. 15.
32. Diary entry, 24 October 1873. Ibid., p. 58.
33. Diary entry, December 1873. Ibid., p. 63.
34. MS. diary, 4 April 1874. Ibid., p. 64.
35. MS. diary, September 1874. Ibid., pp. 65–6.
36. MS. diary, 18 December 1875. Ibid., p. 70.
37. MS. diary, October 1879. Ibid., p. 71.
38. Webb, *My Apprenticeship*, p. 131.
39. Ibid., p. 221.
40. Ibid., p. 239.
41. MS. diary, December 1887. Quoted in Webb, *My Apprenticeship*, p. 272.
42. MS. diary, March and May 1888. Ibid., p. 274.
43. Quoted in Webb, *My Apprenticeship*, p. 300.
44. Webb (1948) p. 35.
45. Beatrice Webb Diary, 16 February 1907. Quoted in Webb (1948) p. 371.
46. Beatrice Webb Diary, 23 July 1909. Ibid., p. 433.
47. Ibid.
48. Ibid., p. 11.
49. Diary of Elizabeth Fry, Twelfth Month 6th, 1806. Quoted in *Life of Elizabeth Fry*, vol. 1 (1847) pp. 126–7.
50. *Life of Elizabeth Fry*, vol. 1 (1847) pp. 281–2.
51. Diary of Elizabeth Fry, Sixth Month 13th, 1822. Quoted in *Life of Elizabeth Fry*, vol. 1 (1847) p. 418.
52. Elizabeth Fry to her eldest daughters. Ninth Month 27th, 1816. Ibid., p. 251.
53. Elizabeth Fry to two of her sons. Ibid., pp. 252–3.
54. Diary of Elizabeth Fry, Second Month 3rd, 1812. Ibid., pp. 183–4.
55. Diary of Elizabeth Fry, Twelfth Month 17th, 1817. Ibid., p. 289.
56. Diary of Elizabeth Fry, Seventh Month 1st, 1818. Ibid., p. 322.
57. Butler (1874) p. 48.
58. Ibid., p. 50.
59. John Grey to his daughter Mme Meuricoffre, n.d. Quoted in Butler (1874) p. 265.
60. Butler (1874) p. 165.
61. Butler (1892) p. 101.
62. Ibid., p. 102.
63. George Butler to Josephine Butler, n.d. Quoted in Butler (1892) p. 120.

64. Walkowitz (1980) p. 119.
65. Butler (1892) p. 216.
66. Ibid., p. 242.
67. Mme Meuricoffre to Josephine Butler, n.d. Quoted in Butler (1892) p. 301.
68. James Martineau to J. E. Carpenter, n.d. Quoted in Carpenter, J. E. (1879) p. 11.
69. Carpenter, J. E. (1879) p. 72.
70. Diary of Mary Carpenter, n.d. Quoted in Carpenter, J. E. (1879) p. 171.
71. Florence Nightingale to Mary Carpenter, n.d. Ibid., p. 387.
72. Mary Carpenter to Mme Olivecrone, May 5, 1874. Ibid., p. 427.
73. Mrs Hill to Octavia Hill, 27 January 1878. Quoted in Maurice, C. E. (1913) p. 358.
74. Octavia Hill to Mrs Hill, 24 March 1878. Ibid., pp. 363–3.
75. Besant (1893) p. 220.

5 A Woman's Place
1. Cobbe (1894) pp. 33, 171.
2. Elizabeth Garrett to Emily Davies, 17 August 1860. Quoted in Stephen (1927) p. 57.
3. Clough (1897) p. 240.
4. Lilias Ashworth 1872. Quoted by Helen Blackburn and in Hollis (1979) p. 7.
5. Florence Nightingale, n.d. Quoted in Cook, vol. 1 (1913) p. 284.
6. Florence Nightingale, private note 1851. Quoted in Woodham-Smith (1950) p. 93.
7. Cook, vol. 1 (1913) p. 40.
8. Quoted in Woodham-Smith (1950) p. 3.
9. Florence Nightingale, *Cassandra*. Ibid., pp. 95–6.
10. Florence Nightingale to Mary Clarke, 1844. Quoted in Cook, vol. 1 (1913) p. 93.
11. Barbara Caine suggests that Beatrice Potter had an especially lonely childhood in a family where both parents had their favourites but neither distinguished her. Caine (1986) pp. 29–50.
12. Webb, *My Apprenticeship*, p. 101.
13. Agnes Jones to a friend, n.d. Quoted in *Memorials of Agnes Jones* (1871) p. 198.
14. Drew (1919).
15. Quoted in Harrison (1978) p. 69.
16. Lucretia Mott on the position of women among Quakers, 1869. Quoted in Butler (1869) p. *xiv*.
17. Journal of Elizabeth Fry. Sixth month 5th, 1817. Quoted in *Life of Elizabeth Fry*, vol. 1 (1847) p. 283.
18. *Life of Elizabeth Fry*, vol. 11 (1847) p. 522.
19. Butler (1869) p. *xxv*.
20. MS. diary, 7 July 1891. Quoted in Webb, *My Apprenticeship*, p. 352.
21. MS. diary, 12 February 1886. Ibid., p. 242.
22. Webb, *My Apprenticeship*, p. 182.
23. Barnett, vol. 1 (1918) p. 38.

24. Ibid., p. 53.
25. Besant (1893) p. 76.
26. Ibid., p. 81.
27. Ibid., p. 82.
28. Florence Nightingale, autobiographical note, n.d. Quoted in Cook, vol. 1 (1913) p. 100.
29. Florence Nightingale, private note, 1846. Ibid., p. 101.
30. Florence Nightingale to Mrs Nightingale, 7 March 1862. Quoted in Woodham-Smith (1950) p. 388.
31. Cobbe, vol. 1 (1894) p. 113.
32. Agnes Jones to an unnamed friend, n.d. Quoted in *Memorials of Agnes Jones*, pp. 197–8.
33. Agnes Jones. Ibid., p. 355.
34. Mary Carpenter, Journal, 31 December 1846. Quoted in Carpenter, J. E. (1879) p. 100.
35. George Eliot to Mrs Peter Taylor, April 1861. Quoted in Cross, vol. 11 (1885) pp. 251–2.
36. Emily Davies to Miss Manning, n.d. Quoted in Stephen (1927) p. 110.
37. Florence Nightingale, private note. Quoted in Cook, vol. 1 (1913) p. 21.
38. Webb, *My Apprenticeship*, pp. 41–2.
39. Ibid., p. 43.
40. Ibid., pp. 45–6.
41. MS. diary, December 1887. Quoted in Webb, *My Apprenticeship*, p. 272.
42. Mary Carpenter to her brother, R. L. Carpenter, April 1848. Quoted in Carpenter, J. E. (1879) p. 134.
43. Carpenter, J. E. (1879) pp. 17, 47.
44. Twining (1893) p. 125.
45. Butler (1869) p. *xxxv*.
46. Delamont and Duffin, p. 46.
47. Basch (1974) p. 10.
48. Carpenter J. E. (1879) p. 158.
49. Mrs Carpenter to her son Philip, 1852. Quoted in Carpenter, J. E. (1879) p. 162.
50. Mary Carpenter to the Rev. R. A. Livermoor, September 1860. Ibid., p. 273.
51. Mary Carpenter, to Dr Guillaume, February 1873. Ibid., p. 405.
52. Octavia Hill to Miranda Hill, 1859. Quoted in Maurice, C. E. (1913) p. 148.
53. Butler (1869) p. *xxx*.
54. Ibid., p. *xxxiv*.
55. Harrison (1978) p. 81.
56. Woodham-Smith (1950) pp. 475–6.
57. *Memorials of Agnes Jones* (1871) p. *xviii*.
58. Florence Nightingale to Mme Mohl, 13 December 1861. Quoted in Woodham-Smith (1950) pp. 385–6.
59. Florence Nightingale in *Fraser's Magazine*, 1873. Quoted in Cook, vol. 1 (1913) p. 97.
60. Florence Nightingale to John Stuart Mill, 11 August 1867. Quoted in Woodham-Smith (1950) pp. 487–8.

61. Florence Nightingale. Draft letter to Dr Jowett, n.d. Ibid., p. 487.
62. Beatrice Potter to her father, November 1885. Quoted in Webb, *My Apprenticeship*, pp. 236–7.
63. Webb, *My Apprenticeship*, p. 304.
64. Beatrice Webb to Millicent Garrett Fawcett, 2 November 1906. Quoted in Webb (1948) pp. 362–3.
65. Caine (1986) p. 116.

6 Religious Experience
1. The second and third volumes of Florence Nightingale's *Suggestion for Thought* are addressed to Searchers after Religious Truth.
2. Woodham-Smith (1950) p. 115.
3. Webb, *My Apprenticeship*, p. 90
4. Journal of Elizabeth Gurney, 7 July 1797. Quoted in *Life of Elizabeth Fry*, vol. 1 (1847) p. 20.
5. Journal of Elizabeth Gurney, 1 August 1797. Ibid., p. 21.
6. Journal of Elizabeth Gurney, 12 August 1797. Ibid., p. 22.
7. Journal of Elizabeth Gurney, 4 February 1798. Ibid., p. 35.
8. Elizabeth Gurney to Joseph Gurney Bevan, April 1800. Ibid., p. 86.
9. Davidoff and Hall (1987) ch. 1 esp. p. 91.
10. Journal of Elizabeth Fry, Eighth Month, 20th, 1808. Ibid., p. 133.
11. Journal of Elizabeth Fry, Seventh Month, 6th, 1806. Ibid., p. 126.
12. Journal of Elizabeth Fry, Third Month, 8th, 1909. Ibid., p. 140.
13. Journal of Elizabeth Fry, Fifth Month, 3rd, 1923. Ibid., p. 453.
14. *Life of Elizabeth Fry*, vol. 11 (1847) p. 470.
15. Private note of Florence Nightingale, n.d. Quoted in Woodham-Smith (1950) p. 171.
16. Florence Nightingale, private notes 12 and 18 May, 1850. Ibid., p. 79.
17. Florence Nightingale to Arthur Stanley, 1852. Quoted in Cook, vol. 1 (1913) p. 57.
18. Florence Nightingale to Mme Mohl, 1853. Ibid., p. 133.
19. Florence Nightingale to Dr Jowett, 1873. Quoted in Woodham-Smith (1950) p. 523.
20. Florence Nightingale, private note, 1873. Ibid., p. 529.
21. Webb, *My Apprenticeship*, p. 50.
22. MS. diary, 23 December 1872. Quoted in Webb, *My Apprenticeship*, p. 55.
23. MS. diary, September 1874. Ibid., p. 66.
24. MS. diary, July 1875. Ibid., p. 68.
25. Webb, *My Apprenticeship*, p. 90.
26. MS. diary, 1926. Quoted in Webb (1948) p. *vii*.
27. MS. diary, 17 January 1909. Ibid., p. 424.
28. MS. diary, 18 June 1909. Ibid., p. 429.
29. MS. diary, 13 March 1910. Ibid., p. 448.
30. Twining (1893) p. 233.
31. Josephine Butler, undated letter. Quoted in Butler, A. S. G. (1954) p. 46.

208   *Notes and References*

32. Agnes Jones to an unnamed friend, *c.* 1860. Quoted in *Memorials of Agnes Jones* (1871) p. 198.
33. Agnes Jones to her aunt, E. March, 1864. Ibid., p. 278.
34. Agnes Jones to a friend, undated letter. Ibid., p. 366.
35. *Memorials of Agnes Jones* (1871) p. 405.
36. Twining (1893) p. 234.
37. Ibid., p. 170.
38. Petrie (1971) p. 40.
39. Boyd (1982) p. 26.
40. Josephine Butlér to her grandson, undated. Quoted in Butler, A. S. G. (1954) p. 180.
41. Butler, A. S. G. (1954) p. 166.
42. Boyd (1982) pp. 34–5.
43. Butler (1892) pp. 218–19.
44. Diary of Josephine Butler, *c.* 1869. Quoted in Butler (1892) p. 223.
45. Josephine Butler to George Butler, March 1871. Quoted in Johnson and Johnson (1911) p. 111.
46. Mr Rylands speaking of Mrs Butler's evidence to the Royal Commission. Ibid., p. 112.
47. Mrs Butler, n.d. Quoted in Butler, A. S. G. (1954) p. 104.
48. Josephine Butler to Miss Forsaith, 1904. Ibid., p. 179.
49. Mrs Butler to Miss Forsaith. Ibid., p. 163.
50. Mrs Butler to her son, *c.* 1900. Ibid., pp. 181–2.
51. Carpenter, J. E. (1879) p. 11.
52. Mary Carpenter to Dr Guillaume (Prison Governor at Neufchatel) August 1872. Quoted in Carpenter, J. E. (1879) p. 395.
53. Carpenter, J. E. (1879) p. 426.
54. Mary Carpenter, diary, 21 March 1832. Quoted in Carpenter, J. E. (1879) p. 29.
55. Mary Carpenter, diary. Ibid., p. 31.
56. Mary Carpenter, diary. Ibid., p. 47.
57. Verses of Mary Carpenter, 1837. Ibid., p. 59.
58. Mary Carpenter to Miss Sandford, February 1845. Ibid., p. 87.
59. Mary Carpenter, diary, 1851. Ibid., p. 146.
60. Mary Carpenter, diary, 23 May 1852. Ibid., p. 167.
61. Mary Carpenter, diary, 31 December 1873. Ibid., p. 423.
62. Octavia Hill to Miranda Hill, 17 September 1854. Quoted in Maurice, C. E. (1913) pp. 33–4.
63. Octavia Hill to Mary Harris, February 1873. Quoted in Maurice, E. S. (1928) p. 106.
64. Octavia Hill to Mary Harris, 19 March 1857. Quoted in Maurice, C. E. (1913) pp. 95–6.
65. Octavia Hill to Miss Harrison, 6 July 1855. Ibid., p. 48.
66. Besant (1893) p. 100.
67. Ibid., p. 89.
68. Dr Pusey to Annie Besant. Quoted in Besant (1893) p. 11.
69. Cobbe (1894) p. 90.
70. Ibid., p. 305.
71. Dr Jowett to Miss Cobbe, n.d. Quoted in Cobbe (1894) pp. 317–18.

7 Social Problems and their Remedies

1. Florence Nightingale, diary, July 1849. Quoted in Cook, vol. 1 (1913) pp. 82–3.
2. Webb, *My Apprenticeship*, p. 130.
3. Ibid., p. 165.
4. Florence Nightingale to Mme Mohl, July 1848. Quoted in Cook, vol. 1 (1913) p. 80.
5. Mary Carpenter to the Rev. Samuel May, July 1848. Quoted in Carpenter, J. E. (1879) p. 125.
6. Hill (1884).
7. Quoted in Mowat (1961) p. 42.
8. Chadwick (1842). Ed. Flinn (1965) pp. 224–5. In Bethnal Green, in 1839, the average age at death of mechanics, servants and labourers was 16 years, compared with 45 for the professional classes. And relative life chances were similar in Leeds and Liverpool.
9. Mary Carpenter to Miss Sandford, February 1845. Quoted in Carpenter, J. E. (1879) p. 87.
10. Octavia Hill to Miss Harrison, 1855. Quoted in Maurice, C. E. (1913) p. 53.
11. Mary Carpenter to Mrs Follen, February 1849. Quoted in Carpenter, J. E. (1879) p. 125.
12. Mary Carpenter to the Rev. John Clay, November 1850. Ibid., p. 144.
13. Mary Carpenter to Lady Byron, June 1853. Ibid., p. 193.
14. Carpenter, M. (1853) p. 5.
15. Ibid., p. 164.
16. Ibid., p. 302.
17. Carpenter, M. (1851) p. 73.
18. Hill (1883) p. 10.
19. Hill, 'Landlords and Tenants in London' (1871), in *Homes of the London Poor* (1883) p. 45.
20. Ibid., p. 47.
21. Twining (1893) p. 171.
22. Hill, 'A Few Words to Volunteer Visitors Among the Poor' (1876), in *Our Common Land* (1877) p. 58.
23. Hill (1883) p. 10.
24. Carpenter, M. (1851) p. 123.
25. Twining (1898) p. 90.
26. Report of Mrs Nassau Senior to the Local Government Board, 1874. Quoted in Twining (1898) p. 17.
27. Twining (1898) p. 154.
28. Lord Lyttleton to Louisa Twining. Quoted in Twining (1898) p. 44.
29. Twining (1893) p. 18.
30. Butler (1871).
31. Butler (1896) pp. 73–4.
32. Ibid., p. 80.
33. Butler (1892) p. 183.
34. Butler (1896) p. *xvi*.
35. Ibid., p. *xx*.
36. Ibid., pp. *xxx–xxxiv*.

37. Ibid., p. *xxxviii*.
38. Ibid., p. 1.
39. Ibid., p. *xxxv*.
40. Hill, 'Cottage Property in London' (1866), in *Homes of the London Poor* (1883) p. 17.
41. Twining (1893) p. 246.
42. Hill, 'A More Excellent Way of Charity' (1876), in *Our Common Land* (1877) p. 80.
43. Twining (1898) p. 121.
44. Mrs Hill to her daughter, Emily, August 1866. Quoted in Maurice, C. E. (1913) p. 224.
45. Florence Hill to her sister Emily, July 1866. Ibid.
46. Hill (1884).
47. Octavia Hill to MH, 1869. Quoted in Maurice, E. S. (1928) p. 204.
48. Octavia Hill to Miranda Hill, n.d. Quoted in Maurice, C. E. (1913) p. 317.
49. Hill, 'Effectual Charity', in *Our Common Land* (1877) pp. 171–2.
50. Briggs and McCartney (1984).
51. See Barnett (1918) for the story of the Barnetts' work at Toynbee Hall.
52. Barnett, S. A. 'Settlement of University Men in Great Towns' (1883), in Barnett and Barnett (1915).
53. Beveridge (1909).
54. Titmuss (1970).
55. Crossman, R. 'The Role of the Volunteer in the Modern Social Services,' in Halsey (1976).
56. Mary Carpenter to the Rev. Samuel May, January 1845. Quoted in Carpenter, J. E. (1879) p. 92.
57. Mary Carpenter to Mrs Follen, February 1849. Ibid., p. 125.
58. Butler (1869) p. *xxxv*.
59. Hill, 'Four Years Management of a London Court' (1896), in *Homes of the London Poor* (1883).
60. Hill, 'Effectual Charity' in *Our Common Land* (1877) p. 153.
61. Hill, 'A More Excellent Way of Charity' (1876), in *Our Common Land* (1877) pp. 73–4.
62. Octavia Hill to Mrs Edmund Maurice, September 1879. Quoted in Maurice, C. E. (1913) p. 393.
63. Hill, 'Cottage Property in London' (1866), in *Homes of the London Poor* (1883) p. 17.
64. Octavia Hill to Florence Hill, February 1867. Quoted in Maurice, C. E. (1913) p. 228.
65. Ruskin to Octavia Hill, August 1870. Quoted in Maurice, E. S. (1928) pp. 179–82.
66. The reference is to William Booth's scheme to rescue and reform the poor by placing them in 'self helping and self sustaining communities, each being a kind of co-operative society, or patriarchal family, governed and disciplined on the principles which have already proved so effective in the Salvation Army'. It is set out in Booth (1890).
67. Hill, 'A Word on Good Citizenship' in *Our Common Land* (1877) pp. 97–8.

68. MS. diary, 17 August 1889. Quoted in Webb, *My Apprenticeship*, p. 338.
69. Webb, *My Apprenticeship*, p. 177.
70. Ibid., p. 178.
71. Webb (1948) pp. 442–3.
72. Ibid., p. 435.
73. Ibid., pp. 43–9.
74. Lord George Hamilton, Chairman of the Royal Commission on the Poor Laws and the Relief of Distress from Unemployment (1905–9). Quoted in Webb (1948) pp. 440–1.
75. Florence Nightingale to Lord Houghton. Quoted in Cook, vol. 11 (1913) p. 284.
76. Parthenope Nightingale to Mme Mohl, January 1853. Quoted in Woodham-Smith (1950) p. 107.
77. Mrs Gaskell to Catherine Winkworth, October 1854. Ibid., p. 128.
78. Florence Nightingale to Mme Mohl, 1853. Quoted in Cook, vol. 1 (1913) p. 133.
79. Osborn, S. G. *Scutari and its Hospitals*, p. 26. Quoted in Cook, vol. 1 (1913) p. 235.
80. Florence Nightingale, May 1855. Quoted in Woodham-Smith (1950) p. 238.
81. Lord Stanley on Florence Nightingale in support of the Nightingale Fund, Manchester, 1856. Quoted in Cook, vol. 1 (1913) p. 272.
82. Florence Nightingale, 1856. Ibid., p. 318.
83. Queen Victoria to the Duke of Cambridge, 1856. Ibid., p. 213.
84. Florence Nightingale, *Notes on the Army*. Ibid., p. 317.
85. Sidney Herbert to Florence Nightingale, August 1857. Ibid., p. 312.
86. Florence Nightingale to Dr Farr, August 1864. Ibid., vol. 11, p. 94.
87. Florence Nightingale to Dr Farr, October 1865. Ibid., p. 92.
88. Lord Stanley to Florence Nightingale, July 1864. Ibid., p. 57.
89. Ibid., p. 60.
90. Florence Nightingale to Mme Mohl, 1865. Quoted in Woodham-Smith (1950) p. 429.
91. Miss Nightingale to Mme Mohl, June 1875. Ibid., p. 530.
92. Dr Jowett to Florence Nightingale, n.d. Quoted in Cook, vol. 11 (1913) p. 433.

Conclusions
1. Stephen (1927) p. 29.
2. Octavia Hill to her mother. Quoted in Maurice, C. E. (1913) p. 363.
3. Webb, Diaries, 16 March 1884. Quoted in Caine (1986) pp. 79–80.
4. Barnett, vol. 1 (1918) p. 34.
5. Young and Willmott (1972).
6. *Social Trends*, no. 17.
7. See especially Heath and Britten (1984) and Goldthorpe (1983) and (1984).
8. Brown and Harris (1978).

Select Bibliography

ABEL-SMITH, B., *A History of the Nursing Profession* (Heinemann, 1960).

ANDERSON, M., *Family Structure in Nineteenth Century Lancashire* (Cambridge University Press, 1971).

ASQUITH, E. M. A., *The Autobiography of Margot Asquith* (Thornton Butterworth, 1920).

BANKS, J. A., *Prosperity and Parenthood* (Routledge & Kegan Paul, 1954).

BANKS, O., *Faces of Feminism* (Martin Robertson, 1981).

BANKS, O., *The Biographical Dictionary of British Feminists, vol. 1, 1800–1930* (Wheatsheaf, 1985).

BARNETT, Mrs S. A., *Canon Barnett: His Life, Work and Friends* (John Murray, 1918).

BARNETT, Canon and Mrs S. A., *Practicable Socialism* (Longman, Green, 1915).

BASCH, F., *Relative Creatures: Victorian Women in Society and the Novel, 1837–67* (Allen Lane, 1974).

BELL, E. M., *Josephine Butler: Flame and Fire* (Constable, 1962).

BELL, E. M., *Octavia Hill: A Biography* (Constable, 1942).

BESANT, A., *An Autobiography* (T. Fisher Unwin, 1893).

BEVERIDGE, W., *Unemployment: A Problem of Industry* (Longmans, 1909).

BOOTH, W., *In Darkest England and the Way Out* (McCorquordale, 1890).

BOYD, N., *Josephine Butler, Octavia Hill, Florence Nightingale: Three Victorian Women who Changed Their World* (Macmillan, 1982).

BRIGGS, A. and MACARTNEY, A., *Toynbee Hall* (Routledge & Kegan Paul, 1984).

BRONTË, A., *The Tenant of Wildfell Hall* (1848) (Penguin Books, 1979).

BRONTË, C., *Jane Eyre* (1847) (Oxford: University Press, 1975).

BROWN, G. W. and HARRIS, T., *Social Origins of Depression: A Study of Psychiatric Disorder in Women* (Tavistock, 1978).

BURDETT-COUTTS, A. (ed.) *Woman's Mission* (Sampson Low, Marston & Co., 1893).

BUTLER, A. S. G., *Portrait of Josephine Butler* (Faber, 1954).

BUTLER, J. E., *Women's Work and Women's Culture* (Macmillan, 1869).

BUTLER, J. E., *The Constitution Violated* (Edmondston & Douglas, 1871).

BUTLER, J. E., *John Grey of Dilston* (Henry S. King, 1874).

BUTLER, J. E., *Recollections of George Butler* (J. W. Arrowsmith, 1892).

BUTLER, J. E., *Personal Reminiscences of a Great Crusade* (Horace Marshall, 1896).

CAINE, B., *Destined to be Wives: The Sisters of Beatrice Webb* (Clarendon Press, 1986).

CARPENTER, J. E., *The Life and Work of Mary Carpenter* (Macmillan, 1879).

CARPENTER, M., *Reformatory Schools* (C. Gilpin, 1851).

CARPENTER, M., *Juvenile Delinquents* (W. & F. G. Cash, 1853).

CHADWICK, E., *The Sanitary Condition of the Labouring Population of Great Britain* (1842); Flinn, M. W. (ed.) (Edinburgh University Press, 1965).

CHAPPLE, J. A. V., *Elizabeth Gaskell: A portrait in letters* (Manchester University Press, 1980).

CLOUGH, B. A., *A Memoir of Anne Jemima Clough* (Edward Arnold, 1897).

COBBE, F. P., *The Life of Frances Power Cobbe* (Richard Bentley & Son, 1894).

COOK, E. T., *The Life of Florence Nightingale* (Macmillan, 1913).

CROSS, J. W. (ed) *George Eliot's Life* (William Blackwood & Sons, (1885).

DAVIDOFF, L. and HALL, C., *Family Fortunes* (Hutchinson, 1987).

DELAMONT, S. and DUFFIN, L. (eds) *The Nineteenth-Century Woman* (Croom Helm, 1978).

DREW, M., *Catherine Gladstone* (Nisbet and Company, 1919).

Memoir of the Life of Elizabeth Fry (ed. by Two of her Daughters) (Charles Gilpin, 1847).

GASKELL, E., *Mary Barton* (1848) (Penguin Books, 1970).

GOLDTHORPE, J. H., 'Women and Class Analysis: In Defense of the Conventional View', *Sociology*, vol. 17, no. 4 (1983) pp. 465–85.

GOLDTHORPE, J. H., 'Women and Class Analysis: A Reply to the Replies', *Sociology*, vol. 18, no. 4 (1984) pp. 491–9.

HALSEY, A. H. (ed.) *Traditions of Social Policy* (Blackwell, 1976).

HARRISON, B., *Separate Spheres* (Croom Helm, 1978).

HEASEMAN, K., *Evangelicals in Action* (Bles, 1962).

HEATH, A. F. and BRITTEN, N., 'Women's Jobs do make a Difference: A Reply to Goldthorpe', *Sociology*, vol. 18, no. 4 (1984) pp. 473–89.

HEWITT, M., *Wives and Mothers in Victorian Industry* (1958) (Greenwood Press, 1975).

HILL, O., *Our Common Land* (London, 1877).

HILL, O., *Homes of the London Poor* (1875) (Macmillan, 1883).

HILL, O., 'Colour, Space and Music for the People', *Nineteenth Century* (May, 1884).

HODDER, E., *The Life and Work of the Seventh Earl of Shaftesbury K.G.* (Cassell, 1886).

HOLCOMBE, L., *Victorian Ladies at Work* (David & Charles, 1973).

HOLLIS, P. (ed.) *Women in Public: The Women's Movement 1850–1900* (Allen & Unwin, 1979).

JOHNSON, G. W. and JOHNSON, L. A., *Josephine Butler: An Autobiographical Memoir* (1909) (Arrowsmith & Simpkin Marshall, 1911).

Memorials of Elizabeth Agnes Jones, by her sister (Strachan, 1871).

KAMM, J., *How Different From Us: A Biography of Miss Buss and Miss Beale* (Bodley Head, 1958).

MACDONALD, J. R., *Margaret Ethel MacDonald* (1912) (Allen & Unwin, 1929).

MAURICE, C. E., *Life of Octavia Hill* (Macmillan, 1913).

MAURICE, E. S., *Octavia Hill* (Allen & Unwin, 1928).

MITCHELL, H., *The Hard Way Up* (Mitchell, G. (ed.)) (Faber, 1968).

MORLEY, E. J. (ed.) *Women Workers in Seven Professions* (George Routledge & Son, 1915).

MOWAT, C. L., *The Charity Organisation Society* (Methuen, 1961).

NEFF, W. F., *Victorian Working Women* (1919) (Frank Cass, 1966).

NETHERCOT, A. H., *The First Five Lives of Annie Besant* (Rupert Hart Davis, 1961).

OWEN, D., *English Philanthropy 1660–1960* (Oxford University Press, 1965).

PARSONS, T., *Essays in Sociological Theory Pure and Applied* (USA: The Free Press, Glencoe, 1949).

PARSONS, T., *The Social System* (USA: The Free Press, Glencoe, 1964).

PETRIE, G., *A Singular Iniquity* (Macmillan, 1971).

PINCHBECK, I., *Women Workers and the Industrial Revolution 1750–1805* (1929) (Frank Cass, 1966).

PROCHASKA, F. K., *Women and Philanthropy in Nineteenth-Century England* (Clarendon Press, 1980).

RATHBONE, E., *William Rathbone: A Memoir* (Macmillan, 1905).

RATHBONE, H. R. (ed.) *Memoir of Kitty Wilkinson of Liverpool, 1796–1860* (Liverpool, 1927).

ROBERTS, E., *A Woman's Place: An Oral History of Working Class Women 1890–1940* (Blackwell, 1984).

ROWNTREE, B. S., *Poverty: A Study of Town Life* (Macmillan, 1901).

RUSKIN, J., *Works*, vol. 1, *Sesame and Lilies* (George Allen, 1880).

SIMEY, M. B., *Charitable Effort in Liverpool in the Nineteenth Century* (Liverpool University Press, 1951).

Social Trends, 17 (Central Statistical Office, HMSO, 1987).

STEPHEN, B., *Emily Davies and Girton College* (Constable, 1927).

STRACHEY, L., *Queen Victoria* (Chatto & Windus, 1959).

TITMUSS, R. M., *The Gift Relationship* (Allen & Unwin, 1970).

TWINING, L., *Recollections of Life and Work* (Edward Arnold, 1893).

TWINING, L., *Workhouses and Pauperism* (Methuen, 1898).

VEBLEN, T., *The Theory of the Leisure Class*, in *Veblen*, Max Lerner (ed.) (New York: Viking Press, 1948).

VICINUS, M. (ed.) *Independent Women* (Virago Press, 1985).

WALKOWITZ, J. R., *Prostitution and Victorian Society* (Cambridge University Press, 1980).

WEBB, B., *My Apprenticeship* (1926), 2nd edn (Longman, Green).

WEBB, B., *Our Partnership* (Drake, B. and Cole, M. I. (eds)) (Longman, Green, 1948).

WEBB, R. K., *Harriet Martineau: A Radical Victorian* (Heinemann, 1960).

WEBB, S. and WEBB, B., *English Poor Law History*, Pt II, vol. 1 (1929) (Frank Cass, 1963).

WILLIAMS, M., *Women in the English Novel 1800–1900* (Macmillan, 1984).

WOODHAM-SMITH, C., *Florence Nightingale 1820–1910* (Constable, 1950).

YOUNG, M. and WILLMOTT, P., *The Symmetrical Family* (Routledge & Kegan Paul, 1972).

Index

women's roles in Victorian England,
12–14, 32–5
  Josephine Butler on, 110–11, 112
  Mary Carpenter on, 111–12
  changing definitions, 193, 195
  Frances Power Cobbe on, 57
  Emily Davies on, 186
  as governesses, 13–14
  in government service, 16
  Octavia Hill on, 112
  Florence Nightingale on, 96–7
  as nurses, 14–15
  in paid employment, 14–20, 193,
    195

  and Parsons' 'pattern variables',
    33–4
  and philanthropy, 35
  Ruskin on, 33
  Beatrice Webb on, 98
  in workhouses and poor law
    administration, 28, 143, 157
women's suffrage, some nineteenth-
century attitudes, 31, 65, 96,
112–13, 114–16

Young, M. and Willmott, P., and
the 'symmetrical family', 193